The Social Psychology of
Collective Action

The Social Psychology of Collective Action:
Identity, injustice and gender

Caroline Kelly and Sara Breinlinger

Taylor & Francis
Publishers since 1798

UK	Taylor & Francis Ltd, 1 Gunpowder Square, London EC4A 3DE
USA	Taylor & Francis Inc., 1900 Frost Road, Suite 101, Bristol, PA 19007

First published 1996

A Catalogue Record for this book is available from the British Library

ISBN 0 7484 0510 0
ISBN 0 7484 0511 9 (pbk)

Library of Congress Cataloging-in-Publication Data are available on request

Cover design by Amanda Barragry

Typeset in 10/12 pt ITC Garamond
by Solidus (Bristol) Limited

Printed in Great Britain by SRP Ltd, Exeter

To John, Joanna and Alex

CK

Kurt and Elaine

SB

Contents

List of Figures and Tables   x
Acknowledgements   xiii

Chapter 1 **Introduction**   1
The Trade Union Movement   3
The Women's Movement   6
Collectivism and Individualism   9
Approaches to Collective Action   11
    Olson's logic of collective action   11
    Resource mobilization theory   13
    Recent micro-sociological approaches   14
Methodology and the Study of Collective Action   16

Chapter 2 **Social Psychological Approaches to Collective Action**   19
Individual Characteristics   20
    Locus of control   20
    Political efficacy   21
    Individualist–collectivist orientation   23
Individual Decision-making   25
    The theories of reasoned action and planned behaviour 26
    Klandermans' expectancy-value model   30
Group Processes   34
    Group membership and self-stereotyping   34
    Deindividuation and crowd behaviour   36
    Relative deprivation theory   38
    Social identity and low status   40
    The five-stage model of intergroup relations   42
    Combining approaches: The moderating role of group
        identification   48
    Applying the social identity framework to gender   51
Concluding Comments   53

Chapter 3 **Social Beliefs and Participation: Exploring Associations**   55
   Study One: Participation in a Trade Union Context   56
      The setting and respondents   56
      The questionnaire   57
      Factor analysis of participation items   58
      Predicting participation   59
      The moderating role of group identification I   60
      Conclusions to study one   62
   Study Two: Participation in a Gender Context   62
      Groups and respondents   62
      Measuring prospective and potential participation 64
      Using social beliefs to predict participation   67
      The moderating role of group identification II   70
      The impact of identification as an activist   72
      Intentions, behaviour and perceived control   72
      The moderating role of group identification III   76
      Identity and its behavioural expression   78
      Conclusions to study two   78
   Comparing the Two Contexts of Action   79

Chapter 4 **Explaining Initial Involvement: Why Join Women's Groups?**   82
   Personal Background and Personal Characteristics   86
      Gender relations in the family   86
      Mothers and daughters   90
      Developing an activist identity   94
   Life Events, Discrimination and Social Support   95
      Experiencing discrimination   95
      Isolation and a sense of 'difference'   102
      Meeting and helping others   104
   Social Beliefs   104
      Collective relative deprivation   105
      Development of a feminist consciousness   105
      Belief in collective action   106
   Group Services   106
   The Role of Chance   107
   Concluding Comments   108

Chapter 5 **Outcomes of Participation**   110
   Group Socialization   111
   Consciousness Raising   113
   Perceived Outcomes of Participation in Women's Groups   118

	Social outcomes	119
	Political outcomes	121
	Personal development outcomes	122
	Professional development outcomes	123
	The Personal and the Political	124
	Exploring Perceived Personal and Political Changes	124
	Comparing New Recruits and Longstanding Members	131
	Comparing Participation and Social Beliefs Over Time	133
	Concluding Comments	134
Chapter 6	**Explaining Non-activism**	136
	Culture, Individualism and Group Membership	136
	Perceptions of Political Minorities and Activists	141
	Non-activism in a Trade Union Context	145
	Non-activism in a Gender Context	151
	Cultural context	155
	Beliefs about women's groups and feminism	157
	Individual-level explanations	164
	Other ways of promoting social change	167
	Concluding Comments	168
Chapter 7	**Conclusions**	171
	Main Themes	171
	Social Identity and Social Movements	176
Appendixes		181
References		196
Index		219

List of Figures and Tables

Figures

Figure 2.1	The theory of planned behaviour	26
Figure 2.2	Klandermans' expectancy-value model of participation	31
Figure 2.3	Taylor and McKirnan's five-stage model of intergroup relations	43
Figure 3.1	Readiness to participate in different types of action in a gender context: Mean ratings	66
Figure 3.2	Explanations for protest behaviour: Percentage of responses	67
Figure 3.3	Social beliefs: Mean scores	68
Figure 3.4	Intentions and behaviours: Mean scores	73
Figure 4.1	Explanations for initial involvement in women's groups	84
Figure 5.1	Perceived outcomes of participation in women's groups	118
Figure 5.2	Participation in a gender context: A comparison according to length of involvement	132
Figure 6.1	Explanations for non-involvement in women's groups: Overview	154
Figure 6.2	Explanations for non-involvement in women's groups: Focus on group level	158

Tables

Table 1.1	Percentages who have and would protest/demonstrate against an unjust bill	10
Table 3.1	Union participation and social beliefs: Mean scores, standard deviations and alpha reliability coefficients	59
Table 3.2	Union participation and social beliefs: Standardized regression coefficients	60

Table 3.3   Union participation and expectancy-value calculations: Standardized regression coefficients   60

Table 3.4   Social beliefs and participation in a gender context: Standardized regression coefficients   69

Table 3.5   Group identification, social beliefs and participation in a gender context: Standardized regression coefficients   71

Table 3.6   The impact of identification as an activist: Standardized regression coefficients   72

Table 3.7   Prediction of intention (whole sample): Standardized regression coefficients   75

Table 3.8   Prediction of behaviour (whole sample): Standardized regression coefficients   75

Table 3.9   Prediction of intention for weak and strong identifiers: Standardized regression coefficients   76

Table 3.10   Prediction of behaviour for weak and strong identifiers: Standardized regression coefficients   77

Table 4.1   Interviewees' explanations for initial involvement: Frequencies   85

Table 4.2   Types of discrimination experienced by women   96

Table 5.1   Perceived outcomes of participation: Frequencies   119

Table 5.2   Items concerning self-reported change   126

Table 5.3   Intercorrelations between self-reported change items   126

Table 5.4   Reported changes in beliefs by less and more active groups: Mean scores, standard deviations and F statistics   127

Table 5.5   Perceived changes: Percentage of total responses from qualitative data   127

Table 6.1   Explaining non-involvement in trade unions   148

Table 6.2   Explaining non-involvement in women's groups: Percentage of total explanations   154

Table 6.3   Beliefs about women's groups: Percentage of total explanations   157

Table 6.4   Ways of promoting women's issues: Responses from activists and non-activists   168

Acknowledgements

Conducting the research described in this book has been a very rewarding experience. We would like to thank all the people who participated, especially those activists in women's groups, who gave up valuable time to take part in lengthy interviews and who were so helpful and enthusiastic about the study. In the interests of confidentiality, we will not name them here but we are immensely grateful to them and hope they will find this book interesting.

Thanks are also due to Rupert Brown for his constructive comments and encouragement and to friends and colleagues for their support, in particular, Tom Bowyer, Justine Breinlinger, Amanda de Ryk, Gen Darbourne, Julie Dickinson, Liz Fincham, Esther Kelly, John Kelly, Sarah Michaels, Liz Newby, Jane O'Connor, Saskia O'Neary, Eva Pascoe, Ann Phoenix, Isobel Radford, Ann Richards and Kate Stainthorpe.

Finally, we would like to acknowledge The Leverhulme Trust, who provided financial support for the study of activism in women's groups, and the British Psychological Society for permission to reproduce Figure 2.3.

Chapter 1

Introduction

> There is no such thing as society. There are individual men and women, and there are families (Margaret Thatcher, interviewed in *Woman's Own*, 31 October 1987).

Since 1979 in Britain successive Conservative governments have promoted a radical individualism, emphasizing individual interests over group interests, individual action over collective action, where the family is the only legitimate source of social identity. The extent to which this aim has been achieved has been the subject of both social scientific and popular discussions during the 1980s and 1990s.

It is 30 years since Europe witnessed a surge of collective organization and activity. For example, from 1968 the trade union movement in Britain passed through a period of spectacular growth, as membership rose by almost three million, peaking at an all-time record figure in 1979 of 13.3 million. Associated with this growing membership of a primarily collective organization was a dramatic resurgence of collective action. Between 1968 and 1974, and again in 1978–79, Britain experienced its biggest waves of strike action for 50 years.

The growth of collective organization and activity was not, however, confined to the industrial relations system, or the economy, but was part of a much more comprehensive 'cycle of protest' (Tarrow, 1991). The 1960s marked the beginnings of the anti-war movement in America, the upsurge of civil rights campaigns by American blacks and Northern Irish catholics, the renewal of the women's movement after a long period of quiescence and the rapid appearance of a politicized and radical student movement in many advanced, capitalist countries. Tarrow (1994) describes a wave of student and labour unrest which swept across Europe between 1968 and 1972, notably in France, Czechoslovakia, Italy, Germany and Poland.

The appearance of such a multiplicity of social movements raised important theoretical and empirical issues which are still the subject of intense debate. Above all, what was the relation between the *old* social movements based on unions and workers' parties and the allegedly *new* social movements with their cross-class constituencies?

Yet even as this issue was being debated, the economic and political context of collective action was being radically transformed. The post-war economic boom ran out of steam and the long years of economic growth, full employment and job security gave way in the 1980s and 1990s to the return of mass unemployment. Politically, Britain and America witnessed significant shifts to the Right as the governments of Thatcher and Reagan came to office, determined to roll back many of the social changes of the postwar period, such as extensive welfare spending and public provision of services. Ideologically, these administrations were concerned above all to promote a rigorous form of individualism and to roll back the collectivist tide. The British government set out to weaken collective organizations, such as trade unions; it introduced restrictions on forms of collective action, such as demonstrations; cut back on collective provision of essential services; facilitated increased individual owner-ship of housing and company shares; and encouraged individuals and their families to become self-reliant and financially independent of others. These political developments were associated with the winding down of Tarrow's 'cycle of protest' as trade union movements went into decline, the women's movement fragmented and the incidence of collective actions, such as large-scale street demonstrations and workers' strikes, fell away, particularly but not exclusively, in Britain and America. In Europe the number of workers involved in strike action fell sharply after 1980, most of all in France, Italy and Belgium.

This in turn led to debates about the decline of collectivism and the rise of individualism. For present purposes, we may define this alleged change as declining identification with, and dependence on, groups outside the family, though as we shall see later, there is much debate about the nature and definitions of individualism and collectivism. Attention focused among other things on whether the alleged decline of collectivism was a product of short-term political and economic circumstances or whether it was the consequence and the symptom of a much deeper shift to a post-industrial or post-modernist era. Equally contentious was the issue of whether all forms of collectivism were in decline or whether it was more specifically the trade union collectivism of organized workers that was being displaced by a more complex pattern of specific collectivisms organized through the 'new social movements' (Crook, Pakulski and Waters, 1992). Finally, there was growing debate about the continued salience of social class as a form of group identity and a determinant of behaviours such as voting (see Crewe and Sarlvik, 1983 and Heath, Jowell and Curtice, 1985, for opposing interpretations of what came to be known as the 'class de-alignment' debate).

We now turn to a more detailed discussion of the two specific social movements which are the contexts for the present empirical research, namely the trade union movement and the women's movement. Subsequent sections focus on the key concepts of collectivism and individualism and the main theoretical approaches which have been developed to study collective interests, organization and action. Finally, in this chapter, we consider the methodological issues which determined our own choice of research strategy.

The Trade Union Movement

Between 1968 and 1979, British trade union membership rose by 2.9 million and strike activity (frequency of strikes, workers involved and days lost) reached levels that had not been seen for almost 50 years. In the years after 1979, the membership gains of the 1970s were completely wiped out and the number of employees in unions fell from the 1979 peak of 13.3 million to just over 8.4 million by the end of 1993. Strike activity showed an equally precipitate decline. Between 1968 and 1979, the annual number of strikes never once fell below 2000 and was often much higher, peaking at just under 4000 in 1970. Since 1979, the annual total has never been above 2000 and has continued to fall way below that figure: In the early 1990s, the annual average number of strikes was about 300–400.

The British miners' strike, which lasted for one year from March 1984 until March 1985, was the longest large strike in British history. At its peak, over a quarter of a million workers were on strike, 10,000 strikers were arrested in the cause of the strike and the number of days lost through the industrial action was over 22 million, the ninth highest annual total since records began in 1893.

Historically, miners had come to be regarded as the vanguard of the trade union movement: In the 1950s, approximately *three-quarters* of all strikes in Britain took place in the coal mines and the national strikes of 1972 and 1974 by the 300,000 strong National Union of Mineworkers (NUM) helped to bring down the Conservative government. The victorious strikes of the early 1970s symbolized both the industrial and political power of the trade union movement and encouraged other groups of workers to emulate their actions.

By contrast, the defeat of the year-long strike of 1984–85 came to symbolize the collapse of union power in the context of economic recession and in the face of a militant, right-wing government. Within ten years of the 1985 defeat, the NUM has seen its membership collapse from 250,000 to just 15,000. In the aftermath of the defeat, strike activity in Britain has fallen significantly, while in the political sphere, the demise of the NUM has greatly weakened left-wing opposition to the moderate wings of the trade union movement and the Labour Party. Not surprisingly given the way in which the strike continues to figure in public consciousness ten years on, an enormous literature has developed around the strike: One study, published in 1989, discovered over 600 published items (books, chapters, journal and magazine articles and pamphlets) (Winterton and Winterton, 1989).

A wide range of economic, political and legal factors have been discussed in the debate about the decline in union membership and activity. One persistent theme, recently restated by a number of very influential writers, is that the current decline of union membership and activity is not just the normal downturn associated with economic recession, but is the product of a deeper, and secular, decline in *collectivism* (see Gallie, 1989).

According to Bassett and Cave (1993), unions are organizations that must operate in two markets: They must recruit employees in one market, but they must also persuade employers to recognize them for the purposes of collective bargaining. Since 1979 the demand for union services has declined in both these markets. Employees are less interested in joining unions, as shown by the figures on membership decline. Employers are also less attracted to unions as shown by the fall in the percentage of the workforce covered by collective bargaining arrangements. Moreover, employers are increasingly seeking to individualize their relations with employees, for instance, by negotiating with them individually rather than collectively. It is argued that in response to employer initiatives, as well as to State policies in the 1980s, employees themselves have become more individualistic and less interested in the traditional, collective services supplied by unions. Flowing from this analysis are a series of proposed reforms of union organization and activity, central to which is the downgrading of collectivism, described by the authors as simply an 'operating technique', not a root principle of trade unionism. In general, they urge unions to concentrate on individual, rather than collective, services to members, such as advice on contracts, legal assistance and financial packages.

H.P. Brown (1990) offers a more historical and wide-ranging analysis of the decline of worker collectivism, arriving nonetheless at very similar policy prescriptions. For Brown, worker collectivism was understood as a sense of interdependence and solidarity with fellow workers. It was rooted in the deprivations of industrialization, in particular, the poverty, job insecurity and lack of rights that were the normal conditions of life for the early working class. This deprivation engendered a powerful sense of collectivism that was reinforced by the concentration of workers in large factories and by their geographical segregation in the poorest areas of large towns and cities. Hence the characteristic pattern of working-class collective organization and activity, common throughout the capitalist world, of trade unions, social democratic parties, strike action and political agitation.

But the development of twentieth-century capitalism has gradually eroded the roots of worker collectivism and contributed to the recent decline of the trade union movement. Affluence has removed the worst excesses of poverty and led to increased financial independence for working-class households. (According to Triandis, 1989, *financial* independence should lead in turn to greater *social* independence as workers become less dependent for their welfare on membership of particular unions or political groups.) The growth of unions and political parties has secured more rights for workers, while the emergence of the welfare state further reduced poverty and ameliorated the worst consequences of job insecurity.

The effects on collectivism of large workplaces and residential segregation have been greatly weakened by the recent sharp fall in the average size of manufacturing workplaces and by the longer term disintegration of working-class communities. The latter has been further undermined by the geographical mobility of the workforce and the expansion of travel-to-work areas. All of these factors further weaken the attachment of individual employees to particular workplace or residential groups and strengthen their individualism. Insofar as trade unionism is the embodiment of worker collectivism, then these developments throughout the twentieth century have gradually weakened its traditional appeal. It is again argued that if unions are to survive at all in the future it will be because of their adaptation to the new, and probably irreversible, tide of individualism and their promotion of individual rather than collective services.

Some of the trends depicted by Bassett and Cave (1993) and Brown (1990) are undeniably taking place: Individualization of pay bargaining, employer resistance to union recognition, geographical mobility, decline of old, working-class communities, decline of workplace size (at least in manufacturing, though not in retail, where the trend is in the opposite direction) and a rise in living standards. However, the argument that these trends are responsible for an erosion of worker collectivism is more controversial. Kelly and Waddington (1995) argue that evidence shows that employees continue to define their interests collectively (see for example, Kelly and Kelly, 1991) and that what has changed since 1979 in Britain is a shift in the balance of power between unions and employers. As union power has declined, so too has perceived union effectiveness. On the plausible and well-supported assumption that people's reasons for joining unions are largely instrumental (Millward, 1990), then a decline in perceived effectiveness is likely to have eroded potential union support amongst employees. In relation to employers, there is indeed declining demand for unions in the employer market, but this is because employers have the power to resist unionization and not because employees have become more individualized.

Brown's argument about affluence, deprivation and collectivism is also problematic. Employees can feel relatively deprived at almost any salary level and can still feel unfairly or unjustly treated (Runciman, 1966). In addition, whereas working-class communities did reinforce a sense of collectivism amongst their members, it is clear from the upsurge of union membership and strike activity in the 1970s, much of it involving white-collar workers, that such communities are not necessary for the genesis of worker collectivism.

In conclusion, there has undoubtedly been a decline in various forms of collective organization and action in the industrial relations sphere, but the extent to which this trend is symptomatic of a deeper decline in collectivism is more controversial and not well supported by empirical evidence. We turn now to consider the other social movement which is the main context for the present research, namely the women's movement.

The Women's Movement

According to Ryan (1992), the rebirth of feminism in the 1960s alongside other social movements can be traced partly to the family-centred years of the 1950s. This was an era which re-established women's place in the home after their brief move into paid employment during World War Two. Although women's labour force participation continued to rise in the post-war period, cultural ideology still defined the wife/mother's role as women's special duty and path to fulfilment. Increasing urbanization and the move away from the extended family network left women isolated. Informal women's groups offered a platform for women's discontent.

As the critical dimensions of women's lives, which traditionally centred on children and domestic labour, were transformed by an urban industrial economy, a new definition of womanhood emerged. During the 1960s there was an increased emphasis on women as workers and less on women as mothers, although in keeping with the ideological contradictions governing women's experience, work outside of the home was still thought to put the child at risk of deprivation (Klein, 1984). However, approval of married women working increased dramatically from 25 per cent in 1945, to 44 per cent in 1967, and to 64 per cent in 1972 (Konek and Kitch, 1994). The traditional view that becoming wives, homemakers and mothers is women's natural destiny was no longer a matter of consensus by 1972. Firestone describes the second wave of feminism as the 'inevitable female response to the development of a technology capable of freeing women from the tyranny of their sexual reproductive roles' (1970: 37). Indeed, with the advent of contraceptive technology, the age of marriage went up and the birthrate decreased. As could be expected, this 'freedom' saw women drawn in increasing numbers into outside employment, yet despite the loosening of traditional roles and an increasing expectation of 'equality' between the sexes, women soon discovered that equality did not always mean equal pay or job opportunities (Randall, 1987).

Opportunities for higher education also expanded in the 1960s and the numbers of highly educated women in both America and Britain rose significantly. Firestone (1970) argues that it is amongst these women that the experience of disparity in status between men and women was most acute and a sense of deprivation *vis-à-vis* male peers most predominant. Increased education and the vocalization of discontent went hand-in-hand. By the early 1970s, the notion that 'the personal is political' came to the fore with more demands for personal liberation through social and political action, which contrasted with earlier beliefs (prevalent in the 1950s) that individual problems required individual, even therapeutic solutions.

In the mid-1970s, divisions within the women's movement became more obvious, particularly over the question of separatism. For example, in 1977 militant radical feminists began calling themselves *revolutionary feminists*, insisting on the total separation of men and women's organizations, at the same time distinguishing their position from *cultural* feminists (Coote and Campbell, 1987).

Despite conflicts between the different factions of the women's movement, by 1980 there were 99 women's groups and 200 refuges; by 1983 *Spare Rib* was listing 20 rape crisis centres in England alone; from the late 1970s there were a series of marches to 'Reclaim the Night' from male attackers, and issues of sexuality and pornography also came to the fore.

During the 1980s, the popular media presented the feminist movement as one in crisis. They suggested that this was reflected in the relative infrequency of protests, demonstrations, marches and the dissolution of many of the early consciousness-raising groups. There was also more audible self-criticism within the movement which may have signalled to some observers that contemporary feminism had little to offer women. It was suggested that we had entered into a post-feminist era where feminism is no longer appropriate or necessary (see Faludi, 1992).

Some argue that it is not the women's movement that became post-feminist; it is the social environment that has become openly hostile to further gains for women (Ryan, 1992). Faludi (1992) argues that paranoia about feminism, particularly in the United States but also in Britain, was orchestrated by the media in perhaps unwitting collusion with government. She argues that attacks on feminism have recurred throughout this century whenever feminism has appeared to be gaining ground and have often taken similar forms, such as 'scares' about working women's poor mental health and diminishing fertility, a 'crisis' in masculinity and a celebration of traditional family values. She sees these as the blatant manufacture of 'trends' which seek to undermine the advances that feminism has made.

Addressing the question of the demise of feminism, as indicated by the relative infrequency of public demonstrations and the like, many argue that although it is true that many of the social movements of the 1960s and 1970s have expired, the feminist movement is one of the survivors (see Ryan, 1992). In terms of how to measure these things, Katzenstein (1987) argues that many of the measures for gauging the health of social movements are not appropriate for feminism. Membership figures, for instance, that give a reasonable indication of the well-being of trade unions tell little of the story of the feminist movement. There are many active feminists, not to mention supporters, who are neither dues-paying or card-carrying members of any particular organizational unit. Where other movements' success has been judged by their very public protests and demonstrations, the women's movement has always made less use of the orthodox tactics of disorder. The feminist agenda targets the private realm along with the public sphere and, in doing so, it has placed a particular reliance on consciousness as a tool of social change. The private realm can only partly be reached through legislation, public policy and judicial action. Consequently, feminism has pursued its often radical agenda in less visible ways through consciousness-raising groups, collectives, caucuses and local organizations. In this sense, any assessment of the well-being of the women's movement must identify the multiple networks through which a feminist consciousness is realized and activism promoted.

Diversity is the striking feature of today's women's movement. It is a decentralized movement covering a wide range of ideologies and activities (see Griffin, 1995). Because there is no fixed form, it is difficult to keep a tab on women's groups and gain precise information for comparison to other periods and geographical locations. This is partly because the resources available to undertake such work are limited and because these organizations are many and constantly changing: Some are local organizations designed to meet a particular need, some merge and/or split into a variety of different groups. Many cease through inadequate funding as very often women's organizations rely on a volunteer staff, and this leaves them vulnerable to the personal circumstances of their key members.

In recent years the number of local and specialist organizations of interest to women in Britain has dramatically increased. There are political interest and pressure groups; women's groups within political parties and unions; education and training groups; groups for women in midlife; professional networks; specialist organizations for older women, younger women and disabled women. They take many forms including discussion groups, self-help and support groups, research and study groups, and local women's centres. In 1983, Bouchier suggested that there were around 300 feminist groups, with a total number of committed activists in the region of 10,000 and an additional 20,000 occasional activists. It is estimated that an active core probably consists of around 2000 each of radical and socialist feminists. In 1992, *The Women's Directory* listed around 400 groups of special interest to women.

As was true in the 1970s, there is no one feminist theory or group. The women's movement then, as now, consists of a number of simultaneous and divergent orientations. This is both the movement's strength and weakness. There has been much talk within the feminist movement over the issue of 'exclusion' in feminist thought. Much of contemporary feminist theory is based on the experience of white, predominantly middle-class women and, as a consequence, 'what we have in common' as women has generally been a description of white middle-class women. It is argued that what has happened in feminist theory is that the condition of this one group has been conflated with the condition of all women (Spelman, 1988). In this sense, any attempt to talk about all women in terms of what we have in common undermines the important differences between women. The problem feminism faces in the 1990s is its need to encompass diversity among women without this focus on difference becoming destructive and demobilizing (see Chapter 7).

In conclusion, over the last decade there has been a decrease in visible signs of collective action by women, as by other social groups. Militant feminism, like militant trade unionism, is commonly regarded as inappropriate and ineffective in bringing about social change and individual forms of action are more socially acceptable. Whether or not this indicates a decline in collectivism *per se* is more difficult to judge and depends very much on how exactly we define collectivism. This brings us to the next section which presents different views on the nature and definition of collectivism.

Collectivism and Individualism

There are a number of ways of conceptualizing these terms and three of these will be discussed here: Collectivism (and individualism) has been discussed as a cultural value (Hofstede, 1980); as a political attitude or cluster of attitudes (Marshall, *et al.*, 1988; Rentoul, 1989); and as a multi-dimensional construct embracing interests, behaviour and organization (Tilly, 1978) and we shall examine each in turn.

For Hofstede (1980), collectivism is a value more or less widely shared by members of a national community which has three components: A perception of interdependence with others; a belief that collective (or group) goals are either synonymous with one's personal goals or should supersede personal goals where the two are in conflict; and finally, a strong sense of ingroups and outgroups. Hofstede argues that advanced capitalist societies are characterized by cultural complexity which means that its members have available to them a wide array of ingroups. This range of choice makes them less dependent on any particular group and hence more independent of the groups to which they belong. This social independence is reinforced by financial independence arising out of affluence and hence the more 'advanced' the society, the more individualist its culture (see Chapter 6 for further discussion; also Triandis, 1989).

Hofstede's work is useful here in offering a conceptualization of collectivism focused on group salience and group boundaries, so that we can begin to make connections with social psychological theory (see Chapter 2). However, in the assumption that cultural values are relatively stable (at least in the absence of rapid economic change or other dramatic events such as war) and are reproduced through successive generations, it is difficult to account for instability, or rapid decline, in collective organization and action, such as that observed in the 1980s.

A second approach to collectivism defines the concept as an attitude or cluster of attitudes (for example, Gallie, 1988; Marshall, *et al.*, 1988; Rentoul, 1989). Collectivism can therefore be measured by examining trends and variations in attitudes to collective provision of services, reasons for joining collective organizations, degrees of identification with collectivities, such as social classes, and willingness to participate in collective action under various conditions. This large and heterogeneous body of evidence has tended to underline the continuing relevance of collectivist attitudes. For example, a growing proportion of respondents (sampled from the whole adult population in Britain) declare that they are willing to pay higher taxes in return for better

Table 1.1: Percentages who have and would protest/demonstrate against an unjust bill

	1983	1986	1989	1991
Have protested/demonstrated	2.0	5.7	8.4	9.1
Would protest/demonstrate	8.0	10.5	14.0	13.6

Sources: Jowell and Airey (1984); Jowell, *et al.* (1987; 1990; 1992)

public services (Rentoul, 1989). People's reasons for joining trade unions centre around a mixture of collective factors, such as wage rises, and more ambiguous items, such as protection at the workplace (protection which can take both individual and collective forms) (Marshall, *et al.*, 1988; 154; see also Gallie, 1989; Millward, 1990 for similar findings). Conversely, the provision of new individual services, such as discount mortgages, appears to have been relatively *unimportant* in persuading employees to join unions in the late 1980s and early 1990s (Kelly and Waddington, 1995). Levels of social class identification appear not to have changed radically through the 1980s, although the time-series data is less than ideal (Marshall, *et al.*, 1988). Finally, evidence from the annual British Social Attitudes Surveys suggests that a *growing* proportion of the population throughout the 1980s has participated in collective action in the form of protests and demonstrations and is willing to do so (see Table 1.1).

The advantage of conceptualizing collectivism as an attitude, as opposed to a cultural value, is that in principle we could account for sudden declines in collective organization and action by reference to changing collectivist attitudes. In practice, matters are more complex since some of the attitudinal data is measured at a high level of generality, making it difficult to derive predictions about specific behaviours or group memberships. For instance, the decline in trade union membership in Britain since 1979 coexists with fairly stable, *general* attitudes to unions (items such as 'Trade unions are essential to protect workers' interests' and 'Trade unions, in general, are a good thing'. See for example, R. Taylor, 1993).

A third approach to collectivism is that of Tilly's (1978) multi-dimensional conceptualization. According to Tilly, collectivism has five components: Collective definition of interests; their transformation into collective organization, understood as both membership of, and identification with, a collectivity; mobilization, by which he means the transformation of individuals into a collective actor; collective action itself (taking a variety of forms); and the opportunity to act, which depends on the balance of power between dominant and subordinate groups, the costs and benefits of collective action and openness of other groups to claims from the subordinate group. Tilly then uses this broad framework to analyse a variety of collective actions, including riots, insurrections, strikes and revolutions.

This conceptualization allows us to recast the debate about the alleged decline of collectivism in a more complex way. A decline in collectivism could mean a decline in any one (or more) of the five components. Moreover, there is no presumption that these components necessarily hang together. We could, for example, observe a decline in collective action, say strike activity, without any corresponding decline in the prevalence of collective interest definition amongst employees. Similarly, in a gender context, women may continue to define their interests collectively without this necessarily being manifest in collective activity or public demonstrations.

Approaches to Collective Action

We turn now to collective *action* and consider the main theoretical approaches to the issue of translating collective interests into collective organizational action. The three approaches we shall consider here are Olson's theory of collective action, resource mobilization theory and recent micro-sociological accounts.

Olson's 'Logic of Collective Action'

Olson's *Logic of Collective Action* was first published in 1965 and is one of the most influential social science monographs of the past 30 years, particularly in economics and political science. The book began with a problem. It was conventional wisdom at the time that if a set of individuals have interests in common, they will form themselves into a group and act collectively to pursue them. Collective interests give rise to collective action. But, according to Olson, there was far less collective organization and action around than this simple model would lead you to expect. For example, trade union density in America was approximately 30 per cent in the early 1960s, i.e., 70 per cent of employees had 'chosen' not to join a union. If voting is treated as a form of collective action, then US Presidential elections normally attracted a turnout of about 50 per cent, with the other 50 per cent not bothering to vote at all.

Olson's analysis of this *lack* of collective action runs as follows: Many collective goals, such as wage rises, are *public goods*, i.e., they are available to everybody in the workplace whether or not they belong to the union that secured the rise. Since everyone gains the wage rise, the rational self-interested person will argue that there is no incentive to join the union. The benefits of unionism can be received without incurring the costs. In any event, any individual contribution to the union's funds and power will add only a negligible amount and, particularly where the union is large, non-joining is likely to go unnoticed. Consequently, the rational individual will choose to free-ride on colleagues, taking the benefits of collective organization but avoiding the costs.

However, if everybody reasons in this way (and Olson assumes that every rational self-interested person does), then *nobody* will join the collective organization and there will be no-one on whom to free-ride. Since we observe that there is *some* collective organization and action, then there must be some other mechanism, apart from collective interests, to bring such organizational action into being. For Olson, that something is *selective incentives*, comprising rewards for group membership and punishments for free-riding. Rewards must be *private* goods, available only to members of an organization, such as legal advice and representation for trade union members that is not available to non-members. Punishments for free-riding can take a variety of forms, but in the world of trade unions, coercion is the principal sanction. Compulsory union membership (the closed shop) forces everybody in a particular bargaining unit to join the union whose benefits they receive, while 'coercive picket lines' ensure that collective action is not undermined by strikebreakers. In the case of trade unions, at least in America, Olson was convinced that their survival hinged on coercion and the major periods of American union growth (1897–1904 and 1935–45) were both associated, he claims, with the widespread use of coercion. Olson does qualify this general argument by stating that the 'logic of collective action' operates most forcefully in large groups, where the contributions of a single individual will make only a negligible difference to the group and where free-riding can easily be undetected. In small groups, neither of these propositions hold, so that the incidence of free-riding is directly related to group size.

It is certainly true that where there is collective organization and action, there is almost invariably free-riding. It is also true that unions in many countries do (or in some cases, did) resort to compulsory membership and do protect strike action with picket lines. It is also undoubtedly true that as the British government from 1980 onwards progressively eroded the closed shop and increasingly restricted the use of strikes and picketing, then both union membership and strike activity dramatically declined. Yet none of these points adds up to a vindication of Olson's theory. A brief survey of relevant evidence and reflection on Olson's concepts suggests that the theory is seriously flawed.

For example, if we examine British trade union growth between 1968 and 1979, we find that total membership increased by 2.9 million. The most authoritative survey of the closed shop in British industry was able to estimate the numbers of employees *coerced* into joining unions in that period by closed-shop agreements and arrived at a figure of 0.25 million (Dunn and Gennard, 1984). In other words, far from being essential for union membership and growth, compulsion was marginal, accounting for just 9 per cent of the total membership rise. If we look at the evidence on strikes and picket lines, we find that in the period 1980–90 less than 35 per cent of strikes were accompanied by picketing. In other words, Olson's mechanism of compulsion in union collective action was absent from the vast majority of strikes. If we turn to the reasons given by workers for joining unions, we find that the overwhelming majority of respondents cite *public* goods, such as wage rises (as well as private goods, such as individual protection), whereas only a minority cite compulsion (Gallie, 1989; Marshall, *et al.*, 1988; Millward, 1990). Similarly, in the context of political activity, Muller and Opp (1986) found that, for the most part, *private* incentives were unrelated to intentions to participate and to participation, which were instead significantly related to *public* incentives.

Conceptually, Olson's theory is open to a number of serious shortcomings. First, if rational individuals are induced to participate in collective organization and action only by selective incentives, how does the organization needed to supply those incentives come into being in the first place? In the case of trade unions, for instance, individuals first starting up union organization in a non-union workplace are likely to incur significant personal costs (various forms of victimization) for few immediate benefits. Why would a rational individual ever act in this way? It seems plausible to follow Marwell and Oliver (1993) and argue that collective organization and action are often started by unusual individuals – activists – who are less self-interested than many of their colleagues, who are willing to bear personal costs and who think they can 'make a difference'. In other words, collective organization and action may well be started, and often sustained, by individuals who defy Olson's logic.

Second, we know from laboratory studies of bargaining and other games, such as Marwell and Ames (1979) that subjects in these settings pursue strategies that reflect combinations of individual self-interest and social norms such as fairness and equality. A theory so firmly rooted in individual self-interest as Olson's almost inevitably treats social norms in a highly unsatisfactory way, as a distortion of 'normal' individualistic behaviour. Just as people have social as well as personal identities, so too do they pursue collective as well as individual interests. In thinking about collective action, 'actors assess what their *group* may gain or lose as well as what they may gain or lose as individuals' (Fireman and Gamson, 1979: 15, italics in original; see also Chase, 1992). For all of these reasons, Olson's theory does not provide a useful starting-point for a social psychological account of collective action.

Resource Mobilization Theory

Resource mobilization theory shares an important premise with Olson's theory, namely the observation that many people are aware of having interests in common with others. Resource mobilization theory takes this point a little further by proposing that many people have grievances that are sufficient to motivate them to act collectively. The key obstacle to be overcome, however, is their lack of resources (financial and personnel) and for this theory the key difference between more and less successful social movements lies in the field of organization. Collective action by a social movement requires the aggregation of resources, and that in turn requires organization. An organization must also seek to involve third parties in its campaigns, as well as mobilizing its own members by an appropriate mixture of costs and benefits (McCarthy and Zald, 1979). This approach proved extremely influential in the 1970s and early 1980s, in part because its focus on organization seemed to fill an obvious gap in Olson's theory. Providing a structural–political framework, it laid out a clear research agenda for analysing the properties of organizations required for successful collective action.

At the height of the 1970s 'cycle of protest' the assumption of plentiful grievances seemed reasonable enough, but as the tide of collective protest began to ebb in the early 1980s, the question of *how* grievances were constructed came to appear increasingly significant and the neglect of this question by resource mobilization theory became increasingly problematic. What combination of social and cognitive processes were involved in persuading women to perceive discrimination at the workplace, or local residents to believe that new road-building programmes were environmentally damaging and illegitimate? These questions became especially apposite with the rise of the so-called new social movements of the 1980s and 1990s, but in particular, the Green movements broadly defined. How was it that movements for animal rights or conservation became attractive to large numbers of, often young, people in a relatively short space of time? Why had these Green movements apparently succeeded in recruiting and mobilizing relatively large numbers of members whereas some larger and resource-rich organizations, such as trade unions, were in decline?

The second line of criticism focused on resource mobilization theory's view of individual mobilization for collective action. Implicit in the argument that individual cost–benefit calculations were critical was a viewpoint not wholly dissimilar to that of Olson. In other words, individuals would participate in collective action if the *personal* costs of doing so could be minimized and the *personal* benefits enhanced. This perspective was increasingly criticized by sociologists and social psychologists who disliked its individualistic bias and its neglect of the growing literature on the nature and significance of social identity. As Morris and McClurg Mueller note:

> In short, the critics charged that RM [resource mobilization] was without
> a social psychology that could explain what real human beings do
> either inside movements or in reaction to them (1992: *ix*).

These two criticisms – the social construction of grievances and the role of social identity in collective action – increasingly coalesced in new approaches to collective action rooted in micro-sociology.

Recent Micro-sociological Approaches

This body of work is as yet relatively ill-defined in comparison with Olson's theory, and resource mobilization theory and its main themes flow directly from critiques of these theories. Echoing the advice of Fireman and Gamson (1979:

8) that sociologists should 'beware of economists bearing gifts', recent writers argue that the rational actor model of resource mobilization theory has been a Trojan horse for social movement theory, bringing with it a radical individualism that assumes an actor devoid of ties to other individuals or social groups and motivated above all else by self-interest (see Ferree, 1992). Gamson (1992) argues that Olson's theory assumes the *absence* of collective identities and neglects the fact that grievances and perceived costs and benefits of action are socially constructed within a collective context.

In developing an alternative approach, many of these writers have adopted a social constructionist perspective. McClurg Mueller argues that three major issues are addressed here:

> They argue, first, that the actor is socially located or 'embedded' in terms of group identities and is rooted in social networks, especially those based on nationality, race-ethnicity, class, gender, or religion; second, that social locations intersect and overlap in providing cultural materials that are drawn upon by a meaning-constructing actor who participates with others in interpreting a sense of grievances, resources and opportunities; and third, that a new model based on shared fate replaces the free-rider paradox as the central problematic to be explained (1992: 7; see Morris and McClurg Mueller, 1992, for a useful collection of essays representing this approach).

In stressing the social embeddedness of social actors and the role of interpersonal communication in interpreting grievances and constructing meanings, this new approach brings the analysis of social movements clearly into the domain of social psychology. In particular, the idea that the social construction of meaning is determined in part by group membership and identity resonates with recent theorizing in mainstream European social psychology into social representations and social identity (see Chapter 2). Melucci (1989) discusses the construction of a collective identity in social movements and the way in which group solidarity may act to blur the distinction between individual and group interests in a way which clearly echoes social identity theory (see Chapter 2), as does the idea of a subjective definition of the self which is linked to a shared social construct.

Unfortunately, these cross-discipline connections are rarely noted by these sociologically oriented writers (see Klandermans, 1989; 1992 for exceptions). This may be because, as Klandermans (1992) notes, scholars of social movements have tended to equate the discipline of social psychology with the study of relative deprivation which, allegedly, paints a disparaging picture of collective action as spontaneous, irrational outbursts by angry individuals. In fact, as we shall see in Chapter 2, social psychological theories have much to offer to the study of collective action. Before we turn to these theories, a brief consideration of methodology in the study of collective action is needed; this follows in the next section.

Methodology and the Study of Collective Action

The move towards a social constructionist approach to studying collective action also has methodological implications and, in particular, encourages the adoption of qualitative methods which are ideal for examining the ways in which meanings are socially constructed. Until quite recently, these qualitative methods have been seen as inappropriate for objective, scientific social psychological research, where theories and hypotheses have traditionally been tested in strict accordance with the canons of Popperian orthodoxy. The perception of social psychology as firmly wedded to positivist quantitative (particularly experimental) methods may be another reason for the lack of integration in the past between sociological and social psychological research into collective action.

However, qualitative methods are now gaining increasing respectability in social psychology (Banister, *et al.*, 1994; Henwood and Pidgeon, 1992; 1994) and there is a greater recognition that both qualitative and quantitative methods can be used to address complementary research questions. Together these methods provide the social sciences with a bifocal lens as they involve different 'ways of seeing' (Andrews, 1991).

Discussing this trend, Henwood and Pidgeon (1992) highlight a number of differences between qualitative and quantitative approaches. The qualitative approach is one where theory and empirical investigation are interwoven. Specifying theory a priori is resisted because of the possibility of introducing a premature closure on the issue to be investigated, as well as the possibility of the theoretical constructs departing from the views of research participants. In this sense, qualitative research 'is marked by a concern with the discovery of theory rather than the verification of theory' (Filstead, 1979: 38). By contrast, the traditional model of quantitative research is one where theories and concepts are the starting-point for investigations, which are then operationalized in order to verify their validity. Having said this, however, the sharp distinction drawn here has been questioned by some commentators, who have suggested that even in traditional experimental studies, theoretical reasoning often occurs towards the end of the research process (Cicourel, 1982) and that such work is often more exploratory and unpredictable in outcome than its description by the advocates of qualitative research implies.

However, in general terms, qualitative methods have tended to be viewed essentially as a preparatory stage of a research project for developing hunches and hypotheses. Such a view treats qualitative research as a second-rate activity by implying that such data cannot stand in its own right and needs to be verified by more rigorous experimental testing. The proponents of qualitative research by contrast see it as an end in itself, in particular because of its capacity to reflect participants' own meanings and interpretations.

A fundamental characteristic of qualitative research is its commitment to viewing actions and events from the perspective of the people who are studied (Blumer, 1969). So by contrast with quantitative methods, where contact with those being studied is fairly fleeting or non-existent, contact with participants in qualitative research is much more sustained. The researcher has to foster some sort of relationship with the respondent and be able to empathize (although not necessarily sympathize) with those being studied, in order to penetrate the frames of reference with which they are operating (see della Porta, 1992; Esseveld and Eyerman, 1992; Kriesi, 1992 for discussion of the issues which this raises in the context of studying collective action). There is a need to get close to the people being investigated, to be an insider, as opposed to the more traditional stance of detached observer. The loss of detachment associated with qualitative research methods is incongruent with the image of the impartial scientist which many quantitative researchers espouse. Discussing the relationship between researcher and researched in in-depth interviewing, Andrews (1991) argues that establishing rapport should not be regarded as a potential source of bias, but as a resource which may enhance the quality of the interview by aiding mutual comprehension (see also Griffin, 1989; Marshall, 1986).

Discussing the expansion of qualitative methods in the study of collective action specifically, Diani and Eyerman (1992a) review a range of different techniques, some more established – participant observation, in-depth interviewing, life histories and the analysis of written documents – and others more innovative – the use of archival sources and of group interviews. These researchers argue that underlying the development of these new techniques has been a questioning of the traditional assumption in social scientific research that action and beliefs can be held distinct and that the latter are a precondition of, and have considerable influence over, the former. This has opened up new research possibilities since, as they put it, 'Viewing values or beliefs as constitutive of action, rather than its precondition, allows one to see action as a social construction' (p. 15). Consequently, more attention has been paid to the qualitative study of culture, meaning and identity processes (see Donati, 1992; Diani and Eyerman, 1992b, for a collection of essays concerning issues involved in studying collective action).

Can qualitative methods and quantitative methods be successfully combined? One view on this issue is to maintain that these approaches constitute different epistemological positions and therefore that they represent incompatible views about the way in which social reality ought to be studied, such as Melucci, 1992. Others feel that some qualitative methods *can* be combined usefully with quantitative methods within a single project to provide a more complete account of the phenomenon under investigation. Diani and Eyerman (1992a) conclude their review by arguing that despite the criticisms which have been made of traditional quantitative survey techniques, no other approach would be able to address certain research questions, such as the relationship between public opinion and social movements.

In the present research, we have employed a combination of questionnaires, where the data is both quantitative and qualitative, as well as in-depth interviews. Both of these types of data are seen as equally important and the combination allows us to both draw some general conclusions about relationships between attitudes, identities and action based on social psychological theories, as well as gaining the insight which comes from qualitative accounts of personal experiences and life-histories. By doing in-depth interviews with our participants, we had the opportunity to be more explorative in our research approach; it enabled us to follow up on topics of personal importance to our interviewees and to deal with issues that were of a sensitive nature, such as personal crises and childhood experiences. It also led us to reflect on the multitude of interlinked events, life histories and personal circumstances that lead to individual involvement in collective action.

In the next chapter, we provide an overview of those theoretical approaches in mainstream social psychology which, in our opinion, have the most relevance to the study of collective action. These are divided into those approaches which focus on aspects of individual personality and cognitive processing and those which focus on group processes. In Chapter 3, a number of these approaches are put to empirical test using the quantitative data derived from questionnaire surveys in both trade union and gender contexts. This data allows us to examine patterns of association between attitudes and action but cannot address questions of cause and effect. This issue is clearly important in this context since involvement in collective action is likely to be both cause and consequence of certain attitudes. The subsequent three chapters are based mainly on qualitative data concerning involvement in women's groups and address the questions of what leads people to involvement in action, how they feel they have been affected by involvement and why others choose not to get involved. Here we can see whether or not the issues which are the subject of social psychological theory emerge in people's own accounts of involvement and how they are combined in individual life stories. We start then in Chapter 2 with a review of social psychological theory which indicates our own theoretical position.

Chapter 2

Social Psychological Approaches to Collective Action

Theoretical approaches to collective action are many and varied. Part of the reason for the heterogeneity derives from the different definitions of collective action which have been adopted. For many social scientists, the term *collective action* encompasses an incredibly broad range of empirical phenomena – 'from raising an army to raising a barn' (Marwell and Oliver, 1993: 1) – whose common elements, these authors suggest, are mutual interests and the possibility of benefits from coordinated action. For those interested specifically in a political context, the term refers to a type of political action which consists principally of 'working through organised or informal groups ... to raise an issue' (Parry, Moyser and Day, 1992: 52).

In the present research, we adopt a more social psychological definition of collective action: 'A group member engages in collective action anytime that he or she is acting as a representative of the group and the action is directed at improving the conditions of the entire group' (Wright, Taylor and Moghaddam, 1990: 995). Even with this very specific definition, there are a number of different social psychological theories on which we can draw in trying to understand individual participation in collective action.

The explanations which have been put forward to address the issue of individual participation may be divided into two types according to the level of analysis adopted. First, there are those explanations which focus on an individual level. These theories describe either individual personality characteristics or individual decision-making processes which lead particular people to get involved in action. By contrast are those theories pitched at a group level of analysis which describe features of the intergroup context and perceptions of that context which promote or inhibit participation in collective action.

This theoretical review chapter will be organized around this key distinction. Of course a full understanding of any particular instance of collective action will in all probability involve both individual and group elements and we would not seek to argue that any one approach provides the *right* answer to the question. However, we would wish to prioritize those group-level explanations which acknowledge the social context of collective action for reasons which we hope will become apparent. We will therefore give more attention to group-level approaches. Within each section, the order in which particular approaches are discussed is necessarily somewhat arbitrary. It is impossible to identify the beginning of the psychological process which leads people to involvement in action, and the elements which we will discuss are often closely related.

We will start with a brief account of three aspects of individual personality which have been considered important in determining participation in collective action. Each will be discussed before making some general comments about the value of a personality approach in this context.

Individual Characteristics

Locus of Control

Locus of control is a generalized expectancy operating over a variety of situations which relates to an individual's beliefs that his or her own actions will be effective in obtaining desired goals (Rotter, 1966). Individuals are said to have an internal locus of control when events are perceived as being a consequence of one's own actions and therefore under personal control. Conversely, individuals with an external locus of control tend to interpret events as being unrelated to personal efforts and beyond personal control. Mirels (1970) argues that the internal–external scale is actually two-dimensional, comprising first, the conviction that one has a command of one's own life (personal control); and second, the conviction that an individual has influence on socio-political institutions (control ideology).

In 1962 Rotter, Seeman and Liverant suggested studying the relationship between internal–external control and socio-political action-taking. They reasoned that 'internals' were more likely to get involved in action-taking than 'externals' because they believe that they can guide events by their own behaviour. Confirming this hypothesis, Gore and Rotter (1963) found in a study of black students from a Southern state in the US that internals were more willing to act on behalf of the civil rights movement and to take part in extreme forms of action.

Twenty years later, Klandermans (1983) reviewed 31 studies which tested this relationship, many of which incorporated Mirel's two factors of control. He found that the results of these studies were rather inconclusive. In some studies it was found that internals participate more than externals, but in others the reverse situation applied and in the majority of studies, no relationship at all was found.

In order to account for these inconsistencies, Klandermans argues that in addition to predicting the greater involvement of internals as formulated by Rotter – the 'efficacy hypothesis' – one can also propose the opposite hypothesis under certain circumstances, i.e. greater involvement by externals – the 'power-formation hypothesis'. Greater participation here may be seen as a way of *gaining* power and control on the part of those individuals who currently feel that they are lacking in these things. It is argued that the power-formation hypothesis will hold true for people who are convinced on objective or ideological grounds that individuals are powerless and the efficacy hypothesis will hold true for people who do not have that conviction. Thus, predicting the relationship between locus of control and action-taking is only possible with a knowledge of an individual's objective social location, such as members of underprivileged or discriminated groups, their ideological orientation and their expectations that participation will or will not be empowering. This is a much more complex view of the role of locus of control which starts to integrate elements of individual decision-making models.

Political Efficacy

Closely related to locus of control is the notion of political efficacy, which is the feeling that the individual can have an impact on the political process. This construct has been incorporated more commonly than locus of control by researchers interested in political participation and with rather more success (see for example, Campbell, Gurin and Miller, 1954).

To begin with, studies have found some clear social and demographic differences in people's sense of political efficacy. For example, both age and level of formal education are positively associated with efficacy and there is some evidence that women have somewhat less efficacious outlooks than men (see Beckwith, 1986 for discussion). Reviewing differences in levels of political efficacy found between the members of different social groups, Parry, *et al.* comment that it is not surprising 'that a *sense* of powerlessness in the political realm goes with being young, female, working class, uneducated, poor and organisationally isolated. These would appear to be the circumstances of *actual* powerlessness' (1992: 176).

Turning to the relationship between political efficacy and participation, there is a fairly large body of evidence to show that people who feel efficacious do indeed participate at a higher level than those who lack such feelings, although Parry, *et al.* found that about half of the relationship amongst their respondents was not so much the product of outlook as of associated background characteristics (for example, education) and group resources. The key aspect of political efficacy which emerged as important in this study was confidence in one's own abilities to exert influence (see also Berkowitz, 1972; Hamilton, *et al.*, 1987; Locatelli and Holt, 1986; Tyler and McGraw, 1983).

One particular context which has attracted research attention into the role of political efficacy is that of anti-nuclear campaigning. This research has suggested that, '[t]he anti-nuclear activist believes that nuclear war is preventable, not inevitable, and that individuals working together can influence government policy to decrease the chance of nuclear war' (Fiske, 1987: 213).

Similarly, Wolf, Gregory and Stephan (1986) argue that the anti-nuclear activist is motivated by a sense of personal political capability combined with a belief in the efficacy of political action. Although activists believe that governments create the risk of nuclear war, they also believe that individuals can and should be responsible for preventing it. Moreover, Milbrath and Goel (1977) found that anti-nuclear activists also tend to participate in other forms of political activity as well, suggesting that their anti-nuclear activity is not a special case but is linked to a broader sense of control in the political arena.

However, the evidence is not entirely consistent. Thus, for example, Schofield and Pavelchak (1989) found that a television film about nuclear war led to a *reduction* in levels of efficacy but an *increase* in intentions to participate in anti-nuclear behaviours. The film appeared to be able to both depress and motivate, perhaps driving home the importance of taking action to prevent a nuclear holocaust, while at the same time suggesting that such action would not necessarily be effective. Tyler and McGraw (1983) found that anti-nuclear activist behaviour was unrelated to judgments about the effectiveness of past political behaviour and suggested instead that activist behaviour is related to a sense of moral responsibility. It was more important that citizens believed that they had an *obligation* to prevent war, and rather less important that they felt they could actually do so. Fox and Schofield (1989) found that efficacy did not have an impact in regression analyses predicting anti-nuclear behavioural intentions. Instead, these were predicted by prior anti-nuclear activity, gender, attitudes towards disarmament and the salience of the issue to the individual.

Some have suggested that the importance of efficacy will vary as a function of the type of behaviour in question. For example, Milbrath and Goel (1977) suggest that efficacy may be more important when considering more demand-ing forms of action, such as political campaigning, community involvement and protest activities (see also Klandermans, 1989). Indeed, the finding that protestors, i.e. those involved in unconventional types of activity, score above average on efficacy casts some doubt on the view that unconventional forms of protest stem from a feeling of powerlessness and dissatisfaction with conven-tional political channels (see Barnes, *et al.*, 1979; Parry, *et al.*, 1992 for discussion).

Finally, some have criticized the way in which perceived control has traditionally been viewed as a property of *individuals*. For example, Andrews argues that:

If one believes, as socialists do, that through collective action, individ-uals can contribute to social and political outcomes, then one might experience a strong sense of control over one's environment, not as an isolated individual, but as a member of an organization (1991: 32).

She argues that a sense of control may derive from understanding the dynamics of power relationships within a society and reasons for oppression, rather than reflecting a position of dominance or advantage. Thus, feelings of efficacy and control may be better understood as associated with membership in – and feelings of identification with – social and political groups, rather than viewed as individual personality characteristics.

Individualist–collectivist Orientation

The final individual characteristic to be discussed is a more recently developed construct, namely individualist–collectivist orientation. While this orientation may be alternatively conceived as a cultural value or a constellation of attitudes (see Chapter 1), it has been recently proposed as an aspect of personality.

An important development in the study of this dimension was Hofstede's (1980) cross-cultural research on work experience, which allowed him to classify countries on the dimension of individualism–collectivism (amongst others), defined as the extent to which one's identity is characterized by personal choices, goals and achievements or by the nature of the groups of which one is a member (see Chapter 1). Smith and Bond (1993) point out that although using culture to explain behaviour can be tautologous (because a culture may be defined in the first place on the basis of the beliefs and actions of its members), it may be possible to claim that a specific value, such as individualism, explains some aspect of social behaviour (see also Rohner, 1984). In this spirit, a number of researchers have examined links between cultural values and aspects of social behaviour, such as cooperation, competition and the subordination of personal goals to group goals.

Since individuals within a given culture will vary in their endorsement of individualism and collectivism, individual-level measures have been developed to set alongside culture-level characterizations such as that provided by Hofstede. Triandis, *et al.* (1988) propose that in order to avoid confusion between these different levels of analysis, we should use different terms, namely *individualism–collectivism* at a cultural level and *idiocentric–allocentric* at an individual level. Similarly, Markus and Kitayama (1991) use the terms *independent* and *interdependent* to refer to people who endorse individualist and collectivist cultural values respectively.

To measure these orientations, Hui (1988) has developed a measure known as the INDCOL scale, where allocentrism/interdependence is related to values such as cooperation, equality and honesty, whereas idiocentrism/independence is related to values such as need for achievement, competition and social recognition. Items measuring these orientations range over cooperation, for example, 'There is everything to gain and nothing to lose for classmates to group themselves for study and discussion'; intragroup consensus, for example, 'My good friends and I agree on the best places to shop'; helping, for example, 'I would help, within my means, if a relative told me that he/she is in financial difficulty'; and the pursuit of personal goals, for example, 'When I am among my colleagues/classmates, I do my own thing without minding about them'. Hui and Villareal (1989) argue that people differing in these orientations are clearly distinguishable in their psychological needs, such that allocentric/ interdependent people have strong needs for affiliation and nurturance, whereas idiocentric/independent people have strong needs for autonomy and social recognition. Triandis, *et al.* (1985) have attested to the construct validity of the scale and examined correlations between INDCOL and other personality scales, such as locus of control and achievement motivation.

Turning to the possible link between these orientations and participation in collective action, Smith and Bond (1993) make the point that *at a cultural level* we cannot assume that collective solutions are always chosen in collectivist societies (nor vice versa). However, one of the features of a collectivist society, according to Triandis, *et al.* (1988) amongst others, is that groups are less easy to leave so that a group solution may be the only way to improve individual status in such a culture. Moreover, the close association purported to exist between personal goals and group goals, and the overwhelming contribution of the group to identity in a collectivist society, also suggest that collective solutions should be more likely in this context than in an individualist society.

At an individual level, there is very little research which directly examines the link between orientation and action, although a number of indirectly related findings are consistent with the idea that allocentric/interdependent people are more likely to get involved. For example, from Smith and Bond's (1993) review of research findings, a picture emerges that such people tend to favour other members of their own group more strongly and treat them more equally, to emphasize ingroup harmony and sharing of resources, to emphasize group over personal goals and to be more susceptible to social influence. All of these factors suggest that they are more likely to get involved in collective action.

Relatedly, Hinkle and Brown (1990) argue that a tendency to favour the ingroup over the outgroup is more prevalent in group contexts characterized first, by a *collectivist orientation*, (i.e. stressing intragroup cooperation, collective achievement and interdependence among fellow ingroup members); and second, by a *comparative or relational ideology*, (i.e. where ingroup evaluation is achieved by social comparison with other groups). In this research, items measuring individualist–collectivist orientation were derived from Triandis, *et al.*'s (1988) scale which focuses on small group processes and cooperation, for example, 'I work best in a group', 'If the group is slowing me down, it is better to leave it and work alone'. In an empirical study, Hinkle, Brown and Ely, (1990) confirm that the link between identification with the ingroup and discrimination against the outgroup is strongest amongst subjects characterized by a collectivist, comparative/relational orientation. All of these findings are consistent with the idea – which also makes intuitive sense – that individuals characterized by a collectivist orientation will be more likely to get involved in collective action.

To sum up, the dimension of individualist–collectivist orientation has attracted much research interest recently but the way in which this construct has been defined and measured has varied considerably across studies. There is also a lack of direct evidence concerning its relationship with participation in collective action at an individual level and therefore more research is needed before conclusions on this issue can be drawn.

In concluding this section on individual personality characteristics, we can say that the linkages between characteristics, such as locus of control, efficacy and individualist–collectivist orientation on the one hand and participation in collective action on the other are not straightforward. The evidence in the former two cases is very mixed and while efforts have been made to reconcile the findings by arguing that relationships will vary according to the individual's social location, beliefs and the action under consideration, the result is that the explanatory power of these variables is considerably reduced. In the latter case, there is very little empirical evidence on which to draw. As with other research in the personality sphere, we can conclude that while individual characteristics have a broad generalized influence on behaviour in a number of different contexts, the value of these factors in predicting participation in any specific instance of collective action is limited (see Ajzen, 1988). In order to fulfil this latter goal, we would need more detailed information about the individual's attitudes towards that specific action and context. This leads us on to models of individual decision-making.

Individual Decision-making

Foremost amongst social psychological models of individual decision-making are expectancy-value models, which have been applied successfully in a number of different contexts (for example, Feather, 1982). Generally stated, expectancy-value models are characterized by the guiding notion that a person's orientation towards a particular course of action is influenced by a) the person's belief that the action will lead to a particular outcome; and b) the person's evaluation of that outcome. In this section, two bodies of research will be discussed both of which are based on the expectancy-value model: First, research conducted around the theories of reasoned action and planned behaviour, which have relevance to many different areas of social behaviour; and second, Klandermans' expectancy-value model of individual participation in collective action. A review of each will be followed by a general critique.

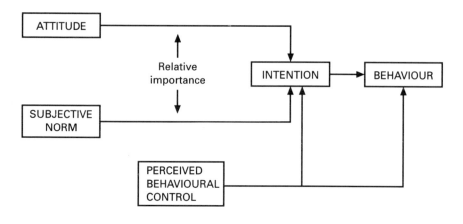

Figure 2.1: The theory of planned behaviour

The Theories of Reasoned Action and Planned Behaviour

One of the most influential examples of an expectancy-value approach in social psychology has been Ajzen and Fishbein's (1980) theory of reasoned action, and its successor, the theory of planned behaviour (Ajzen and Madden, 1986), which concern the relationship between attitudes and behaviour (see also Ajzen and Fishbein, 1977). In both cases, the immediate precursor of behaviour is intention, whose determinants in turn comprise attitudinal and normative factors. It is proposed that attitudinal and normative factors are derived from the summed products of beliefs about the outcomes of performing that behaviour and evaulations of those outcomes. In the theory of planned behaviour, a further factor is also incorporated, namely perceived behavioural control, which feeds into intention and directly into behaviour (see Figure 2.1).

Here, the attitudinal component comprises personal beliefs about the possible positive or negative outcomes of performing the behaviour and evaluation of those beliefs. Importantly, the focus is not a generalized attitude towards a *general* behaviour, such as helping others, but concerns a particular behavioural act, such as doing the shopping for a neighbour at a specified time. Normative beliefs refer to social pressures to perform or not perform that behaviour, together with the motivation to comply. Generally, attitudinal and normative factors are assumed jointly to determine behavioural intention, although the relative importance of these factors will vary according to the context and the individual. Reviewing this evidence, Ajzen (1988) found that, in general, attitudinal factors are somewhat more important, except in relation to some very personal behaviours, such as decisions to have an abortion, where normative factors are stronger predictors of intention than are attitudinal factors.

Even where very precise and specific measures of attitudinal and normative components are obtained, their ability to predict intention or behaviour is likely to be less than perfect because the conditions which facilitate or make the behaviour possible are also important. The incorporation of behavioural control into the theory of planned behaviour is a way of taking into account some of the realistic constraints that may prevent performance of a behaviour which is otherwise well supported by attitudinal, normative and intentional factors. A behaviour is said to be completely under a person's control if the person can decide at will to perform it or not to perform it. The more a behaviour is contingent on internal or external resources, the less the behaviour is said to be under volitional control. The most extreme case of behaviour not under a person's control is provided by addictive behaviours, such as smoking, where a person's best intentions to give up the habit may not be realized. Most behaviours fall between the two extremes of control.

In his review of the control factors which may intervene between intention and behaviour, Ajzen (1988) distinguishes two types. The first refers to internal factors, such as an individual's skills, abilities and knowledge; and the second refers to external factors, such as time, opportunity and dependence on others. Although Ajzen concedes that it may be difficult to assess *actual* control prior to behaviour, the theory of planned behaviour asserts that *perceived* behavioural control can be measured, i.e. the person's beliefs about how easy or difficult performance of the behaviour is likely to be. This perception will be based on past experiences as well as on anticipated impediments and obstacles.

Ajzen and Madden (1986) propose two versions of the theory of planned behaviour. The first version indicates that the effect of perceived behavioural control is completely mediated by behavioural intention and that intention is the immediate antecedent of behaviour. The second version indicates a direct effect from perceived behavioural control to behaviour, as well as an effect via behavioural intention. The direct effect of perceived behavioural control is expected only when the behaviour is not under the individual's complete volitional control, such as in the case of addictive behaviours, and only when the individual's perception of behavioural control accurately reflects the actual control the individual has over performance of the behaviour.

By incorporating control-related variables, the theory of planned behaviour expands the boundary conditions of the theory of reasoned action. It is hypothesized that the inclusion of the control-related variables should result in more accurate prediction of behaviour under conditions of imperfect control. If, however, the behaviour is under complete volitional control, then the theory of reasoned action should be adequate in predicting behaviour. Confirming their hypothesis, Ajzen and Madden (1986) found that the incorporation of the behavioural control component allowed for a more accurate prediction of behaviour in a study of students' class attendance and course achievement compared with the theory of reasoned action. The perception of practical impediments, such as transport problems getting to lectures, stood in the way of behaviour which was well supported by attitudinal and normative factors. Further studies have also indicated that the effects of behavioural control are most vivid when attempting behaviours which present some problems with respect to control (see for example Kimiecik, 1992; Madden, Ellen and Ajzen, 1992; Netemeyer and Burton, 1990; Netemeyer, Burton and Johnston, 1991).

In sum, it is argued that people intend to perform a behaviour if their personal evaluations of it are favourable, if they think that important others would approve of it and if they believe that the requisite resources and opportunities will be available.

In further theoretical developments, a number of factors have been suggested as moderators of the attitude–behaviour relationship (see Ajzen, 1988 for a review). One such factor is personal involvement, where it has been argued that people with a strong vested interest in a behaviour are more likely to act on their attitudes than people with little vested interest in the behaviour (see Regan and Fazio, 1977; Sivacek and Crano, 1982). Another example is the level of effort required to perform a behaviour. In an experiment manipulating students' access to reading material, Bagozzi, Yi and Baumgartner (1990) found that when behaviour required substantial effort, the mediating role of intentions was strong and attitudes only had indirect effects on behaviour consistent with the theory of reasoned action. Conversely, when the behaviour required little effort, attitudes had a more significant effect on behaviour and the mediating role of intentions was reduced. In addition, Bagozzi and Yi (1989) found that the degree to which intentions are well-formed affects relationships with behaviour. Their findings indicate that when intentions are well-formed, they completely mediate the effects of attitudes on behaviour, in keeping with the theory of reasoned action. However, when intentions are only poorly formed, their mediating role is reduced and, in this situation, attitudes have a direct effect on behaviour.

In addition, many researchers have pointed out the need to consider past experience as an important predictive element of a person's behaviour. For example, Bagozzi's (1981, 1982) studies on blood donation revealed that past behaviour tended to reduce the impact of intentions on behaviour. Similarly, Echebarria-Echabe, Rovira and Garate (1988) conducted a study aimed at predicting voting behaviour where past experience was measured by asking subjects if they had voted for one of these parties in previous elections. Predictive power was significantly improved when past experience was taken into account. They argue that where there is a long time gap between measurements of intention and behaviour, past experience will improve predictions of behaviour (see also Fazio and Zanna, 1981; Montano and Taplin, 1991).

Finally, there has been some recent debate regarding the role of identity in theoretical models of the attitude–behaviour relationship. Charng, Piliavin and

Callero (1988) suggest that repeated behaviours influence a person's self-concept, which then becomes an important factor in itself, so that carrying out behaviours consonant with this identity 'conveys meaning over and above the positive or negative attitudes we may hold toward performing the behaviour itself' (p. 304). In their study into blood donation, they found evidence to suggest that role identity as a blood donor influenced intentions to donate blood independently of attitudes, where role identity is defined as, 'a set of characteristics or expectations that simultaneously is defined by a social position in the community and becomes a dimension of an actor's self' (p. 304). Their study also suggested that the salience of this identity increases with increments in the frequency of blood donation.

Further evidence comes from a study by Biddle, Bank and Slavings (1987) into students' decisions to stay in, or withdraw from educational courses. Again, findings suggested that identity, or 'self-referent identity labelling', had an effect on behaviour which was independent of the effect of individual preferences. The authors argue for the role of identity as a generative force behind behaviour independent of attitudinal and normative factors. Finally, in the context of voting behaviour, Granberg and Holmberg (1990) investigated the impact of identity on intentions and behaviour. They found that amongst weak party identifiers, identity (as a Liberal, Conservative, etc.) exerted only an indirect effect on behaviour through intention, whereas for strong party identifiers, identity exerted a strong direct effect on behaviour. Indeed, amongst this latter group, identity proved the strongest predictor of voting behaviour.

Others have been more critical of the idea that identity has an independent impact on intentions and behaviour. Sparks and Shepherd (1992) argue that a person's identity should be reflected in their beliefs, values and attitudes and that it is unlikely that there is a causal link from identity to intentions which is independent of the effect of attitudes. Criticizing the methods used in previous studies of this link, they suggest that where independent effects are found, we should consider the possibility that attitudinal factors have been inadequately measured or that moral factors, which are embodied in identity, have not been tapped by attitudinal factors. However, the impact of their argument is reduced somewhat by the fact that in their own study of 'green' consumer behaviour, they also found support for the independent role of identity and concluded that the role of this factor merits further study.

To conclude here, the theories of reasoned action and planned behaviour have been tremendously influential in many areas of social psychological research. Broadly speaking, the main contribution of these approaches has been to direct researchers' attention to the principle that in order to accurately predict a specific intention to act – and a specific behaviour – one needs specific measures of attitudinal, normative and control factors. A more global measure of attitudes will allow a crude prediction of general behavioural tendencies – in much the same way offered by a knowledge of personal characteristics – but is less useful in trying to predict a specific act. We turn now to the application of the expectancy-value approach to the study of individual participation in collective action.

Klandermans' Expectancy-value Model

The most influential attempt to use an expectancy-value model specifically for the study of individual involvement in collective action has been undertaken by Klandermans (1984a; b; 1986a; b). His work has been aimed mainly, though not exclusively, at the attempt to understand participation in trade union action. His model has two components: A theory of consensus mobilization and a theory of action mobilization.

Consensus mobilization is the process by which a union familiarizes its members with the objectives of intended action and tries to win their support for those objectives. This process is necessary but not sufficient for action to occur because rational workers will think not only about the desirability of a given objective but also about the costs and benefits of achieving it. Hence the need for action mobilization in which the union tries to persuade its members that the benefits of action will outweigh the costs and that they should participate. Klandermans describes three motives for participating in action: Goal motives, social motives and reward motives. In each case, expectancies are multiplied by values (see Figure 2.2).

Here the connections with Ajzen and Fishbein's theory of reasoned action become clear. Mapping directly onto the normative component of that theory, Klandermans proposes social motives, which are the expected reactions of significant others to involvement, multiplied by the value assigned to those reactions. The attitudinal component from the theory of reasoned action is broken down here into reward motives and goal motives. Reward motives concern the worker's assessment of the personal costs and benefits of action (for example, in terms of time and money) multiplied by their value. Finally, under the heading of goal motives, Klandermans argues that workers must believe the following in order to participate: That a high level of worker participation is necessary for the success of the proposed action; that other workers will participate (i.e. that any costs of participation will be spread over a large number of workers); and that the action will lead to the achievement of the objective. Again, expectations are multiplied by the value of the intended goal.

The individual's willingness to take part in collective action is a *weighted sum* of these three motives, weighted because the three motives can take different weights for different individuals and can also compensate for one another. One worker may have strong goal motives and weak social and reward motives, whereas another may have the opposite pattern of motives. In addition, the weights of the different motives may vary with the type of action. In particular, Klandermans suggests that calculations of effectiveness will be most important for relatively costly forms of action, such as strike participation.

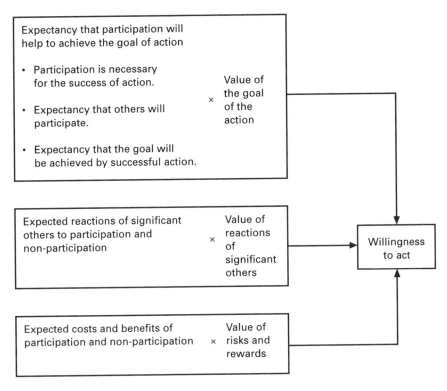

Figure 2.2: Klandermans' expectancy-value model of participation. Taken from: Kelly, J. and Kelly, C. (1992) Industrial action. In Hartley, J.F. and Stephenson, G.M. (Eds) *Employment Relations: The Psychology of Influence and Control at Work*, Oxford: Blackwell, pp. 246–68 (Figure 11.1).

In his words, 'success expectations will be more important if participation demands more of people' (1989: 121). This relates to a point made earlier in the discussion of political efficacy, where it was similarly suggested that the perceived effectiveness of action-taking is more important when considering more demanding forms of action.

A number of pieces of evidence may be cited in support of the expectancy-value approach in this trade union context. For example, Brett and Goldberg (1979) found a positive correlation between miners' perceptions of the effectiveness of strikes (goal motives) and the incidence of pit level strike activity (see Kelly and Kelly 1992 for further examples). More important are those few studies which have sought to provide a comprehensive test of all the elements of Klandermans' model.

Klandermans himself has conducted a number of studies in which the expectancy-value model is applied in the context of strike participation. He reports on three studies of Dutch trade union campaigns in the late 1970s and early 1980s over work reorganization, manning agreements and the shorter working week. He found that interplant variations in willingness to participate in strikes were closely correlated with differences in all three motives and reported that between 40 per cent and 60 per cent of the variance between plants and overtime in willingness to participate could be accounted for by the expectancy-value approach (see Klandermans, 1984a; 1986b). Those who were willing to participate were more optimistic about the numbers who would take part, about the positive reactions of fellow workers, about the likely personal costs and about the probability of the action achieving its objective. He also reports that goal motives were the most important predictors of participation and, in particular, the expectation that one's own participation in union meetings would make a difference to the outcome.

Klandermans also raises an interesting issue about the relationship between moderate and more militant forms of action (for example, one-day strikes versus indefinite strikes). Conventional wisdom has it that the more militant the action, the more difficult it is to mobilize people. However, Klandermans found that while militant action was indeed seen as more costly, it was also seen as more effective and so it may actually be easier to mobilize people behind a more costly but effective tactic than one which is seen as less costly but less effective.

Further evidence in support of an expectancy-value approach was found by Flood (1993), who confirms that goal motives accounted for between 26 per cent and 35 per cent of willingness to attend a union general meeting. However he also found, contrary to Klandermans' theory, that a *pessimistic* estimate of the likelihood of others participating in meetings was associated with increased participation amongst union activists. Similarly, Oliver (1984) argues that participation is often determined by the sentiment, 'If you don't do it, nobody else will'. In her study of participation in neighbourhood collective action, she found that active individuals were more *pessimistic* about their neighbours' willingness to make active contributions. These findings contrast with Klandermans' suggestion that people with a high willingness to act are optimistic about the chances of achieving their goals.

In their discussion of this approach, Kelly and Kelly (1992) put forward three criticisms of the expectancy-value model of industrial action. The first point is that in many studies in this area, researchers use *current* measures of cost–benefit calculations to explain *past* behaviour. In this case, explanations for participation which are consistent with the expectancy-value model may in fact be *rationalizations* for behaviour after the event rather than rational reflections which precede decisions. Thus, evidence from Hartley, Kelly and Nicholson (1983) concerning the 1980 steel strike in Britain showed that strikers would often decide on actions and then justify them by retrospectively criticizing the other options.

Second, there is some evidence which suggests that consensus mobilization may be sufficient to generate action. For example, Turnbull, Woolfson and Kelly (1991) report that during a meeting of shop stewards to discuss industrial action, one worker declared that if he did not strike to protect jobs he would feel ashamed: 'I wouldn't be able to live with myself, I wouldn't be able to look my kids in the face'. Similar moral defences for strike action are reported in other case studies (Beynon, 1984; Fantasia, 1988; Gouldner, 1954; Woolfson and Foster, 1988). In these cases it appears, contrary to the expectancy-value approach, that decisions were not based on individual calculations of costs and benefits but on an overriding belief in the justness of the cause.

Third, it seems that once consensus mobilization has succeeded and workers believe in the justness of their demands, they may become insensitive to personal costs and simply accept that collective action involves sacrifices. Woolfson and Foster (1988) report one striker as saying, 'I'm here as long as it takes – suppose it be another nine weeks or another nine months, I'll still be here' (p. 164). The assumption of individual rationality is tested to the limits in the cases of long-drawn-out strike action such as the 1984–85 British miners' strike (see Winterton and Winterton, 1989), where many individual strikers suffered acute financial hardship as well as sustained criticism in the media and propaganda about the impossibility of victory. It is hard adequately to account for their continued commitment to the action on the basis of individual calculations of costs and benefits. A similar point is made by Hirsch (1990) who argues that increased costs do not always result in decreased participation; protesters often respond to threats and repression by developing a greater willingness to ignore personal costs in favour of the collective goal. He concludes that even the most sophisticated rational choice models cannot account for group solidarity because they neglect the role of group processes, such as consciousness-raising and collective empowerment which together create a sense of group identification.

This last point raises a fundamental criticism of Klandermans' model of participation in industrial action and expectancy-value models in general, which is their emphasis on individual decision-making processes and neglect of social processes. Schrager argues that Klandermans' approach is insensitive to the way that attitudes develop in interaction with people and in the course of historical experience. As she puts it, '[c]ollective action is more than the sum of economistic calculations; social and ideological factors figure powerfully in people's willingness to act' (1985: 859). In particular, she argues that the low salience of collective goals in the particular campaign studied by Klandermans (1984b) led participants to adopt a more calculative approach than they might have done had they been more strongly moved (but see Klandermans, 1985).

Of course one way of dealing with the importance of social factors is to build them into the social motives component of the expectancy-value model. Any number of new variables can be added in and weighted with the benefit of hindsight but the explanatory power of the model is reduced as it becomes more and more unwieldy. Giving due importance to the significance of social factors involves a shift in the level of analysis away from individual decision-making processes to the group level of analysis and this requires a wholly different theoretical approach to collective action.

Indeed, in a more social formulation of his theory, Klandermans emphasizes the social construction of protest behaviour: 'Grievances and success expectations are not objective entities. Grievances must be interpreted. People must be convinced that the resources they provide can be employed effectively' (1989: 121–2; see also Klandermans, 1992). This analysis raises important questions about the way in which the meanings of actions are socially constructed in interaction with others. In situations of collective action, meanings will be constantly negotiated by the parties involved in formal and informal settings. As Klandermans acknowledges, one important factor in this negotiation of meaning is social categorization. Social identification with a relevant category makes people susceptible to social influence processes (Kelly, 1993) and makes it possible for people to develop a sense of group discontent. In Klandermans' (1989) words, 'social categorization points to the socially constructed reality protest behaviour is embedded in' (p. 122). It is to this group level of analysis that we now turn.

Group Processes

Group Membership and Self-stereotyping

The approaches which have been discussed so far locate the psychological origins of action in individual processes of personality and cognition. However, central to recent theorizing in social psychology is the distinction which can be made between personal and social identity. In other words, an important part of our sense of self derives from the groups and categories to which we belong and these group memberships will influence behaviour just as much as will individual personality characteristics or cognitive processes. This distinction between personal and social identity is central to social identity theory and self-categorization theory. It is argued that personal and social identity can be located on a continuum and that it is rarely the case that one is functioning to the complete exclusion of the other.

Research has been conducted into the determinants of group salience, where a salient group membership is defined as,

> one which is *functioning psychologically* to increase the influence of one's membership in that group on perception and behaviour, and/or the influence of another person's identity as a group member on one's impression of and hence behaviour towards that person (Oakes, 1987: 118, emphasis in original).

Building on Bruner's (1957) ideas, it is argued that a categorization will become salient where it has a high degree of accessibility and fits observed similarities and differences between individuals or their actions in a direction which is consistent with the normative content of the categorization. Turner, *et al.* argue that one consequence of a salient social identity is depersonalization, or 'self-stereotyping', whereby 'people come to perceive themselves more as the interchangeable exemplars of a social category than as unique personalities defined by their individual differences from others' (1987: 50). Depersonalization represents a *change* from personal to social identity and may be seen as representing a *gain* in identity, since it is a mechanism 'whereby individuals may act in terms of the social similarities and differences produced by the historical development of human society and culture' (p. 51). This stands in contrast to some previous theorizing which represented situations of depersonalization as a *loss* in identity (see Zimbardo, 1969).

It is further argued that depersonalization is the basic process underlying group processes, such as collective action and social influence. Depersonalization would be expected to promote participation in collective action by making self-esteem more dependent on social comparison and social identity; by increasing ingroup cohesion and intergroup differentiation; by facilitating social influence processes within the group; and by promoting perceived commonality of interests with fellow ingroup members, thereby promoting intragroup cooperation. In relation to this latter point, perception of one's interests as interchangeable with other ingroup members is an important step on the road to collective as opposed to individual actions. As Turner, *et al.* argue, 'To the degree that the self is depersonalized, so too is self-interest' (1987: 65; see also Brewer and Schneider, 1990; Chase, 1992; Kramer and Brewer, 1984).

Evidence for depersonalization comes from a number of experimental studies. For example, Hogg and Turner (1987) found that under conditions in which sex-category membership was expected to be salient, subjects perceived themselves to be more typical of their sex and described themselves more closely in line with certain (positive) aspects of their situation-specific own-sex stereotype. Interestingly in this study, gender salience increased self-esteem for males but decreased self-esteem for females. In related research, Reicher (1984a) found that in experimental conditions which emphasized group membership, individuals expressed attitudes which were more in line with the stereotypical response of their group. Finally, Kelly (1989) found that in a situation where political group membership was made salient, both ingroups and outgroups were perceived as more homogeneous along group-relevant dimensions (see also Judd and Park, 1988; Mullen and Hu, 1989; Simon, 1992; Simon and Brown, 1987; Simon and Mummendey, 1990; Wilder, 1984).

The depersonalization hypothesis provides theoretical integration for research spanning a number of different aspects of group processes and allows the study of collective action to be explored in the broader context of social identity and social influence processes. In situations where the members of low status groups come together to challenge the status quo, their actions cannot be divorced from the intergroup context and their perceptions and understandings of that context.

Deindividuation and Crowd Behaviour

One area in which this theorizing has been applied is that of crowd behaviour. Thus, Reicher (1987) argues that crowd behaviour results from self-categorization and the internalization of stereotypical ingroup norms. In situations in which social identity is made salient – perhaps by the physical presence of other ingroup members in crowds – the result is collective behaviour, which both conforms to and is limited by the ingroup stereotype, thereby accounting for the homogeneity of behaviour in crowds.

Not only is there the experimental research discussed above to support this view, but Reicher has also conducted field studies of crowd and riot situations. In his research into the street disturbances in Bristol in 1980, observation and interview data suggested a clear pattern to events with strict limits as to what was deemed appropriate behaviour which is consistent with the idea of self-stereotyping (Reicher, 1984b). In addition, participants stressed the sense of collective purpose, the meaningfulness of crowd action and the solidarity and positive emotional feelings associated with group membership (see also Reicher, 1987; 1993; Reicher and Potter, 1985).

Reicher's emphasis on the rationality and shared meaning of crowd behaviour is very different from the traditional social psychological approach to crowd behaviour which can be traced back to the work of Le Bon (1895) and McDougall (1921) (see Foster, 1991 for a review). These early theorists paint a very unflattering portrait of the crowd which emphasizes the irrationality and unconscious processes underlying crowd action. The aspect of Le Bon's theorizing which attracted the most attention from social psychologists was the idea of submergence in the crowd which was equated with a *loss* of personal identity and referred to as *deindividuation*. This topic was subsequently taken up by Zimbardo, whose findings showed that individuals who were deindividuated showed higher levels of aggression (see, for example, Zimbardo, 1969). Translated to a crowd situation, it is argued that aggression in crowds is explained by deindividuation, whose antecedents are anonymity and the diffusion of responsibility. The irrationality of collective behaviour stressed in these accounts contrasts with the meaningfulness of crowd action emphasized by Reicher (and even more so with the rationality of the expectancy-value approach to collective action which has been discussed).

Despite methodological shortcomings of many of the experimental studies into deindividuation, the idea has had strong appeal within and beyond the psychology community. Zimbardo himself has recently used ideas of deindividuation to explain the violence and destruction in Los Angeles in 1992 following the unexpected acquittal of police officers involved in the videotaped beating of a black motorist. He argues that the background factors of poverty and racism are necessary but not sufficient explanatory factors and that what translates a sense of injustice into aggressive collective behaviour is a mental state of deindividuation, a feeling of 'no-one really knows who I am or cares' (Zimbardo, quoted in McDermott, 1993: 458).

Taking this one step further, the concept of deindividuation has been used to try to defend individuals accused of violent acts in crowds and this has attracted most attention in the context of a number of recent South African murder trials. With the introduction of the law of 'common purpose' in South Africa, defence built on a case that the defendant did not strike the fatal blows was insufficient since the law specified that the defendant need simply have been a willing party to the will of the crowd. Instead, defence lawyers turned to the argument that their client should not be punished for the action taken by members of the crowd because of diminished personal responsibility. This strategy paved the way for a social psychological account of the processes which operate in crowds and the effects on individual consciousness (see Colman, 1991).

However, use of the psychology of deindividuation in defence of individual actions sparked some debate which centred around problems with the concept of deindividuation itself and the political implications of using it as extenuating circumstances in particular contexts.

In relation to the former, Reicher and Potter (1985) draw attention to a number of problems with the traditional approach to crowds based on deindividuation (see also Reicher 1982; 1987). It is argued that assuming irrationality of crowd action neglects the meaning which the event may have for ingroup members and reflects the perspective of the outsider. Consequently, there is an overwhelming emphasis on the negativity of crowd events and an abstraction of crowd episodes from their intergroup context. It is suggested that this latter problem is comparable to shining a torch on a crowd of strikers so that only the crowd is visible (and not the police), making its actions seem inexplicable and irrational.

Underlying the debate about deindividuation is the question of the rationality or otherwise of crowd action. The deindividuation account stresses the irrationality of collective behaviour and conjures up images of the 'mindless mob.' Indeed, some have commented on the historical context in which Le Bon developed his idea of deindividuation when there was more interest in how to get rid of crowds than how to understand them (Holton, 1978; Reicher, 1987). In using the idea of deindividuation to extenuate the actions of individuals in crowds, to what extent must one deny the rational political motivation which might underlie their action? In this respect, Reicher argues that using the deindividuation card to defend individuals does raise some wider issues and problems. The whole idea of extenuation in this context is based on presenting collective action as irrational: 'not only have the individual accused been criminalised, but also the entire collectivity has been pathologised' (1991: 488).

Thus, while the successful deployment of the deindividuation principle may help in the defence of individuals, the unintended cost may be a discrediting of the collective action in general.

In considering this issue, a distinction should perhaps be made between the proximal and the distal determinants of collective behaviour. The proximal determinants concern those features of the immediate social environment in crowd situations which may lead people to extreme behaviour, whereas the distal conditions are those factors, such as deprivation and poverty, which bring people together in the first place. Approaches to crowd behaviour based on the idea of deindividuation neglect the wider meaning of actions for the individuals involved and the ways in which those actions may be expressions of social identity. We turn now to those more distal determinants of action which bring people to the collective arena in the first place.

Relative Deprivation Theory

The traditional starting-point for social psychological approaches to collective action is the individual's perception of inequality in either current or future intergroup status relations. This emphasis on perceived inequality is found most clearly in the study of relative deprivation. A number of attempts have been made to find empirical support for a direct link between feelings of deprivation, relative to other individuals or groups, and participation in protest activities (see Olson, Herman and Zanna, 1986; Walker and Pettigrew, 1984).

The concept of relative deprivation was originally proposed by Stouffer *et al.* in 1949 and was developed in a later study which examined the relationship between people's class, status and power positions and their feelings of deprivation (Runciman, 1966). Runciman proposes that a person is relatively deprived of some valued object when four necessary and taken together, sufficient, conditions are present: The person does not have it; the person sees other people as having it (which may include self in the past); the person wants it; and the person sees it as feasible that he or she should have it. Crosby (1976) suggests that the critical factor in relative deprivation is the feeling of entitlement and hypothesizes that people feel resentment only when they think that they deserve better outcomes. Similarly, Folger, Rosenfield and Robinson (1983) argue that feelings of resentment are produced by a combination of three factors: Outcomes are below the desired level with little hope of change in the foreseeable future; there is awareness of at least one instance of outcomes at the desired level being generated by contrasting circumstances or arrangements; and there is insufficient justification why actual outcomes are not as high as desired outcomes (see also Folger and Martin, 1986; Folger, *et al.* 1983).

An important distinction is made in this literature between *personal* relative deprivation, where the individual feels deprived relative to other individuals, and *collective* relative deprivation, where the individual feels that his or her group is deprived relative to other groups. This distinction maps onto that between personal and social identity. Walker and Pettigrew (1984) argue that these different levels of comparison have quite different behavioural consequences, namely that personal relative deprivation is associated with individual responses, whereas collective relative deprivation is associated with collective responses.

This difference results in part from the different causal attributions associated with personal as opposed to group disadvantage. For example, Appelgry and Niewoudt (1988) argue that personal relative deprivation is usually attributed to one's own limitations, the consequence of which is to motivate an individual towards individual efforts. If, however, the individual believes that other members of his or her group share this fate, then the probability of external attribution is greater. The problem then becomes a group problem which is improved only by improving the lot of the entire ingroup relative to the outgroup. Causal attributions are thus an integral part of the genesis of personal and collective deprivation. Consideration of the role of causal attribution will be taken up again in later discussion.

It is generally argued that since collective action involves a sense of group identification, the prime motivator of protest will be the perceived gap between *ingroup* and *outgroup* attainments – collective relative deprivation – and not the perceived gap between *personal* expectations and attainments. The idea is that people protest not so much when they are dissatisfied with their personal situation, as when they experience discontent as a result of a disadvantageous comparison between the ingroup and an outgroup. Research conducted in a number of different contexts has confirmed that it is the perception of collective relative deprivation which has the most impact on participation in collective action, although the relationships have not always been strong (see Abeles, 1976; Birt and Dion, 1987; Cook, Crosby and Hennigan, 1977; Dubé and Guimond, 1986; Guimond and Dubé-Simard, 1983; Vanneman and Pettigrew, 1972; Walker and Mann, 1987).

Another distinction made in this literature is between cognitive and affective components of relative deprivation (Cook, *et al.*, 1977). These researchers refer to these two components as the distinction between the magnitude (cognitive) and the intensity (affective) components of relative deprivation. The former refers to the *perception* of deprivation, whereas the latter involves the *value and emotional significance* of that perceived deprivation. In reviewing the literature, Cook, *et al.*, note that, 'a major difficulty in defining relative deprivation . . . is to know how intensity and magnitude should be related together' (1977: 309). For example, is the mere knowledge that the ingroup is deprived relative to the outgroup sufficient to account for collective action or is it necessary to assess individual feelings of discontent?

Recent researchers argue that perceptions of inequality alone do *not* necessarily produce intense feelings of dissatisfaction and that it is mainly those people who are unhappy or angry about perceived inequality who endorse militant acts, certainly doing so to a greater extent than those who merely acknowledge its existence. Birt and Dion (1987) found that affective collective relative deprivation was a better predictor of social outcomes than either cognitive or personal alternatives (see also Guimond and Dubé-Simard, 1983; Tougas and Veilleux, 1988; 1989). However, Petta and Walker (1992) argue that the four types of relative deprivation – personal, collective, cognitive, affective – are not independent, either conceptually or empirically, and that relative deprivation involves both the perception of inequality *and* the dissatisfaction associated with that perception.

It also seems likely that a perceived inequality will only arouse passion when the comparison dimension is highly valued or when the comparison directly involves personal or social identity. A similar point is made by Martin and Murray (1983), who argue that consideration of the affective dimension is essential for predictions based on collective deprivation. They note that most of the relevant research has concentrated on group contexts with long histories of conflict. Temporary or emotionally neutral group identifications are 'unlikely to tap the deep anger which underlies feelings of fraternal [i.e. collective] deprivation' (Martin and Murray, 1983: 193).

The social psychological focus on relative deprivation as the starting-point for understanding participation in collective action has been the subject of criticism over the years, because of the relatively weak empirical support often found for relationships between perceived deprivation and behaviour (see McPhail, 1971), because it has been argued that the approach downplays the rationality of collective behaviour (see Martin, Brickman and Murray, 1984) and because the concept is seen as insufficiently social (Smith and Gaskell, 1990; see also Gurney and Tierney, 1982, for a critical review of relative deprivation research). However, with more recent theorizing comes acknowledgment of the importance of the individual's sense of identification with the group (Tougas and Veilleux, 1988) and of the ways in which grievances are socially constructed in group contexts (Klandermans, 1989). Connections can thus be made with social identity theory which shares many assumptions and principles in common with relative deprivation theory (see Lalonde and Cameron, 1994).

Social Identity and Low Status

An important part of social identity theory is the assumption that, '*society comprises social categories which stand in power and status relations to one another*' (Hogg and Abrams, 1988: 14, italics in original), where *status* refers to the outcome of intergroup comparison. Membership of a high status group will confer on the individual a positive sense of social identity and self-esteem, in addition to the greater material and social benefits which may be associated with high status. By contrast, membership of a low status group will confer a negative social identity. How then can the individual respond to this situation?

In their formulation of social identity theory, Tajfel and Turner (1986) suggest three possible strategies in the pursuit of a positive social identity: Individual mobility (physical or psychological); social creativity; and social change/competition.

Individual mobility refers to the strategy of actually quitting – or, where this is not possible, psychologically dissociating from – the low status group. It represents an attempt to achieve upward individual mobility and improve individual status without bringing about any change in the status positions of the groups as a whole. Thus, it represents a personal but not a group solution to status inequality. As Hogg and Abrams (1988) point out, it is a very convenient strategy as far as dominant groups are concerned since it leaves present status relations unchanged.

By contrast, the strategies of *social creativity* and *social change/competition* are both group solutions. The former does not entail any actual change in the positions of the groups; instead group members are encouraged to change the nature of the intergroup comparisons, emphasizing new outgroups, new dimensions or new values. In this way, a social identity which was viewed as negative is seen in a more positive light.

It is only the third strategy of social change/competition which seeks to bring about any actual change in material circumstances and objective social locations. It is this third strategy which entails collective action to challenge the status quo, though Condor (1989) argues that in his original formulation of the theory, Tajfel (1975) uses this term to refer to self-perception and consciousness rather than to transformation of ideas and social structures.

What are the factors which will lead group members to adopt one or other of these different strategies? One factor which can be distinguished is an individual's level of identification with the group. Ingroup identification has been shown to be positively related to conflictual intergroup *attitudes* (see Kelly, 1988; 1990a), although the strength of this relationship varies in different group contexts (see Hinkle and Brown, 1990 for a review). With regard to conflictual intergroup *behaviour,* it can be hypothesized that individuals who identify strongly with a group will be more likely to get involved in collective action on its behalf, whereas individuals who identify only weakly with a group might be more likely to engage in individual action to try to improve personal status (but see Condor, 1986). There are clear links here with the notion of individualist–collectivist orientation and with research into depersonalization discussed earlier.

According to Tajfel and Turner (1986), the crucial factor in determining responses to low status is whether *cognitive alternatives* to the status quo are available – whether other outcomes are conceivable. Where status relations are perceived as immutable, a part of the fixed order of things, then social identity is described as 'secure'. If social change is inconceivable, then the only way to improve social identity is through individual mobility. If instead it is possible to conceive an alternative to the status quo – because the status hierarchy is perceived as illegitimate or unstable – then a strategy of social change/ competition is made more likely. Tajfel and Turner regard the combination of illegitimate and unstable intergroup relations as the most powerful cause of competition between groups, though Turner and Brown (1978: 209) argue that these two dimensions may vary independently.

Beyond this formulation of the awareness of cognitive alternatives to the prevailing intergroup relationship, social identity theory provides no precise hypotheses concerning the conditions that will determine which of the alternative responses will ultimately be preferred and also fails to indicate which variables might lead disadvantaged group members to perceive the intergroup situation as illegitimate and unstable in the first place. For further guidance on these questions we must turn to approaches which have been developed from social identity theory.

The Five-stage Model of Intergroup Relations

In an attempt to develop this aspect of social identity theory, Taylor and McKirnan (1984) propose a five-stage model of intergroup relations. The model traces a developmental sequence in the relations between high and low status groups (see Figure 2.3) and will be discussed in some detail since it allows some precise hypotheses derived from social identity theory to be empirically tested.

The sequence begins with rigid social stratification (based for example, on race or sex) (Stage 1), then moves to an individualistic ideology (Stage 2) and individual social mobility (Stage 3), where some low status group members pass into the advantaged group. Others fail to do so and, perceiving group boundaries as largely impermeable, initiate consciousness-raising in their original group (Stage 4) which leads to collective action (Stage 5). It is argued that all intergroup relations pass through the same stages in the same sequential manner, though the length of time spent at any one stage will depend on specific historical and social realities.

It is argued that acceptance of one's social position usually occurs when social stratification is based on inherent characteristics, such as sex or race. Where rigid social systems exist, there is no legitimate basis for questioning the status differences which exist. However, with the advent of industrialization, social stratification based on ascribed membership is seen as increasingly illegitimate and is replaced with a view of stratification based on individual achievement or worth. Within this new structure, it is legitimate to challenge the higher status group on the grounds of individual worth and merit. The crucial factor in promoting collective action is a shift in causal attribution on the part of disadvantaged group members from internal attributions for lack of success,

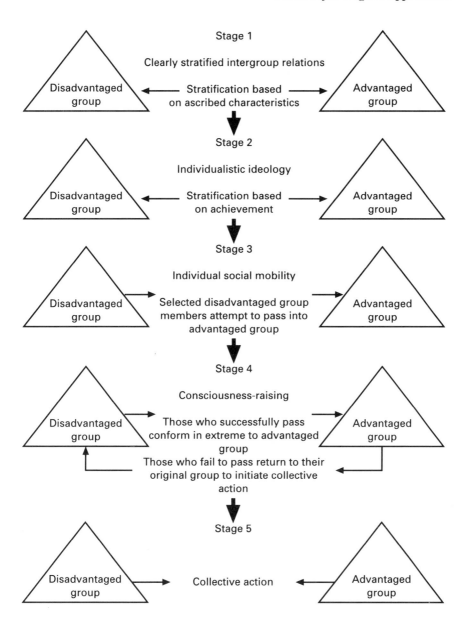

Figure 2.3: Taylor and McKirnan's five-stage model of intergroup relations. Taken from: Taylor, D.M. and McKirnan, D.J. (1984) A five-stage model of intergroup relations. *British Journal of Social Psychology*, **23**, 291–300 (Figure 1).

for example, insufficient ability, to external attributions, such as discriminatory actions of the dominant group.

Here again then, causal attribution is identified as one of the key processes underlying changes in intergroup relations over time. There is some empirical evidence to support the role of causal attributions here. A study by Rappaport (1977) indicated that those young American blacks most likely to get involved in collective action were those that made external causal attributions for their past and present status combined with an internal attribution for their future status. In an earlier study, Gurin, *et al.* (1969) found that young American blacks who judged economic or discriminatory factors as more important causes of their social position than individual skill and personal qualities were more ready to engage in collective action than were blacks who did not make such attributions (see also Hewstone and Jaspars, 1982). It appears that the ways in which individuals come to explain intergroup relations and differences is intimately tied to how they will respond to social inequality. Moreover, these explanations will be crucially affected by cultural context.

In relation to this point, it has been suggested that an ideology of individualism in western cultures leads individuals to privilege internal over external attributions (see Al-Zahrani and Kaplowitz, 1993; Miller, 1984; see Hewstone, 1989 for a review). In fact it was Ichheiser in 1943 who first identified the 'fundamental attribution error', or tendency to privilege internal attributions, when he argued that concepts like success and failure are based on a belief in the personal determination of behaviour and are built into the ideology of our society. More recently, researchers interested in social representations – defined as 'the contemporary version of common sense' (Moscovici, 1981: 181) – argue that a social representation of individualism ensures that the dominant way of accounting for individual outcomes, such as in contexts of poverty and unemployment, is in terms of personal characteristics rather than illegitimate social practices and prejudices. Not only does such an explanation accord with the dominant ideology, but it may also be reassuring to believe that the world is a just place, where misfortune only occurs to those who deserve it (Lerner, 1980). Those with a stronger belief in a just world are less likely to get involved in individual or collective action (Hafer and Olson, 1989; 1993).

The five-stage model of intergroup relations allows a number of specific hypotheses to be tested, relating to characteristics of the perceived intergroup situation and individual characteristics. In relation to the intergroup situation, predictions revolve around the nature of group boundaries. It is hypothesized that when entrance to an advantaged group is perceived to be completely open (permeable boundaries), individual action will ensue, and that when entrance to the advantaged group is perceived to be completely closed (impermeable boundaries), collective action will result.

The significance of group boundaries relates directly to Tajfel and Turner's notion of cognitive alternatives. According to an *individual mobility* belief structure, higher status may be realized through individual upward mobility to another group, as in an *equal opportunities* society where, in principle, each person achieves the status he or she deserves. Group boundaries in such a system are *permeable*. By contrast, in a very rigidly stratified society (or a collectivist society, in Triandis, *et al.*'s (1988) terms), where group boundaries are impermeable, people have no realistic alternative to their current group membership. Since there is no opportunity to change one's group affiliation, identification as a group member may therefore seem inevitable. Van Knippenberg and Ellemers (1990) argue that, 'impermeable boundaries force group members to seek collective solutions' (pp. 140–1).

In order to test the effects of group status, permeability of group boundaries and perceived instability and illegitimacy of status relations on people's tendency to identify as ingroup members, Ellemers and her colleagues conducted a series of experimental studies (see Ellemers, 1993; Van Knippenberg and Ellemers, 1993 for reviews). An experimental procedure was devised whereby group hierarchies were created in a laboratory setting and aspects of the intergroup situation were manipulated. These experiments are important in providing empirical tests for some of the principles which may be derived from social identity theory.

In the first of these experiments, Ellemers, *et al.* (1988, exp 1) found that group members are generally more satisfied and identify more strongly with high status groups than with low status groups and that levels of satisfaction and identification were particularly low amongst the members of low status groups with permeable boundaries. It is argued that permeable group boundaries present the possibility of individual mobility and thereby serve to reduce levels of identification with the low status group. A further experiment showed that this decreased level of group identification was more pronounced when group members had high individual ability. For these individuals, the opportunity for upward mobility constituted a realistic prospect. In a related experiment, Taylor, *et al.* (1987) found that by far the most negative feelings arose among subjects whose low status was perceived to be illegitimate and who were close to gaining entry to the advantaged group. These subjects were more likely to endorse collective action in response.

In relation to *perceived stability* in status relations, Ellemers, Van Knippenberg and Wilke (1990) found that unstable group status resulted in lower satisfaction with present low group status and evoked the aspiration to achieve a higher position for the group as a whole. To summarize, while permeable group boundaries were associated with individual mobility and lower group identification, unstable status relations were associated with collective attempts at status improvement and higher group identification.

Turning to the perceived *illegitimacy* of status relations, Ellemers, Van Knippenberg and Wilke (1993) differentiate between the effects of an unjustly low status position of the ingroup in the social structure on the one hand, and the effects of illegitimate inclusion of specific individuals in a low status group on the other hand. Results from their study showed that an illegitimate assignment of the subject's *group* to a low status position resulted in strong identification with the ingroup, especially when group status was unstable and group boundaries impermeable. By contrast, a perception that one has been unfairly assigned to a low status group results in lower identification with the group and a concern with *individual* status. Interestingly, however, examining subjects' *behaviour* in these experiments shows a different pattern, in that they were guided less by legitimacy considerations and more by the *feasibility* of the different strategies; group members tended to pursue those strategies that were most likely to succeed in the specific context.

Further research into group boundaries has been conducted by Taylor, *et al.* (1987). These researchers created three types of group boundary dividing high and low-status groups: Open; almost closed (tokenism); and completely closed. Findings provided some support for the hypothesis that subjects perceiving open-group boundaries would pursue individual action, whereas subjects faced with a completely closed group would show a greater interest in collective action. In fact in this study, subjects showed a strong preference for individual action even where access to the advantaged group was restricted to tokenism. Wright, *et al.* (1990) argue that,

> If a member of a disadvantaged group is primarily concerned with personal advancement, then as long as there remains even the slightest possibility for personal advancement ... there is little appeal in improving the status of the entire disadvantaged group through collective action (p. 1001).

Implicit in the argument that low status group members will show a general preference for individual mobility over collective action is the assumption that behaviour is driven ultimately by self-interest. Wright, *et al.* (1990) go on to argue that even when individuals do engage in collective action, this may not necessarily reflect a collective consciousness, but just the realization that this is the only way to improve personal status. Studying the role of self-interest as a determinant of action, Taylor, *et al.* (1987, exp 1) used the distinction between *distributive* injustice (concerned with resource distribution among individuals) and *procedural* injustice (involving the manner in which distribution is arrived at). They argued that the latter, which concerns the collectivity, would be more likely to provoke collective action in response. However, results indicated that an unjust procedure alone was insufficient to produce collective action but had to be coupled with an unjust distribution which affected the actor personally. The significance of personal consequences as a determinant of action received further support in Wright, *et al.*'s (1990) study. Here, individuals *near* to access to the advantaged group were provoked into action to a greater extent by an arbitrary change in procedures than were subjects *distant* from the advantaged group for whom the change had no personal consequences (see also Taylor, *et al.*, 1987, exp 2).

This evidence suggests that individuals are concerned first and foremost with their own personal status and accords with a basic assumption underlying the five-stage model, which is an initial preference on the part of low status group members for individual action:

> A key assumption underlying the five-stage model is that because intergroup comparisons are deemed inappropriate by the overriding social philosophy of stratification on the basis of individual perform-ance, attempts at individual upward mobility – an individual normative response – are always the first strategy attempted by members of the disadvantaged group. It is only when these individual attempts are blocked that the overriding social philosophy is questioned and the advantaged group is perceived to be closed to the disadvantaged group members. And it is only then that collective action will be initiated (Wright, *et al.*, 1990: 996; see also Tajfel and Turner, 1979).

Further supporting evidence comes from an experimental study by Lalonde and Silverman (1994) who found a widespread preference for individual action, even under closed boundary conditions. However, subjects in their study were more likely to take collective action when social identity was made salient, and the researchers relate the widespread preference for individual solutions to the idea that in many real life cases of injustice, social identity is *not* salient and attributions are made internally leading to greater acceptance of the situation. More generally, this is related to a *Zeitgeist* of individualism in North American culture.

Thus, the accumulated evidence which has been described suggests that collective solutions and improving the position of the whole group is under-taken as a last resort when personal mobility is not possible. These principles have been developed primarily on the basis of experimental research using *ad hoc* laboratory groups, although not exclusively. For example, Taylor, *et al.* (1982) found evidence of a high preference for an individualistic coping strategy even in the face of collective threat in the context of ethnolinguistic intergroup relations.

However, some researchers have disputed the universal applicability of these ideas. For example, Moghaddam and Perreault (1992) suggest that one reason why student subjects acting as minority group members in laboratory simulations can abandon their groups fairly readily is perhaps due to the fact that ties of sentiment with the ingroup have had little opportunity to develop. Findings from their own study, using first-generation, visible ethnic minority immigrants in Canada, conflict with predictions from the five-stage model of intergroup relations. Specifically, it was the respondents with *low* self-esteem who were most likely to endorse a strategy of individual mobility (assimilation into the majority group), rather than those with high self-esteem as would be suggested by the five-stage model. Relatedly, Dube and Guimond (1986) found that it was not individuals' concern for their own well-being which motivated participation in mass protest, but their defence of highly symbolic principles.

Moghaddam and Perreault are critical of the individualistic assumptions underlying the five-stage model which suggest that individuals will always give preference to individual mobility. In comments which are reminiscent of the criticisms made of expectancy-value models of action discussed earlier, they argue that the approach does not give sufficient importance to the role of group loyalty: 'Taylor and McKirnan adopted a model of humankind that assumes individuals to be mobile and untouched in any important ways by group ties and loyalties' (Moghaddam and Perreault, 1992: 352). It is suggested that the model has been influenced by the 'self-contained individualism' (Sampson, 1977) which pervades North American culture and that in many other cultures a greater emphasis on collectivism would make the model less appropriate. They conclude that the five-stage model is perhaps of greatest value for understanding the behaviour of minority groups who are not held together by strong bonds. Where groups have stronger cohesion and unity, the individualistic assumptions of the five-stage model may not apply so well.

In further related criticism, Andrews argues that placing emphasis on the possibilities presented for individual self-advancement does insufficient justice to the complexities of real socio-political environments and multiple social identities. As she argues, 'If an individual is class conscious, the fact that some people have successfully risen out of their class (and thus that social boundaries have some degree of permeability, however small) need not alter her political convictions' (1991: 31). Andrews draws a distinction between macro- and micro-social perceptions, such that one can simultaneously believe that mobility is possible at an individual level, while also believing that the only way to change conditions more generally is through group action. Thus, the potential for individual mobility need not eliminate a sense of group loyalty. The relevance of theoretical principles derived from social identity theory to *real* groups and categories will only become clear with the adoption of a wider range of methods situated outside the laboratory.

Combining Approaches: The Moderating Role of Group Identification

One way to combine these different theoretical approaches is to examine the possible moderating role of group identification. As stated previously, underlying social identity theory is a continuum which runs from personal identity to social identity. In certain situations, social identity is more salient with the result that actions are determined primarily by the implications of group membership; in other situations, personal identity is more salient and behaviour is governed primarily by personal concerns. This distinction emerges as important in much of the recent theorizing and research in group processes (see for example, Brewer, 1994).

Thus, one possible way forward in considering participation in collective action is to suggest that the desire for self-advancement will be most strongly felt where personal rather than social identity is salient. The readiness with which individuals were ready to quit their experimental groups for personal advancement in the studies which have been described may not be representative of behaviour where individuals feel a strong sense of identity and solidarity with other low status group members.

Others have also suggested that strength of identification may play a moderating role in determining collective or individual behaviour. Kawakami and Dion (1992) propose an integrative model of social comparisons bringing together the theories of relative deprivation, social identity and self-categorization. Accordingly, the model begins with the determinants of category salience which influence whether personal or group identity is salient. Personal identity salience is associated with intragroup comparison, where negative and illegitimate outcomes lead to personal relative deprivation, a negative personal identity and individual actions. Conversely, group identity salience is associated with intergroup comparison, where negative and illegitimate outcomes lead to group relative deprivation, a negative group identity and group actions.

Some support for this model is described by Kawakami and Dion (1993) in a study in which salient self-identities and the outcomes of intragroup and intergroup inequalities were varied experimentally with a role-play design. A classroom context was chosen and salience was varied by accentuating the characteristics of the student (personal salience) or the student's tutorial group (group salience). Individual student's and tutorial group's grades were manipulated so as to result in perceptions of large versus small intragroup and intergroup inequalities.

Findings showed that people whose group rather than personal identities were salient were less satisfied and perceived less justice in intergroup comparisons. These people were also more likely to take positive collective actions, such as asking for help, compared with people whose personal identities were salient – who were more likely to take negative individual actions, such as quitting the group. More unexpectedly, it was found that subjects who were told that large intergroup inequalities existed were less likely to take positive collective action than subjects who were told that small intergroup inequalities existed. The authors suggest that if the inequality is perceived as being too large in a group situation, the possibility of improving the group standard through collective hard work and help may not be seen as viable. Individuals may intend to take positive group action only if they see the size of the gap between their own group and an outgroup as bridgeable. This relates to Ellemers, *et al.*'s (1993) finding that in relation to *behaviour,* people are guided primarily by considerations of feasibility.

Other researchers have also found evidence of the moderating role of group identification. Haselau, *et al.* (1991) found that feelings of relative deprivation (personal and collective) predicted activist intentions amongst pro- and anti-abortion lobbies *only* amongst subjects who strongly identified with an abortion-related group. Similarly, Struch and Schwartz (1989) found that the impact of predictor variables, such as perceived value dissimilarity, on inter-group aggression was particularly strong amongst respondents who identified highly with their own group.

Tougas and Veilleux also argue that the concepts of relative deprivation and social identity must be interrelated. 'It could be said that social identity and its underlying psychological processes are responsible for the genesis and function-ing of collective relative deprivation' (1988: 17). These researchers argue that if a person belongs to an underprivileged group and strongly identifies with it, he or she will engage in social action only if he or she feels dissatisfied with the group's situation. In other words, collective relative deprivation's affective component acts as a mediating variable between identification and promotion of changes designed to improve the situation (see also Tougas and Veilleux, 1989). Others stress the opposite direction of causation, namely that collective relative deprivation heightens identifications with the group (Petta and Walker, 1992).

Group identification may also moderate relationships between individual characteristics, individual decision-making and participation in collective action. Whereas group processes, such as collective relative deprivation, may be particularly important motivators for strong identifiers, individual processes may be more important for weak identifiers. For example, Kelly and Kelly (1992) argue that the sort of individual calculations which lie at the heart of expectancy-value models of behaviour will be relatively more important as determinants of action amongst individuals who do not identify very strongly with the group involved. By contrast, for those individuals who feel a strong sense of group identification, feelings of loyalty and solidarity may override any perceived personal costs of collective action. Relatedly, recent debate in the context of the theory of planned behaviour (discussed earlier) has focused on the way in which identity may have an impact on intentions and behaviour which is independent of attitudinal and normative considerations (see Biddle, *et al.*, 1987; Charng, *et al.*, 1988; Granberg and Holmberg, 1990; Sparks and Shepherd, 1992).

It may thus be useful to consider group identification as a variable which not only has a direct effect on participation in collective action, but also serves to moderate the relationship between that behaviour and other predictor variables. Where personal identity is salient (i.e. group identification is weak) behaviour will be determined mainly by individual characteristics and calcula-tions of the costs and benefits associated with action. Where social identity is salient (i.e. group identification is strong) behaviour will be determined mainly by group processes, such as perceptions of inequality in intergroup relations. This is not to say that personal identity is associated *exclusively* with individual processes, and social identity *exclusively* with group processes, but rather that privileged relationships exist between the concepts within each of these domains.

Applying the Social Identity Framework to Gender

Finally in this chapter, we will turn to a consideration of the application of social identity theory to gender relations, since much of the research to be presented was conducted in a gender context. The first discussion of this issue was by Williams and Giles (1978), who argued that the strategies of individual mobility, social creativity and social change/competition reflect women's different responses to status inequality, ranging from psychological dissociation from the category of women, promoting the greater value of traditionally 'female' qualities, such as sensitivity and interpersonal skills, and finally, challenging the status quo through involvement in feminist groups and collective action. Breinlinger and Kelly (1994) present empirical evidence which supports the conceptual distinctness of individual mobility and social change/competition ideologies in this context.

A number of criticisms have been made of the attempt to use the social identity framework to understand relations between men and women. Skevington and Baker (1989) make three main points. First, they argue that Williams and Giles,

> make the mistake of assuming that womanhood is perceived by all women in the same way, using the same consensual (and unfavour-able) dimensions when comparing themselves to men. So womanhood is presented as a unified social category whose characteristics are well known and accepted (p. 5).

Similarly, Breakwell (1979) stresses in her own analysis of women's social identity that it is *lack of consensus* as to what characterizes 'womanhood' at any one time that gives rise to an unsatisfactory social identity for women, rather than unfavourable comparisons with men.

The second point stressed by Skevington and Baker concerns the relationship between group identification and strategy adoption. They refer critically to the assumption made by Williams and Giles that only those women who reject the sex-role status quo will identify strongly as a group and so adopt the collective strategy of social change to improve their group's status. By contrast, Condor (1986) and Gurin and Townsend (1986) argue that the extent of gender group identification is not necessarily dependent on group consciousness, i.e. on beliefs about the group's position of power and status in the intergroup context. Thus, Condor (1986) found that 'traditional women' accepted the sex-role status quo and yet identified strongly with their group, seeing their roles as preferable to those of men. Gurin and Townsend (1986) found that gender group membership may be a central aspect of the self-concept without necessarily involving any awareness of the low status of women as a group.

The third point made by Skevington and Baker is that the competitive orientation which underlies social identity theory may not be appropriate for understanding women's responses to low status. Following Williams' (1984) analysis, they suggest that women may emphasize a *communal* social identity, sustained by relationships within the ingroup, rather than an *agentic* social identity, which is sustained by intergroup competition and, it is argued, is more characteristic of men (see also Archer, 1984; Gilligan, 1982). However, even apart from the problem of lack of empirical backing for this distinction in a social identity context, there is also the problem raised by Breakwell (1990) that this distinction, drawn on by some feminists, assumes the reality of these different orientations by men and women which may itself be seen as part of gender stereotyping.

Much of the debate in this area focuses on the relationship between gender identity and gender consciousness, where, '[i]dentity connotes the member's awareness of membership and feelings attached to being a member, while consciousness refers to the member's ideology about the group's position in society' (Gurin and Townsend, 1986). Group consciousness has been defined multidimensionally to involve a sense of collective discontent over the group's relative power or material resources, an appraisal of the legitimacy of the social structure by which the group is advantaged or disadvantaged and the belief that collective action is required to realize the group's interests (Gurin, Miller and Gurin, 1980; see also Miller, *et al.*, 1981).

Studying the correlates of collective discontent, Gurin and Townsend (1986) examined three aspects of social identity: Centrality of group identity in the self-concept; perceived similarities in the personal characteristics of group members; and an awareness of common fate in the way in which group members are treated in society. Findings from telephone interviews with several hundred women found that all three properties of identity influenced collective discontent. It is argued that each heightens the salience of group boundaries and increases the use of categorical distinctions in social comparison. 'Collective discontent requires a categorical, intergroup focus. Women cannot become discontented with the status and power of women unless they compare women with men' (1986: 146). A sense of common fate was the property of gender identity that proved most consistently and strongly implicated in gender consciousness.

In line with other research which has been discussed, the authors argue that thinking about causation plays a key role in the development of gender consciousness. A major premise behind the consciousness-raising groups that flourished in the early 1970s was the need to help women counter the impediments to group consciousness posed by an ideology of individualism and associated attributional biases favouring internal explanations. Moreover in the context of gender, it is argued that categorization processes are inhibited by the frequency and intimacy of women's relations with men and their interdependence with men in families. Appreciation of the extent to which men and women are treated categorically may consequently be obscured. The slogan, 'The personal is political', adopted by many consciousness-raising groups, symbolizes the tie between common fate and criticism of legitimacy. Through comparing personal experiences, participants understood that the personal was in fact shared. Discussion of common fate was the mechanism that made the personal political (see also Gurin, 1985; Gurin and Markus, 1989; Gurin, *et al.*, 1980; Miller, *et al.*, 1981).

In the discussion of gender relations then, many of the same themes emerge which have been discussed earlier in this chapter, such as the links between group identification and action and those between a cultural context of individualism and internal attributions for low status which discourage participation in collective action.

Concluding Comments

In this chapter we have discussed a great range of different theoretical perspectives which are relevant to the question of individual participation in collective action. These approaches were categorized into those focusing on elements of individual personality and cognition and those focusing on aspects of group processes and intergroup relations. As is apparent at several points, there are important connections between these different approaches. Moreover, drawing conclusions about causality is difficult, if not impossible. All of the factors which have been discussed may be *outcomes* of participation as well as *determinants* – and are probably both. For example, group identification may function as a determinant of action and it is also likely to be strengthened by involvement in collective action. Similarly, Milbrath and Goel (1977) argue in the case of political efficacy, that participation in politics and feelings of efficacy reinforce each other producing a circularity of effects. In particular, favourable interactions with authorities are likely to enhance one's sense of efficacy. In recent discussion, Klandermans stresses the need to view collective action as both a dependent and an independent variable: 'On the one hand, the social construction of meaning precedes collective action and determines its direction; on the other, collective action in its turn determines the process of meaning construction' (1992: 82).

Once involved in collective action, it is likely that a person will develop a new social identity as an activist, increasingly seeing herself as 'someone who gets involved'. Kelly (1993) suggests that this identity itself may be sufficient to motivate further involvement short-circuiting any other psychological determinants. Some evidence for this comes from Lydon and Zanna's (1990) study, where value relevance was shown to predict commitment in the face of adversity. Under conditions of high adversity, those who saw their values as relevant to their personal projects felt more committed than those who saw their values as less relevant. Once an activist identity has formed, individuals may continue to participate in collective action to the extent that such action is seen as relevant to their social identity and values. Further evidence comes from studies, which have been described earlier as the attitude–behaviour relationship, which show that identity has an impact on behavioural intentions which is independent of attitudinal factors (Biddle, *et al.*, 1987; Charng, *et al.*, 1988; Granberg and Holmberg, 1990; Sparks and Shepherd, 1992).

The idea that participation in collective action can be related to an activist identity is also supported by interview material obtained from longstanding political activists, which suggests that involvement is part of an activist's personal repertoire of behaviour which is undertaken to reinforce a valued social identity, as well as being related to perceptions of illegitimacy and instability in status relations. This theme emerges clearly from Andrews' interview study in 1991 of 15 British men and women, aged between 70 and 90, who had spent their lives working for social change and justice. She argues that over the years, these individuals have come to define themselves through their activism: 'Activism is not merely something which the respondents do, nor even just a part of them. It is them' (1991: 164).

Basing her analysis on social identity theory, Andrews argues that self-definition for these activists revolved crucially around identification as a socialist and that this identification was continually being restated and recreated in the actions of daily life. Socialist identification here is conceived as comprising both a sense of *being* (indicating consciousness) and *doing* (performing actions consonant with beliefs). Interview findings pointed to the important connections made by activists between perceiving a problem and taking action to try to do something about it, which Andrews refers to as a 'culture of responding'. It represents a feeling of responsibility, that one cannot simply see a problem and do nothing about it. As a result of this constant interplay between identity, beliefs and action, individuals who have been involved in political activity over a period of time are likely to continue to do so:

> Political action, however, is not unreflective, but rather has built into it
> a history of past actions, and incorporates their underlying purpose as
> part of its own. In this way actions past, present and future are part of
> a larger, self-perpetuating continuum of purposeful, directed action
> (Andrews, 1991: 164).

In the chapters which follow, theoretical principles discussed in this chapter will be applied to the study of participation in trade unions and women's groups. Social identity theory will provide the main theoretical framework. The next chapter will describe quantitative data derived from questionnaires which is used to explore relationships between identity, beliefs and action and to test some of the theories which have been discussed.

Chapter 3

Social Beliefs and Participation: Exploring Associations

Chapter 2 set out a number of social psychological approaches to the study of collective action. According to the theories discussed in that chapter, there are a number of ways in which we might expect more active individuals to differ from less active individuals. For example, we would expect individuals who are more highly involved in collective action to express higher levels of identification with the group in question, as well as higher levels of political efficacy, collective relative deprivation and collectivist orientation. In accordance with the expectancy-value models of social behaviour, we would expect that more active individuals would associate greater benefits and fewer costs with participation than less active individuals.

In the present chapter, the aim is to test some of the theories of activism which have been described using quantitative data obtained by questionnaires. This methodological approach allows us to examine associations between social beliefs and levels of participation, but of course does not allow us to draw any conclusions regarding causation. Thus should an association be found between activism and relative deprivation for example, we cannot conclude that relative deprivation *causes* participation since it may just as plausibly be an *outcome* of this behaviour. Establishing associations is therefore just the first step on the way to exploring the relationships between social beliefs and participation, although some cross-lagged analysis will also be possible.

Despite this limitation however, questionnaire data is valuable in allowing us to pursue some more specific questions arising from the review of previous research. For example, how do associations with social beliefs vary according to the type of action? Does group identification moderate the relationship between social beliefs and activism? What is the relationship between intentions to participate in collective action and actual behaviour? These and other such questions will be the focus of the present chapter.

Data will be presented from two different contexts of action where similar questionnaire measures were employed. The first of these contexts concerns participation in trade unions; the second, and more extensive, study concerns participation in a range of activities aiming to bring about social change in the context of gender relations. As discussed in Chapter 1, the trade union movement and the women's movement represent two very important contemporary contexts for collective action. Data presented in this chapter will allow us to draw some comparisons between the correlates of participation in these two contexts.

Study One: Participation in a Trade Union Context[1]

Trade unions offer the opportunity for many different types of involvement in pursuit of their aim to defend and promote the terms and conditions of all their members. It is generally the case that unions are run at local level by a small number of activists; a large proportion of the membership is inactive, at most attending occasional meetings, voting in elections and taking part in informal activities, such as reading union journals (Fosh, 1993).

While the topic of trade union participation has been of some interest to occupational psychologists, the correlates which have been studied have generally been demographic variables, such as age, gender, education, seniority, employment status and job satisfaction, and relationships have generally proved weak or inconsistent (for example Barling, Kelloway and Fullager, 1992; Gallagher and Strauss, 1991; Huszczo, 1983; McShane, 1986). The present study, with its emphasis on the social psychological correlates of participation, therefore represents a significant departure from this tradition.

The Setting and Respondents

The present study was carried out in a local government authority in London which employed approximately 4500 staff in the grades covered by the white-collar union NALGO (National and Local Government Officers' Association). Of these staff, approximately 2000 belonged to the union, giving it a density of around 40 per cent. Staff belonged to a wide range of departments, including social services, education, housing and leisure. Occupations were as diverse as clerical assistants, social workers, auditors, administrators and departmental managers. NALGO may therefore be described as a vertically organized trade union, which includes junior white-collar workers as well as their managers.

Industrial relations in the authority had deteriorated in recent years as councillors were forced to make expenditure cuts by among other means freezing vacant posts. Staff were involved in a national strike of local authority workers two years previously and there had been occasional local stoppages within particular departments. Nationally, NALGO has acquired a growing reputation for being a politically left-wing union and one that is willing to back industrial action by its members (see Lawrence, 1994 for a short history of NALGO).

The present study was conducted using a questionnaire which was mailed out through the union to 894 randomly selected members along with a covering letter from the local union officials explaining the purpose of the study and assuring confidentiality of responses. Exactly 350 completed questionnaires were returned directly to the researchers in stamped addressed envelopes representing a response rate of 39.15 per cent. (This response rate is comparable with previous research of this kind, see Nicholson, Ursell and Blyton, 1981.) The sample contained 190 females and 140 males. (There were 20 non-replies on this question of gender, reflecting a relatively large number of respondents who chose not to complete the section concerning personal characteristics. Some of these respondents commented that they did not wish to give information which might allow them to be identified by management in what were sometimes quite small departments. This is perhaps an indication of the insecurity which many respondents were feeling at work.)

The mean age of respondents was 37 years. Respondents were all employed in white-collar occupations and worked in a range of local government departments. In terms of duration of union membership, respondents were fairly equally distributed across response categories ranging from 'Less than 2 years' to 'Over 10 years' of union membership. Only 13.1 per cent were office-holders in the union.

The Questionnaire

All questions were answered on seven-point Likert scales. The first section of the questionnaire comprised ten questions relating to prospective participation ('over the next 12 months') in both formal and informal types of union activity. The sections which followed contained questions concerning a number of possible social psychological correlates of action: Group (union) identification; collectivist orientation; perceived intergroup conflict; personal and collective relative deprivation; and political efficacy.

In addition, interest in expectancy-value models of action was reflected in a number of questions relating to Klandermans' theory of union participation (see Chapter 2) and measures were computed in accordance with previous research in this area. Goal motives were measured by items concerning the desirability of more union influence in the workplace, perception of the degree to which the individual's participation would make any difference to this aim and the degree to which it was felt that more union influence would lead to better terms and conditions of employment. Total goal motive was a multiplicative function of scores on these three items.

Social motives were measured by asking about the perceived reactions of friends, family, colleagues and superiors to the individual becoming a union activist and then asking about the value placed on the reactions of each of these four groups. An expectancy-value score was computed for each significant other by multiplying the expectancy and the value score. The sum of these four expectancy-value scores formed the total social motive.

Reward motives were assessed by a number of items asking about possible costs of participation (reputation as a troublemaker, damage to promotion prospects, time and effort) and possible rewards (getting to know people, expressing your beliefs, influencing other people). Following reversal of some items so that high scores always indicated rewards, total reward motive was then calculated as the sum of the scores across all items.

The next section comprised eight attitude statements covering a range of industrial relations issues and selected from Allen and Stephenson (1983). For each item, respondents were required to give their own opinion and then to say how they thought 'a typical manager' in their organization would respond to that item. Subtracting perceived outgroup (management) scores from own scores provided a measure of the degree to which outgroup members were perceived as different in their attitudes from self. Reversing the scoring on some of the items ensured that a traditionally managerial perspective was always scored in the same direction. Resulting 'difference' scores were then aggregated to produce a total 'outgroup stereotyping' score.

Finally, respondents were asked to supply some background information about themselves, such as age, sex, occupation, duration of union membership and details of any union office-holding.

Factor Analysis of Participation Items

Factor analysis was conducted on the participation items and this showed that two main types of participation could be distinguished (see Appendix 1). These could be broadly interpreted as referring to first, more *easy* forms of activity, comprising informal items, such as 'Reading union journals', and items where the individual is not readily visible or identifiable, such as 'Voting in union elections'; and second, more *difficult* forms of activity, where the individual is more visible, such as 'Speaking at union meetings' and items relating to office-holding. This finding is comparable with previous research into this question which has likewise distinguished between voting activity on the one hand and administration/office-holding activities on the other, with the possible addition of a separate third factor relating specifically to meeting attendance (McShane, 1986; Nicholson, *et al.*, 1981).

Scores from items loading on each of these two factors were aggregated to provide two composite measures of participation which were used in subsequent analyses. Mean scores and internal reliability scores are displayed in Table 3.1.

Table 3.1: Union participation and social beliefs: Mean scores, standard deviations and alpha reliability coefficients

Variable	Mean	SD	Alpha
Easy forms of participation[a]	4.71	1.46	.84
Difficult forms of participation[a]	1.88	1.24	.81
Group identification[a]	4.23	1.45	.87
Collectivist orientation[a]	4.82	0.92	.72
Perceived intergroup conflict[a]	4.57	1.38	.79
Outgroup stereotyping[b]	2.46	1.50	.86
Personal relative deprivation[a]	3.59	2.03	–
Collective relative deprivation[a]	3.43	2.03	–
Political efficacy[a]	5.15	1.44	.54
Goal motives[c]	121.23	107.67	.69
Social motives[d]	79.38	30.94	.64
Reward motives[e]	30.27	5.43	.60

Key:
- [a]Range: 1–7; [b]Range: 1–6; [c]Range 1–343; [d]Range:4–196; [e]Range: 6–42
- Each relative deprivation variable was measured by a single item and hence there are no alpha reliability scores

Predicting Participation

Multiple regression analyses were conducted where the dependent variables comprised the two measures of participation. In first analyses, independent variables comprised group identification, collectivist orientation, perceived intergroup conflict, outgroup stereotyping, personal and collective relative deprivation and political efficacy. Standardized regression coefficients relating to this analysis are displayed in Table 3.2.

Results from these analyses indicate that in the case of the *easier* forms of participation, significant correlates were group identification, outgroup stereotyping and collectivist orientation. In other words, the stronger the respondent's sense of identification with the union, the more that management were perceived in a stereotypical way and the more collectivist the individual's general orientation, the greater the intention to participate in union activities in the future. In the case of the more *difficult* forms of participation, the only factor significantly associated with intention to participate was group identification. Thus, there is strong support from these findings for the idea that group identification is not only associated with more conflictual *attitudes* towards outgroups (see Kelly, 1988), but also with more conflictual *behaviours*, or to be precise, *behavioural intentions*. In the present case, intention to get involved in a range of union-related activities is the behavioural expression of the individual's identification with, and commitment to, the group.

Table 3.2: Union participation and social beliefs: Standardized regression coefficients

Independent variables	Dependent variables	
	Easy forms of participation	*Difficult* forms of participation
Group identification	+54 **	+62 **
Collectivist orientation	+15 **	−09
Perceived intergroup conflict	−06	−02
Outgroup stereotyping	+19 **	+07
Personal relative deprivation	−02	−02
Collective relative deprivation	+06	+07
Political efficacy	−01	−05
R^2	0.54	0.33
F	46.85 **	20.07 **

Key:
** $p < 0.01$
Decimal points have been omitted from regression coefficients

This combination of significant independent variables, at least in relation to the *easier* forms of participation – group identification, outgroup stereotyping and collectivist orientation – suggests a picture of the potential activist as a person who is firmly committed to a 'them and us' representation of intergroup relations, having a strong sense of identification with the ingroup and a clear perception of differences between ingroup and outgroup members, grounded in a general collectivist orientation.

In further analyses testing the expectancy-value model, goal, social and reward motive variables were entered into equations as independent variables (see Table 3.3).

Table 3.3: Union participation and expectancy-value calculations: Standardized regression coefficients

Dependent variables	Independent variables				
	Goal motives	Social motives	Reward motives	R^2	F
Easy forms of participation	+45 **	+10 *	+12 **	0.27	41.73 **
Difficult forms of participation	+35 **	+08	−01	0.14	18.05 **

Key:
* $p < 0.05$; ** $p < 0.01$
Decimal points have been omitted from regression coefficients

Both equations were highly significant and it is clear that of the three motives for participation, goal motives were easily the most important, in accordance with previous research findings (Klandermans, 1984a; b; 1986b), though both social and reward motives did reach significance for the dependent measure relating to *easier* forms of participation. In a further set of analyses relating to each individual measure of participation, goal motives proved highly significant in all ten equations, unlike the other two motives, which were significant in only a small number of cases. We can conclude that the most important type of expectancy-value calculation in this context seems to be that relating to the perceived effectiveness of the action in achieving a desired goal.

When expectancy-value calculations were entered into regression equations along with social beliefs, the former failed to show any significant relationships with either type of participation. As in analyses already described, *easier* forms of activity were related to group identification, collectivist orientation and outgroup stereotyping and more *difficult* forms were related only to group identification. Thus, whereas expectancy-value calculations, particularly goal motives, were significant when entered alone in regression analyses, they were completely overshadowed by the more group-oriented social beliefs.

The Moderating Role of Group Identification I

Finally, in order to examine the possible moderating role of level of group identification on the other correlates of participation, the sample was divided into strong identifiers and weak identifiers by using a median split. Repeating the regression analyses with all other independent variables revealed a broadly similar pattern of results across the two sub-samples in relation to both social beliefs and expectancy-value calculations, reflecting the pattern of associations which has been described already.

However, comparing the contributions of the independent variables across the two sub-samples did suggest two possible sources of difference. First, collective relative deprivation appeared to be rather more important as a correlate of participation for strong than for weak identifiers, in accordance with some previous research findings (see Haselau, *et al.*, 1991). Second, the opposite seemed to be true for political efficacy, which appeared to be somewhat more important for weak than for strong identifiers. However, the significance of these trends was not supported by further regression analyses in which interaction terms were entered as independent variables. The percentage of variance explained was no better in these subsequent analyses. The possible moderating role of group identification will be put to further test in the second context to be discussed in this chapter.

Conclusions to Study 1

The present findings confirm the important role of group identification as a correlate of participation in collective action. Taking part in collective action in a trade union context is strongly associated with the individual's sense of subjective identification with the group and perception of the relationship between ingroups and outgroups. Perception of the outgroup in stereotypical terms and expression of a collectivist orientation are also bound up with action.

A test of the expectancy-value model of action showed that the most important type of calculation was that relating to the perceived effectiveness of the action in achieving a desired goal, i.e. Klandermans' notion of goal motives. Whereas the perceived reactions of significant others (social motives) and the perceived costs and benefits of participation (reward motives) played some part as correlates of intentions to participate in *easier* forms of action, their impact was overshadowed by the more significant role of goal motives. However, even the measure of goal motives ceased to be significant when it was pitted against the group-oriented variables of identification, outgroup stereotyping and collectivist orientation.

We turn now to our second context of collective action, concerning gender relations, before drawing comparisons between the findings.

Study 2: Participation in a Gender Context

Groups and Respondents

In this more extensive study, which also forms the basis for most of the next three chapters, the focus was on women's participation in a range of activities aiming to bring about some social change in the context of gender relations. Data was obtained in a panel study using questionnaires at two different times. The first time, information was gathered regarding social beliefs and readiness to participate in various forms of action. One year later, a sub-group of the same respondents was asked to report on the extent to which they had *actually* engaged in those behaviours and to provide further measures of social beliefs.

To reach women activists, questionnaires were distributed through over 120 different women's groups and campaigns. Groups were selected which, according to their stated aims and objectives, were committed to achieving some social change for women as a group, though the precise context and scope of that change varied widely. Some were single-issue groups; others had very broad aims. Some group goals were explicitly political, working towards the removal of discrimination and encouraging the effective participation of women in public life; others were less outspokenly political, combining support needs with an attempt to bring about some social change.

Out of our activist sample of women, 87 per cent belonged to groups which could be categorized according to context as follows:

Context	Number of respondents
Work/management	83
Work/other professional	50
Health/childbirth/children	46
Party political	45
Work/trade union	43
General/umbrella groups	34

The remaining respondents came from groups concerned with issues such as ethnicity, age, crime, pornography, the environment, peace, international relations, religion and local community groups (see Appendix 2 for a list of groups).

Groups were contacted by letter and phone and the aims of the study were discussed and approved in group committee meetings before questionnaires were sent out, sometimes along with regular mailings. The communication networks and overlapping membership which exists in this context became clear when questionnaires were returned from members of groups which we had not contacted in the first place!

For the purpose of comparison, we also required a less politically active sample. Questionnaires were distributed to women enrolled on a variety of primarily postgraduate courses, where students tended to be from professional occupational groups seeking further qualifications, who would provide a good match with our more active group. More and less active groups were matched on educational and occupational status, ethnicity, general political orientation (on a Left–Right spectrum) and whether or not they had children. We also sought to ensure that they came from a similar population in terms of certain gender-related attitudes. A single item on the questionnaire was used to eliminate from the total sample any women who disagreed with the statement, 'There is still a lot of prejudice and discrimination which prevents women achieving their full potential'. Sixteen respondents were excluded on this basis. This step ensured that non-activism could not be explained as simply arising from a different, possibly more traditional, set of gender-related attitudes and allows us to address the question, given that *all* of our sample think that women suffer prejudice and discrimination as a group, why are *some* prepared to get involved in action to try to change things?

All questionnaires were accompanied by a covering letter which was explicit about the aims of the research. Respondents were told that we were interested in why some women get involved in groups and campaigns aiming to promote women's issues and others choose not to do so.[2] Questionnaires were returned in stamped addressed envelopes. Respondents willing to participate in the second stage of the study provided their names and addresses so that they could be contacted one year later.

At time one, 610 completed questionnaires were returned, representing a response rate of 51 per cent. The enthusiasm of our activist sample was particularly striking. Unusually for social psychological research, we were contacted by groups and by individuals who had heard about the research and who wanted to be included in our sample. Activists clearly welcomed the opportunity to give their views on these issues and to tell the stories of their own participation.

One year later, at time two, we contacted 459 of the same participants (activists and non-activists) who had indicated that they would like to be involved in the follow-up. Three hundred and eighty-seven of these second questionnaires were returned, representing a response rate of 84.3 per cent.

Of the 610 respondents at time one, 347 stated that they were 'actively involved in a women's group or campaign' and the rest stated that they were not. This distinction forms the basis of a crude categorization into *activists* and *non-activists*.[3] Of the activists at time one, 53 per cent could be thought of as longstanding activists, having been involved for a period of more than three years; and 50 per cent could be considered to be highly committed, spending at least several hours a week on activities related to the group. At time two, 252 of the 387 women reported that they were actively involved in women's groups or campaigns, including 36.7 per cent longstanding activists and 32.3 per cent highly committed activists as previously defined.

As regards the demographic characteristics of our sample, the average age was 35–44 years and nearly all (90 per cent) described their ethnic origin as white/British. In terms of occupational status, they were predominantly (67.6 per cent) drawn from professional and white-collar categories and two-thirds of them (66.9 per cent) had higher educational qualifications. Whether or not this reflects the profile of activists as a whole is difficult to say, though it has been suggested that white, middle-class, university-educated women are over-represented in women's groups and campaigns and in feminism as a movement (Andrews, 1991: 38; Randall, 1987; Spelman, 1988).

Measuring Prospective and Potential Participation

All questions were answered on five-point scales. At time one, respondents were asked to rate how likely it was that they would be engaging in six different types of action over the next 12 months. These actions covered formal and informal aspects of participation and provided measures of *prospective participation*. Respondents were then asked to imagine a situation (details unspecified) in which the government was proposing to introduce a new law which was considered harmful to women's interests. They were asked to assess how prepared they would be to engage in six different forms of protest action covering conventional and unconventional forms. These provided measures of *potential participation.*

Responses to these 12 measures were subject to a single factor analysis, which resulted in four factors: Participation in women's groups; collective protest; informal participation; and individual protest (see Appendix 3). Mean scores for individual items (for the whole sample) are shown in Figure 3.1. (It should be noted that there were no significant differences here or elsewhere across the different categories of activist group, for example, party political, work/trade union, etc. In fact, it was striking how similar were the responses from members of groups with such diverse aims and structures.)

Figure 3.1 shows that the highest scores (as in Study 1) were given to informal items, such as reading articles or watching films about women's issues, closely followed by items concerned with individual protest, such as contacting MPs. Lower participation scores were found for items relating to participation in women's groups and collective protest, in particular breaking the law. Reluctance to engage in any unlawful behaviour was also reflected in responses to an open-ended question where respondents were invited to explain their ratings concerning potential participation. By far the largest category of responses (29.8 per cent) were those stating that they would not want to break the law, although some stated that it would depend to some extent on the precise circumstances and the precise issue (see Figure 3.2).

Correlations were computed between the various aspects of behavioural intention, as well as self-perception as an activist, where respondents rated the extent to which they would describe themselves as 'someone who is actively involved in promoting women's issues'. This latter measure provides an indication of identification as an activist. Analysis showed that the strongest correlation was between this identification and participation in women's groups, suggesting that people's own definition of activism is strongly bound up with participation in these sorts of formal activities. By contrast, participation in collective protest activities was much less strongly associated with identification as an activist. It seems that the longer term commitment and responsibility associated with formal activities feed more strongly into a sense of identity than the short bursts of activity associated with attending rallies and demonstrations.

One year later at time two, respondents were asked to report to what extent during the previous 12 months they had *actually* engaged in the different forms of action which had been listed at time one as prospective participation items. Factor analysis of these subsequent scores revealed that all items at time two loaded on a single factor which can be called *overall participation* (see Appendix 4).

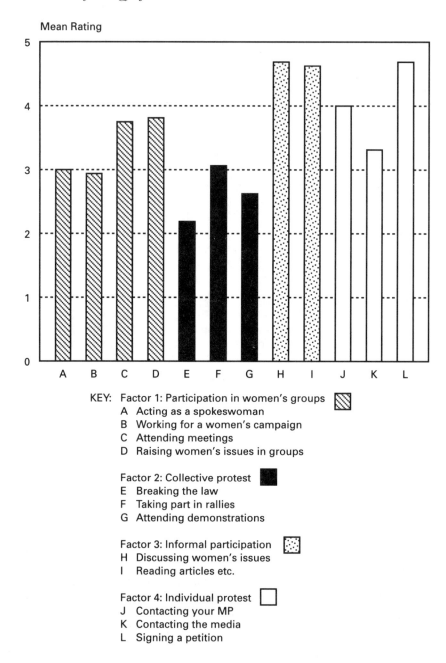

Figure 3.1: Readiness to participate in different types of action in a gender context: Mean ratings

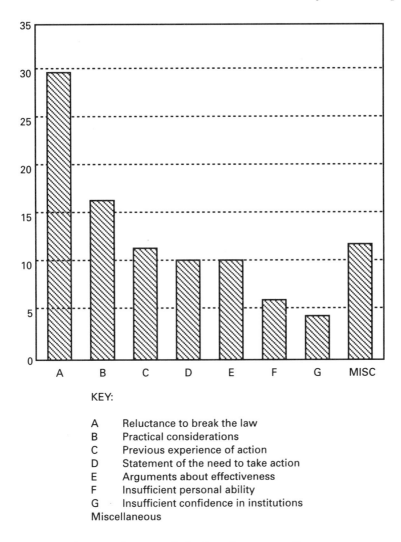

KEY:

A   Reluctance to break the law
B   Practical considerations
C   Previous experience of action
D   Statement of the need to take action
E   Arguments about effectiveness
F   Insufficient personal ability
G   Insufficient confidence in institutions
Miscellaneous

Figure 3.2: Explanations for protest behaviour: Percentage of responses

Using Social Beliefs to Predict Participation

As in Study 1, questions to be used as independent measures ranged over a
number of possible social psychological correlates of participation. Again, as
in Study 1, we will begin by examining social beliefs concerning group
identification, (collective) relative deprivation, political efficacy and collectivist
orientation and then move on to consider expectancy-value calculations. In
relation to the former, factor analysis extracted five factors which mapped onto
the sets of items comprising relative deprivation, gender identity, political

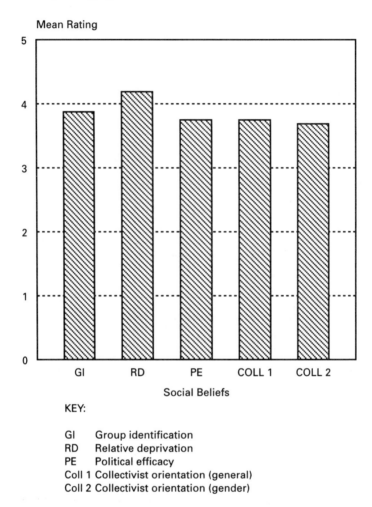

Mean Rating

Figure 3.3: Social beliefs: Mean scores

efficacy, collectivist orientation (concerning gender relations specifically) and collectivist orientation (general) (see Appendix 5). Mean scores for these composite factors are displayed in Figure 3.3.

Relationships between these social beliefs and participation were analysed using multiple regression as in Study 1. The five variables comprising gender identity, relative deprivation, political efficacy and collectivist orientation (both gender and general) were entered as independent variables and the four measures of participation (in women's groups, informal, and individual and collective protest) as dependent variables. Results are shown in Table 3.4.

Examining the contributions made by the different social beliefs in these equations shows that gender identity was the most powerful variable, being

Table 3.4: Social beliefs and participation in a gender context: Standardized regression coefficients

Independent variables	Dependent variables			
	1^1	2^2	3^3	4^4
Gender identity	37 **	28 **	36 **	19 **
Relative deprivation	05	23 **	23 **	13 **
Political efficacy	20 **	10 **	05	18 **
Collectivism (general)	09	05	–02	06
Collectivism (gender)	06	11 **	–01	04

Key:
[1] Participation in women's groups:
$R^2 = .31$; $F(5,593) = 54.25$; $p < 0.01$
[2] Collective protest:
$R^2 = .31$; $F(5,593) = 55.18$; $p < 0.01$
[3] Informal participation:
$R^2 = .27$; $F(5,593) = 44.96$; $p < 0.01$
[4] Individual protest:
$R^2 = .16$; $F(5,593) = 24.20$; $p < 0.01$
Decimal points have been omitted from regression coefficients
**$p < 0.01$

highly significant in all equations, especially those relating to participation in women's groups and informal participation. Thus, a strong sense of identification with other women as a group is associated with a readiness to participate in a range of activities on behalf of the group, just as identification with the union, in Study 1, was associated with a readiness to act on its behalf.

Turning to the other social beliefs, relative deprivation was significantly related to all forms of participation except participation in women's groups. By contrast, political efficacy emerged as a powerful correlate of participation in women's groups, as well as of individual protest. It is the belief that getting involved *does* make a difference which distinguishes more from less active individuals. Those less inclined to these types of activity were much more likely to feel that there's no point in participating, that it won't make any difference. Accordingly, a number of respondents commented on the questionnaire that they felt that the government and political institutions in Britain have become increasingly unresponsive throughout the 1980s and that nobody will pay any attention to lobbying by women's groups and campaigns.

The present findings show that feelings of powerlessness are associated with *inaction* on all the dimensions measured here. There is no suggestion that disaffection with conventional political channels encourages participation in unconventional or illegal activities. It is the same women who are prepared to get involved in conventional activities, such as writing to MPs over gender-related issues, who are also more likely to take part in protest rallies and demonstrations. Involvement in women's groups is not an expression of political disaffection for these women, but a commitment to do something positive to help bring about social change depends on a feeling that such change is a real possibility.

Neither of the variables relating to collectivist orientation was a powerful contributor to these equations. In fact, the *only* significant relationship was that women expressing a more collectivist orientation in a gender context also expressed greater readiness to get involved in collective protest activities.

Finally, we can undertake some cross-lagged analysis to address the question of causality. Correlations between social beliefs$_{(t1)}$ and total reported behaviour$_{(t2)}$ were in all cases greater than those between total behavioural intention$_{(t1)}$ and social beliefs$_{(t2)}$. The differences were small but consistent across all variables as follows: gender identity (.47 > .45); relative deprivation (.33 > .32); political efficacy (.29 > .20); and collectivist orientation (general) (.24 > .23). (Collectivist orientation (gender) was not measured at time two.) There is thus some evidence here of a slightly stronger causal connection from social beliefs to behaviour rather than the other way round.

The Moderating Role of Group Identification II

Further regression analysis was conducted to examine the possible moderating role of group identification. Using the gender identity variable, the sample was divided by a median split into relatively weak and strong identifiers. Analysis was then conducted where the independent variables comprised relative deprivation, political efficacy and the two measures of collectivism, and dependent variables comprised aggregate measures of total prospective participation (time one) and total actual participation (time two). Results are displayed in Table 3.5.

These results show some clear differences in the patterns of association for weak and strong identifiers in this context, particularly in the equations relating to reports of actual participation at time two, where the patterns of statistical significance were exactly opposite for the two sub-groups. In other words, for the weak identifiers, political efficacy and collectivist orientation (both gender and general) were significantly associated with reported participation but relative deprivation was not; whereas for the strong identifiers, relative deprivation was the *only* social belief which was significantly associated with reported participation. The differences were not quite so striking in the equations relating to prospective participation, where political efficacy and relative deprivation were significant correlates for both groups. However, differences relating to collectivist orientation remained, with both types being significantly related to prospective participation for weak but not for strong identifiers. These analyses suggest that group identification does play some role in moderating relationships between participation in collective action and other social beliefs.

Table 3.5: Group identification, social beliefs and participation in a gender context: Standardized regression coefficients

	Weak group identifiers	Strong group identifiers
Time 1 Intentions to participate (total)[1]		
Relative deprivation	18*	22**
Political efficacy	18*	23**
Collectivism (general)	19**	06
Collectivism (gender)	20**	10
Time 2 Reported participation (total)[2]		
Relative deprivation	11	18*
Political efficacy	21**	13
Collectivism (general)	19**	06
Collectivism (gender)	16*	08

Key:
[1] Weak group identifiers: R^2 = .18; $F(4,178)$ = 10.91; $p < 0.01$
Strong group identifiers: R^2 = .12; $F(4,193)$ = 7.97; $p < 0.01$
[2] Weak group identifiers: R^2 = .15; $F(4,178)$ = 8.89; $p < 0.01$
Strong group identifiers: R^2 = .06; $F(4,193)$ = 4.04; $p < 0.01$
Decimal points have been omitted from regression coefficients
*$p < 0.05$, **$p < 0.01$

Further support for this role comes from comparisons with regression analyses in which interaction terms were entered as independent variables. In analyses where the social beliefs variables were entered *separately* as independent variables (gender identity, relative deprivation, political efficacy, collectivist orientation) to predict total prospective participation$_{(t1)}$ and total actual participation$_{(t2)}$ (for the whole sample) the percentage of variance explained was 33 per cent and 21 per cent respectively. In the case of prospective participation, entering interaction terms (gender identity with collectivist orientation and with political efficacy) increased the percentage of variance explained to 34 per cent in both cases. An interaction term comprising gender identity with relative deprivation made no difference to the percentage of variance explained. In the case of actual participation, entering interaction terms (gender identity with relative deprivation, with political efficacy and with collectivist orientation) increased the percentage of variance explained to 23 per cent in all cases. Although these improvements were small, they are in line with findings from other research which has explored the role of interactions in regression (see Hirsch, 1990: 251).

Further investigation of the moderating role of group identification comes from analysis of the expectancy-value items to which we will turn shortly. Before this however, we will examine the impact of one further variable, namely identification as an activist.

Table 3.6: The impact of identification as an activist: Standardized regression coefficients

	Time 1 intentions to participate (total)[1]	Time 2 reported participation (total)[2]
Gender identity	16**	10
Relative deprivation	07	04
Political efficacy	05	06
Collectivism (general)	01	04
Collectivism (gender)	06	06
Identification as an activist	62**	50**

Key:
[1] $R^2 = .63$; $F(6,374) = 109.01$; $p < 0.01$
[2] $R^2 = .40$; $F(6,374) = 43.89$; $p < 0.01$
Decimal points have been omitted from regression coefficients
**$p < 0.01$

The Impact of Identification as an Activist

Self-perception as a political activist is likely to be an important factor in understanding political participation. In order to test this idea, regression analyses were conducted where dependent variables comprised the total measure of prospective participation (time one) and the total measure of reported actual participation (time two). This time, identification as an activist was included as an independent variable along with the other social beliefs. Results are displayed in Table 3.6.

This analysis shows that the addition of identification as an activist had the effect of eclipsing all other independent variables. In the case of prospective participation (time one), only gender identity maintained its significance in the equation; and in the case of reported actual participation (time two), all other variables ceased to be significant. Thus, reported activism at time two was accounted for *only* in terms of self-perception as an activist at time one. That respondents differed in the extent to which they felt a sense of activist identity was further confirmed in comments made in response to an open-ended question inviting women to explain their activism or non-activism. A number of activists referred to a sense of themselves as 'a doer', 'a natural campaigner', 'an action-oriented type person', 'someone who wants to do something positive for women'. This issue will be explored in subsequent chapters.

Intentions, Behaviour and Perceived Control

We can now look in more detail at the relationship between people's intentions to participate at time one and their actual behaviour as reported one year later at time two.

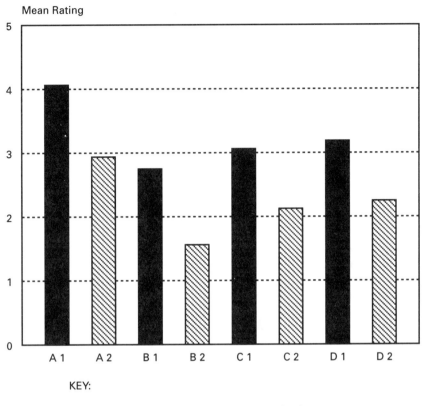

KEY:

A1/2   Attending meetings (Intention/Behaviour)
B1/2   Taking part in rallies (Intention/Behaviour)
C1/2   Working for a women's campaign (Intention/Behaviour)
D1/2   Acting as a spokeswoman (Intention/Behaviour)

Figure 3.4: Intentions and behaviours: Mean scores

Mean scores for intended and actual behaviour are shown in Figure 3.4.

Why were intentions not fully realized? One possibility is that social beliefs changed. In order to test this idea, we examined respondents' social beliefs measured at time two, which were a sub-set of those measured at time one relating to relative deprivation, group identification, political efficacy and collectivist orientation. Examining the scores revealed that the first three of these items showed slight *increases* over time whereas collectivist orientation showed a slight decrease. None of these changes was statistically significant. Consequently, this does not seem a likely explanation for the discrepancy between intentions and behaviour.

Another possibility concerns the prevailing political context. The period over which the research was conducted (1992–93) was not one of great political activity over gender relations at a societal level and many respondents commented themselves that they felt that the political climate was hostile to single-issue campaigns (see Chapter 6 for further detail). Perhaps as a result, respondents were less involved in collective action than they had anticipated.

A third possibility concerns the roles of opportunity and practical constraints, which are encapsulated in the notion of 'perceived behavioural control' in the theory of planned behaviour (Ajzen and Madden, 1986; see Chapter 2). To investigate this possibility, we carried out a complete test of this model and its predecessor, the theory of reasoned action, on the present data. This analysis also represents a test of the expectancy-value approach in this context.

We thus concentrate on three factors – *attitudinal* (mapping onto Klandermans' reward motives); *normative* (mapping onto Klandermans' social motives); and perceived behavioural control. (Measures relating to Klandermans' notion of goal motives – as employed in Study 1 – cannot be meaningfully included here because of the varied nature of the groups' goals and activities.)

Attitudinal factors were measured in relation to two possible outcomes of group participation. They were first, getting to know lots of other like-minded women; and second, doing something positive to help bring about change for women. In each case, respondents were asked at time one to assess the expectation that group participation would be associated with this outcome and to assess the value attached to that outcome. The two products from these ratings were averaged to provide the attitudinal component (internal reliability .72). The normative component comprised the expected reactions at time one of first, friends and second, family to participation by the respondent in a women's group or campaign multiplied in each case by the values attached to those reactions. These two products were averaged to produce the normative component (internal reliability .54).

Perceived behavioural control was measured also at time one by the single item, 'Women's meetings are often too difficult to get to', which emerged from pilot interviews as a common way in which control beliefs were expressed. Attendance at group meetings was seen as central to involvement; the item also covers a range of possible practical impediments, such as lack of time, transport and childcare facilities which would inhibit involvement.

In order to test the theories of reasoned action and planned behaviour, regression analysis was employed where attitudinal, normative and control factors (measured at time one) were used to predict intention (at time one) and then intention and control (both at time one) were used to predict behaviour (at time two). Table 3.7 shows the results of hierarchical regression analysis for the first of these analyses, namely the prediction of intention.

In this analysis, attitude and subjective norm were entered in the first step as specified by the theory of reasoned action. The attitudinal component was very strongly related to intention, whereas the normative component made a much weaker contribution to the equation, only just reaching statistical significance. In the second step, perceived behavioural control was incorporated into

Table 3.7: Prediction of intention (whole sample): Standardized regression coefficients

	r	Beta	R^2
Step 1 (Theory of reasoned action)			
F(2,369) = 82.58**			
Attitude	55**	52**	
Subjective norm	26**	09*	.31
Step 2 (Theory of planned behaviour)			
F(3,368) = 57.46**			
Attitude		51**	
Subjective norm		09*	
Perceived behavioural control	15**	10*	.31

Key:
*p < 0.05; **p < 0.01
Decimal points have been omitted from correlation and regression coefficients

the equation as specified by the theory of planned behaviour. As can be seen from Table 3.7, the contributions of the attitudinal and normative components were largely unchanged and perceived behavioural control made a small contribution to the equation which was comparable to that of the normative component. The value of R^2 was unchanged.

Table 3.8 shows the results of hierarchical regression analysis for the prediction of behaviour. In this analysis, intention was entered in the first step in accordance with the theory of reasoned action and perceived behavioural control in the second step in accordance with the theory of planned behaviour.

Results show a strong relationship between intention and behaviour and a much weaker (though still just significant) relationship between control and

Table 3.8: Prediction of behaviour (whole sample): Standardized regression coefficients

	r	Beta	R^2
Step 1 (Theory of reasoned action)			
F(1,372) = 435.27**			
Intention	74**	74**	.54
Step 2 (Theory of planned behaviour)			
F(2,371) = 223.21**			
Intention		71**	
Perceived behavioural control	19**	08*	.54

Key:
*p < 0.05; **p < 0.01
Decimal points have been omitted from correlation and regression coefficients

behaviour. The addition of the control variable made no difference to the overall R^2 value. There is thus little evidence here that the sort of practical impediments represented by the control variable were responsible for the discrepancy between intentions and behaviour, though of course it is possible that a more complex measure of control would have picked up other considerations.

The Moderating Role of Group Identification III

A further possibility is that the relative importance of attitudinal, normative and control factors will vary according to the degree to which the activity in question is relevant to the individual's identity (see Chapter 2). To test this idea, the sample was divided according to strength of identification as an activist using a median split. This provided groups of relatively weak and strong identifiers. Regression analyses were repeated on each sub-group separately. Results for the prediction of intention are shown in Table 3.9.

Results for the weak identifiers show that the attitudinal component was significantly associated with intention, though the normative component was not, and that the addition of perceived behavioural control in Step 2 made little difference to the pattern of relationships or to the overall R^2 values. The pattern for strong identifiers was rather different. None of the variables in Steps 1 or 2 showed a significant relationship with intention and consequently, the overall R^2 value was much lower than that for the weak identifiers. Thus, it appears that

Table 3.9: Prediction of intention for weak and strong identifiers: Standardized regression coefficients

	r	Beta	R^2
Step 1 (Theory of reasoned action) Weak identifiers: $F(2,186) = 29.41^{**}$ Strong identifiers: $F(2,180) = 3.67^{*}$			
Attitude	47** (19**)	45** (15)	
Subjective norm	24** (13)	11 (09)	.23 (.03)
Step 2 (Theory of planned behaviour) Weak identifiers: $F(3,185) = 20.78^{**}$ Strong identifiers: $F(3,179) = 3.00^{*}$			
Attitude		45** (13)	
Subjective norm		09 (11)	
Perceived behavioural control	14 (11)	11 (10)	.24 (03)

Key:
Figures outside parentheses refer to weak identifiers; Figures inside parentheses refer to strong identifiers
$^{*}p < 0.05$; $^{**}p < 0.01$
Decimal points have been omitted from correlation and regression coefficients

the contribution of the attitudinal component in the equation for the whole sample (Table 3.7) can be accounted for largely by the responses from the weak identifiers.

In analysis using the whole sample, if just the attitudinal component was used as an independent variable, the percentage of variance explained was 30 per cent; if just identification as an activist was used, this figure went up to 47 per cent; if these two variables were both entered, 52 per cent; and if an interaction term composed of these variables was used, 53 per cent of variance was explained. In other words, the percentage of variance explained was higher in the equation with only the interaction effect than with the main effects entered separately or together.

Turning to the prediction of behaviour, Table 3.10 shows the results of hierarchical regression analysis for the two sub-groups. The results here were very similar for the two sub-groups. In both cases, intention was very strongly associated with behaviour and the addition of the control factor made hardly any difference to the overall R^2 value. There was no direct relationship between control and behaviour for either group. The use of interaction terms in analysis using the whole sample did not improve the amount of variance explained.

To sum up, results from these analyses show, first of all, strong support for the theory of reasoned action rather than the theory of planned behaviour in this context. In other words, the addition of behavioural control, as specified by the theory of planned behaviour, added little to regression equations, suggesting that the type of behaviour under consideration here is under high volitional

Table 3.10: Prediction of behaviour for weak and strong identifiers: Standardized regression coefficients

	r	Beta	R^2
Step 1 (Theory of reasoned action)			
Weak identifiers: $F(1,187) = 88.48^{**}$			
Strong identifiers: $F(1,183) = 102.73^{**}$			
Intention	57** (60**)	57** (60**)	.32 (.36)
Step 2 (Theory of planned behaviour)			
Weak identifiers: $F(2,186) = 45.69^{**}$			
Strong identifiers: $F(2,182) = 54.08^{**}$			
Intention		55** (59**)	
Perceived behavioural control	17* (18*)	09 (12)	.32 (.37)

Key:
Figures outside parentheses refer to weak identifiers; figures inside parentheses refer to strong identifiers
$^*p < 0.05$; $^{**}p < 0.01$
Decimal points have been omitted from correlation and regression coefficients

control and is therefore adequately accounted for by the theory of reasoned action. Although ratings of perceived control were significantly related to intentions and behaviour, these relationships were relatively weak by comparison with the predictor variables from the theory of reasoned action, particularly the attitudinal component. Attitudinal considerations were also found to be especially important for those individuals who identified themselves relatively weakly as political activists.

Identity and its Behavioural Expression

Finally, can we bring together expectancy-value and the other social beliefs (group identification, relative deprivation, political efficacy, collectivist orientation) to produce an overall activist profile? When all of these variables were analysed together, only one of the expectancy-value variables (attitudinal or normative) retained its significance in the resulting equation, namely the expectation and value attached to 'a feeling of doing something positive for women'. Indeed, this variable emerged as the only one (of all the social beliefs) which was significant across all forms of behavioural intention at time one, as well as reported behaviour at time two. The importance of this feeling also emerged in interviews (to be discussed in more detail in subsequent chapters) where many activists said that although they sometimes had doubts about the effectiveness of their actions in terms of actually bringing about any social change, they nevertheless had a sense that it was important to stand up and be counted, to do *something* rather than nothing. The next most powerful factor overall was identification with other women – a strong sense of gender identity. The desire to *do* something for women can be seen as the behavioural expression of this identity. These themes will be explored more fully in subsequent chapters.

Conclusions to Study 2

This study into women's participation in a gender context has shown a number of interesting findings from the questionnaire data. Results from factor analysis revealed four types of participation: Participation in women's groups; collective protest, such as attending rallies and demonstrations; informal participation, such as discussing women's issues with friends; and individual protest, such as signing petitions. Of these different types of participation, those concerned with collective protest received the lowest scores and comments made by respondents suggested a dislike of mass confrontation and a very widespread reluctance to engage in any unlawful behaviour.

Examining the correlates of participation in these different forms of activity showed support for a number of the theoretical constructs discussed in Chapter

2, namely group identification, collective relative deprivation, political efficacy and collectivist orientation. The strength of the associations between these variables and intentions to participate varied somewhat across the different types of participation, though a sense of group identification with other women stood out clearly across all types. Cross-lagged correlations showed slightly stronger connections from these social beliefs to behaviour than the other way round. In addition, two other factors emerged as important. The first was derived from the expectancy-value variables and concerned the importance attached to doing something positive for women. The second concerned self-perception as an activist which overshadowed all other variables when it was incorporated into analyses. These results point to the central role of identity and the desire to give that identity some behavioural expression.

Group identification not only has a direct relationship with participation; it also plays an important moderating role. A number of differences emerged between the correlates of participation for relatively weak and strong group identifiers. Indeed, in some cases the patterns of association were completely different. In relation to reported actual behaviour, collective relative deprivation was the only significant correlate for strong identifiers and conversely, the only social belief which was *not* a significant correlate for weak identifiers. In relation to the expectancy-value variables, it was found that attitudinal factors were much more important in predicting intentions amongst weak than strong identifiers. For strong identifiers, participation in collective action is central to their social identity and calculations of costs and benefits are of less significance. It seems valuable then to examine the way in which different variables interact to promote participation in collective action. This point will be pursued in subsequent chapters where qualitative data from this same sample of respondents will be presented.

Comparing the Two Contexts of Action

A number of points can be made in comparing the correlates of behavioural intention across the two contexts – trade union and gender – though there is not a perfect match between the specific measures used in the two studies. One factor which does stand out however is the importance in both contexts of the individual's sense of group identification. Individuals express intentions to get involved in collective action to the extent that they feel a sense of identification with the group in question, be it a trade union or a gender category. Where individuals do feel a strong sense of group identification, achieving collective goals becomes a matter of personal concern.

The role of group identification as a moderating variable was much more evident in the gender context, though a similar relationship with collective relative deprivation was hinted at in the trade union study as well. Since this interaction has been found in previous research as well (see Haselau, *et al.*,

1991; Kawakami and Dion, 1993), it may be safe to conclude that a sense of collective relative deprivation is indeed a more important correlate of action for individuals who identify strongly with the group.

It is interesting that if we consider the direct relationship between collective relative deprivation and intentions to participate (regardless of level of group identification), this was found to be non-significant in the context of trade union involvement and in the context of intentions to participate in women's groups (although it was significantly related to other forms of participation in the gender context). It seems that a sense of collective injustice is not a strong predictor of involvement in formal group activities, though as we have noted already, it is a more important factor for some people than others.

Two factors which were measured in both studies – collectivist orientation and political efficacy – showed inconsistent results. The former was associated with intentions to participate in the *easier* forms of trade union action but was not a strong correlate of activity in the gender context. The latter showed no significant associations in the trade union context, whereas in the gender context it was significantly associated with all forms of behavioural intention apart from informal activities where a weaker relationship would be expected anyway. Furthermore, the possibility of an interaction with group identification which was suggested in the first study, with efficacy being a more important consideration for weaker identifiers, was not confirmed in the second study, where no clear pattern emerged in this respect.

Drawing further comparisons across the two contexts is difficult because of the somewhat different measures which were used. Expectancy-value calcula-tions were assessed in both studies though (necessarily) there were some differences in the precise measures employed. In both cases, significant associations were found in analyses where expectancy-value calculations were used alone as independent variables, but the significance of these factors was considerably reduced when they were pitted against the more group-oriented variables in a single analysis. In the gender context, expectancy-value calcula-tions were found to be particularly important for individuals who did not have a strong sense of themselves as activists.

One interesting difference between the two studies is that in the trade union context, considerations of the effectiveness of action (as measured by goal motives) proved to be a particularly important part of respondents' expectancy-value calculations. By contrast, in the context of gender, women stressed the importance of 'doing something positive for women' almost regardless of the perceived effectiveness of the action in actually bringing about some social change. Here, involvement in collective activities is partly a way of expressing support and solidarity with other women, giving a behavioural expression to gender identity, as well as bringing about social change. While there are undoubtedly trade union activists whose involvement is undertaken in a similar spirit, it is possible that most trade union members most of the time have a more instrumental orientation to action and will only get involved in costly action if this is perceived to be effective in bringing about some change. The particular support and solidarity functions of women's groups will emerge in later chapters as well. To conclude here, we can suggest that the nature of the group will, in all likelihood, have an important bearing on the factors which lead group members to get involved in collective action.

The quantitative analysis undertaken in these two contexts has provided evidence relating to a number of the theoretical approaches discussed in Chapter 2 and has suggested that the central elements of participation are self-perception as an activist, identification with a social group and the desire to give some behavioural expression to that sense of identification through collective action. The following chapter will focus on respondents' own accounts of what led to their involvement in women's groups and we can examine the extent to which factors discussed in this chapter are reflected in respondents' own accounts.

Notes

1   This study was conducted by Caroline Kelly and John Kelly and is also described in: Kelly, C. and Kelly, J.E. (1994) Who gets involved in collective action?: Social psychological determinants of individual participation in trade unions. *Human Relations,* **47**, 63–88.

2   Use of the term *women's issues* in questionnaire items is not meant to imply that we feel that these issues *should* be exclusively women's concerns but we could think of no other term which would encompass the enormous range and diversity of issues covered by the different groups and be meaningful to our respondents.

3   While the terms *activist* and *non-activist* have been used here and elsewhere in other chapters, we are nevertheless sympathetic to the view that there are many different *types* of activist and that many people who are not involved in formal activities may nevertheless be involved in informal activities. Where we use the terms here, they refer specifically to responses on this question of self-reported current involvement in women's groups and campaigns.

Chapter 4

Explaining Initial Involvement: Why Join Women's Groups?

In Chapter 3, data was presented which showed clear differences between the social beliefs of individuals involved to varying extents in collective action in trade union and gender contexts. Clear differences emerged relating to social identity, relative deprivation, collectivist orientation, political efficacy and the perceived costs and benefits associated with participation. Having established these differences, the next step concerns the causal connections – to what extent are these beliefs causes or effects of involvement? The present chapter will focus on reasons for initial involvement and will make use of qualitative data concerning involvement in women's groups which illustrates and develops the themes discussed in Chapter 3.

Explanations for involvement to be discussed here are taken from two sources. Firstly, in-depth interviews were carried out with 30 women activists who had volunteered to be interviewed from a questionnaire mail-out (see Chapter 3 for details). Interviewees were members of a range of different groups and had been involved for varying lengths of time. Interviews were conducted on a one-to-one basis by a female interviewer in respondents' homes and were tape-recorded and fully transcribed. Interviews lasted between one and three hours and followed a semi-structured format. The second source of data to be discussed here were responses to an open-ended question on the questionnaire which invited respondents to explain why they had got involved in women's groups or campaigns. On the questionnaire, 327 activists provided explanations for their involvement ranging from a couple of sentences in length to several paragraphs (and in some cases, pages). These comments were fully transcribed.

Qualitative data obtained by means of interviews and questionnaires was analysed by both researchers, initially working independently and then coming together to arrive at a mutually agreed set of coding categories. These categories were constantly revised in the light of the data until a final satisfactory set was achieved. All the data was then coded by both researchers, again working independently and then together (see Chapter 1 for methodological discussion).

Asking people to provide accounts of their lives and to explain actions taken some time – even years – previously raises particular methodological issues. In her adoption of a life-history approach to social research, Andrews (1991) defends the approach against the criticism that the data gained is based on biased or faulty recollections of the past and is therefore invalid. Instead, she argues that the inevitable selectiveness of memory for life events is not a problem for researchers – unless they are documenting a strict chronological biography. For researchers interested in social psychological processes, the way in which a respondent reconstructs his or her past and the events seen as significant are interesting in their own right. Indeed, Andrews argues that it is impossible to distinguish a single, objectively correct account of a person's life, quoting DeWaele and Harré:

> The individual's past is not a relic ... Quite the contrary, it is part of the living present ... what is remembered of it is inevitably subject to continuous modification ... the past not only makes us, but we also make it by putting pieces together into a more or less coherent whole (1979: 180–1; see also Becker and Geer, 1979).

Andrews echoes this dialectical perspective on the passage of time: 'Individuals are constructed by their pasts, but at the same time they are constantly involved in reconstructing, reinterpreting and re-membering that past' (p. 65).

Consequently, in conducting research where we ask participants to provide accounts of their lives or, as in the present case, to explain how they first came to get involved in collective action, the data gathered represents current perspectives and interpretations of events. The connections made between events are made possible with the benefit of hindsight and with the perspective of a personal and social identity which has developed subsequently. Thus, 'reconstructed memory provides the rememberer with some sense of continuity in her life' (Andrews, 1991: 65). In the present research, we should bear in mind that the data represents respondents' current interpretations of the factors which led to their initial involvement in collective action.

To give some idea of the demographic characteristics of our interviewees, Appendix 6 provides a profile according to questionnaire responses showing the type of women's group to which the respondent belonged, for example, work/professional, party political, etc., duration of membership in that group, membership of other women's groups, ethnicity (as described by the respondent), age, occupation and whether or not she had children. A comparison of scores on variables relating to participation and social beliefs (see Chapter 3) showed that our interviewees were representative of our wider activist sample.

From analysis of the qualitative data, six distinct themes emerged in the explanations which were given for initial involvement in women's groups. These were: the respondent's *personal background* and *personal characteristics, social beliefs, life events, services offered by the group* and an element of *chance.* Each of these major categories comprised a number of specific sub-themes and here we can look for correspondence with the social beliefs discussed in Chapter 3. The explanations provided for initial involvement are illustrated in Figure 4.1.

Of course there are important connections between these various themes – emphasized by the links made between the first four categories in Figure 4.1 – and the coding process rests ultimately on judgments about where the conceptual boundaries lie within a set of statements. The frequencies with

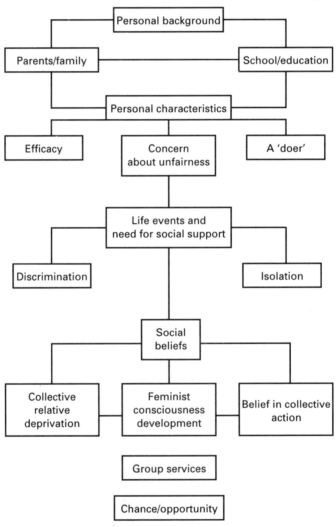

Figure 4.1: Explanations for initial involvement in women's groups

Table 4.1: Interviewees' explanations for initial involvement: Frequencies

Category	Number of comments (n = 143)	Number of interviewees (n = 30)
Personal background/characteristics	49 (34%)	22
Life events and social support	42 (29%)	24
Social beliefs	26 (18%)	16
Group services	8 (6%)	8
Chance	18 (13%)	18

which the major categories were drawn upon *in interview* is represented in Table 4.1.

In all, there were 143 distinct comments (or units) which emerged from the 30 interviews as explanations for initial involvement. The length of these units varied enormously from short statements to lengthy discussions on a particular theme. Categorization into coding units is a subjective judgment. Thus, each respondent was providing on average between four and five different explanations, sometimes drawing on different categories and sometimes on different sub-themes within the same overall category. The fact that respondents were drawing on more than one explanation suggests that it is important to look at the constellations of factors and the interactions between them rather than search for a single cause of activism. Table 4.1 also shows the number of interviewees who drew (at least once) on each of the main categories. For example, the first column shows that in total 49 comments were made relating to aspects of personal background/personal characteristics (34 per cent of the total number of comments); the second column shows that 22 of the 30 respondents referred to such factors. (Data relating to these two factors has been aggregated because respondents clearly linked aspects of their personal background with the development of various personal characteristics.)

As we can see, nearly two-thirds of the explanations centre around aspects of personal background/personal characteristics and life events. However, it is worth noting that when this interview data is compared with the data obtained from the questionnaire (482 explanations in all), the numbers of responses referring to personal background/personal characteristics and life events dropped dramatically to 4.2 per cent and 13.1 per cent respectively. In the questionnaire, by far the largest categories of response referred to social beliefs and group services. (Although the frequencies in the various categories differed for the questionnaire data, the categories themselves were the same.) To explain this difference, it is possible that the more impersonal questionnaire approach encourages a response which is itself rather impersonal and is easier and quicker to give. An in-depth one-to-one interview by contrast encourages the respondent to reflect on personal factors and to provide the interviewer with an account which places political activism within the broader context of the individual's life-history. Thus, when considering the present findings we should be alert to the fact that the explanation given for involvement depends to some extent on the context in which the question is asked. Of course, it is also possible that the women who volunteered for interview were different in some way from the rest of the sample though, as stated previously, a comparison of scores on the questionnaire items showed no differences at least in this respect.

If we turn then to the factors displayed in Figure 4.1, we can see that all of the social beliefs discussed in Chapter 3 (social identity, collective relative deprivation, political efficacy, collectivist orientation) are represented in some form or other. In the discussion which follows it will be possible to see the precise form which these beliefs take in this context and how they are interrelated. Each factor will be discussed in turn drawing on both questionnaire and interview data for the purpose of illustration. Extracts are referenced by respondent numbers. As each factor is discussed, related themes and relevant previous research will also be described.

Personal Background and Personal Characteristics

The first cluster of responses concerns personal background and personal characteristics. Personal background comprises parents/family on the one hand (the main element discussed by respondents) and (to a much lesser extent) school/education on the other. In relation to the former, respondents' parents were very mixed in terms of their own *level* of political activity. Some respondents said that their parents were activists and that political activism was very much a part of their upbringing, for example, 'a "speak out against evil where you see it" kind of background' (434). Some respondents even referred to their grandmothers' involvement in the Suffragette movement as evidence of the family tradition of political activism in the area of gender.

On the other hand, just as many other respondents commented that their parents had *not* been politically active and that their own activity was a reaction or compensation for their parents' inactivity, for example, 'My reaction was that it's better to get in there and try and do things than just to be sitting at home feeling upset or guilty or angry' (431), 'We've never been the kind of family to take a stand on anything, anything for a quiet life' (230). We cannot conclude therefore that level of general parental political involvement will predict own involvement in any simple fashion.

Gender Relations in the Family

More important than parents' *level* of political activity was the set of attitudes which they encouraged in their daughters regarding gender relations. Two contrasting patterns emerged here. On the one hand, were respondents who referred to perceived inequalities in the treatment of boys and girls in the family and to the sense of injustice which this engendered. These stories of perceived injustice in the family are worth quoting at some length since they convey a strong sense of the women's emotional responses:

... coming from a very patriarchal Jewish religion, really resenting that, really feeling like a second class citizen and not being willing to accept that, feeling really very strongly about that. I used to go to the synagogue with my father, I adored my father and then when you're seven, you're thrown up into the women's gallery, you're not allowed to sit with the men anymore. And the sense of exile and outrage, not being able to sit with my father any more and not having a sense of place and security. I knew if I'd been a boy, I wouldn't have been sent up there (311);

I think my ideas were formed at quite an early age and basically they haven't altered all that much, because I could see that my brother was getting a much better education than I was, simply because he was a boy. My parents spent money on him but they didn't on me and that didn't strike me as fair at the time and it still doesn't strike me as fair now (325);

I know that even when I was a little girl, I went around saying 'It's not fair.' I was forever seeing things that weren't fair. I was the eldest and I had a brother, and my mother absolutely adored my brother. And because he was a boy he used to get lots of privileges – he was allowed endless slices of the white bread we were brought up on – with butter – but I was only allowed two slices with butter and then I had to have margarine, which was pretty diabolical in those days! Little things like that – he didn't have to do the washing up and I did. I grew up really grumbly because of this brother, who got all those privileges that I didn't get and I think I got an anger about things that aren't 'fair' and that is quite a motivation I think for me. If I see an injustice, I want to do something about it. Who knows if it's about having that brother and the slices of bread and margarine (422);

I think it's my family experiences really. My uncles, my cousins, my male cousins – they always had to do things that I wasn't allowed to do. I remember I wanted a bike for my birthday and my Dad said 'No, you can't, you're a girl' and my cousin got a bike, and I said 'Why did you get a bike?' and I felt really sick about that. And ever since, he was always treated differently, he was always thought of as more than I was, and I thought 'Why am I treated as more inferior than he is?' Because he's a male. It was quite a crazy thing, that they thought less of you because you were a woman. In your own family as well. Even my mother, which I could never forgive her for, she always thought that being a man was much better than being a woman (596).

This sense of injustice engendered in childhood provides one clear route to subsequent activism on behalf of women as a group. The personal injustices described were obviously very keenly felt and these experiences broadened out into a wider sense that women as a group are disadvantaged.

There was a second contrasting route to activism which was also engendered in personal background. These were respondents who commented that they were brought up to believe that gender is *not* an issue, that men and women are obviously equals and that they, as women, could achieve anything they wanted. This feeling was very much reinforced at school. Many of these respondents attended all-girls schools (and sometimes colleges) where they not only saw women in responsible positions and became used to talking over personal problems with other women, but were also given confidence and a very positive feeling that they could do and achieve anything they wanted and that it was nothing to do with gender. The clear way in which this theme emerged from our data suggests that this feeling of early confidence or personal efficacy is an important part of the life history of some female activists. It was when this confidence was shattered by the experience of discrimination in later life that many of these women were led to political activism. For example,

Until I went to [college], I don't think I ever felt discriminated against because usually I'd been in situations where it just didn't occur and I think that's probably why it was such a shock to me facing blatant discrimination that then I felt I had to do something about it (431);

I went to art school and after the first year we had an interview with the principal who flatly told me that I couldn't go into creative art because people in advertising agencies only took men, women left and had babies. That was my first encounter. So I was what then, I was 19, coming up 20. That was my first encounter of the block which was a bit shattering because my parents had always been open-minded and my father especially had always said you can do whatever it is that you want to do (296);

I grew up with very conservative parents who did not encourage me towards feminism at all. I went to a girls' school and thought it was fine to be clever and female. It was only when I got to university that I discovered that it wasn't fine at all after all. The sexism I discovered shocked and paralysed me for a bit before I realised that I was not the only woman feeling that way (328).

This second route contrasts with that concerned with early experiences of unfairness. Indeed, a related feature of the second route is that many respondents in this group commented that their parents encouraged a general concern about unfairness and a sympathy for people getting a rough deal. This combination of factors promoted in respondents' upbringing – personal efficacy and a general concern about unfairness – set the stage for a second route to later political involvement. This is one place where we can see the role of efficacy which emerged as a significant characteristic of activists from the analyses presented in Chapter 3.

To summarize, our data shows two distinct patterns of family experience. The first refers to those respondents who felt a sense of personal injustice through family experiences when they felt that they were not receiving the same treatment as brothers and other male relations. Here, a number of respondents provided accounts of incidents from childhood when they felt that they had been treated unfairly. Many of the incidents, while apparently trivial, were strongly felt and vividly remembered. Respondents argued that it was such incidents which led them to feel that women as a group are not treated equally. The second route refers to the opposite state of affairs in childhood, namely, to the idea encouraged by parents that women can do whatever they want to do in life and are no different from men. This engendered a sense of confidence which was shaken by subsequent experience of discrimination. What links these different patterns is clearly the experience of discrimination and the feelings of injustice which arise from it; what is different about the accounts is the stage in life at which these women first perceived unfair treatment on the basis of sex.

These two patterns confirm the important role of perceived injustice and support some previous theorizing as to the origins of a sense of relative deprivation. In his discussion, Brown (1988) describes two ways in which a sense of relative deprivation may develop: first, through social comparisons with similar others (Runciman, 1966); and second, through experience and the expectations which develop as a result (Davies, 1969). The two routes to activism which have been identified here map onto these two ideas, where the first relates to social comparisons made in the family (between self and brothers, male cousins, etc.); and the second relates to the expectations built up in childhood concerning equality of treatment.

The role of childhood experiences was also explored by Banks (1986) in her study of the social origins of 'first wave' feminism. In common with the second route to activism identified in the present research, she found that these feminists often had parents – fathers in particular – who were radical in their politics, who encouraged independence in their daughters and who provided a role model which emphasized achievement rather than dependence (see also Stewart and Gold-Steinberg, 1990). She suggests that this pattern was particularly common where the mother–daughter relationship was weak and notes that there were fewer close and affectionate relationships with mothers than with fathers in her sample. Mothers were more likely to have discouraged their daughters in their ambitions largely, she suggests, because the mothers had more conventional attitudes to the position of women than the fathers. We turn now to look in more detail at relationships between mothers and daughters.

Mothers and Daughters

A tendency for some women to feel critical of their mothers has been noted by some feminist commentators. For example, Briscoe (1994) argues:

> While men talk about the inspiration – or pressure – their fathers' success has meant for them, women often seem desperate to be as different from their mothers as possible. Mothers and homemakers are wimps in the eyes of so many daughters, particularly amongst the generation for whom the feminist movement intervened (p. 37).

Others have also argued that the reality of mother–daughter relationships does not reflect the popular and idealized belief that such relationships are characterized by an intrinsic closeness. For example, O'Connor (1990) conducted an interview study with 60 women and found that less than a third of them described their relationships with their mothers as very close. Relationships with sisters were frequently reported to be more rewarding and to be characterized by an intimate sharing quality not typical of relationships with mothers. O'Connor concludes that the idea that mother–daughter relationships are very close is a reflection of prevailing definitions of femininity and an idealized view of the mother role (see also Baruch and Barnett, 1983; Boyd, 1989; Fischer, 1981; Henwood and Coughlin, 1993 for a review).

However, in their study, Henwood and Coughlin (1993) found a strong preference among their interviewees to describe mother–daughter relationships as very close or intimate – but the meaning of these terms varied widely, in some cases referring to global feelings of fondness or affection, in others to ease of interaction, and in others to a feeling of 'we-ness' or 'one-ness'. Where women did describe relationships with their mothers as conflictual, they often drew on images, such as the mother 'clutching onto' the daughter, as a way of understanding and communicating their experiences.

In the present research, it was notable that in discussing their family backgrounds, respondents tended to focus particularly on their past and present relationships with their mothers and the ways in which relationships with mothers had shaped their views. Respondents talked in particular about the extent to which their views on gender relations were similar or different from those of their mothers. Their comments reveal both the points of connection and difference between generations, on the whole, painting a picture of perceived difference in terms of lifestyle and outlooks. In this respect, they point to the particular difficulties of maintaining solidarity between different generations of women. More generally, the comments allow us to reflect on interaction across the generations and the ways in which individuals (in this case, mothers and daughters), are influenced by the attitudes and behaviours of each other's generation. They illustrate the ways in which, through interaction with others, we are constantly involved in revising and renewing our beliefs.

Five themes emerged from analysis of these responses (taken from interviews with activists and non-activists), two of which expressed broadly positive sentiments towards mothers, whereas the remaining three were broadly negative, expressing a seemingly unbridgeable gulf between the generations. Each theme will be briefly described with illustrating extracts from interviews.

'There's a lot of my mother in me'

This theme is the most positive in its emphasis where respondents stressed the similarities between themselves and their mothers, at least in terms of beliefs if not in terms of lifestyle. Although a number of respondents pointed to the differences in the material circumstances of their lives as compared to their mothers, they perceived a basic correspondence of outlook and a sharing of belief. Respondents here expressed positive and affectionate feelings towards their mothers, arguing that their own beliefs were influenced in a positive way by those of their mothers. For example, 'She's quite a fighter – if she doesn't like what she's been out and bought at the greengrocers, or if there's a kettle she's bought that doesn't work, she will take things back and complain. She won't be shortchanged' (592).

Statements of similarity were often accompanied however by acknowledgement of difference, so that, for example, the same respondent who stated that there is 'a lot of her mother in her' also stated that, 'I'm much more like my father' (592). This sense of difference usually referred to a perception that respondents' mothers' lives were more narrow or circumscribed, more focused on the home and family. Although some respondents said that their own lives had started off on a similar track, events, such as marriage breakdown, had caused the direction of their lives to change making their current circumstances very different from those of their mothers.

'I'm not a feminist but . . .'

Respondents here were arguing that although their mothers would not want to call themselves feminists, their views on a number of issues do reflect a feminist perspective. Thus, one woman said, 'She sort of dismisses it all [feminism] as nonsense. But if I talk to her about individual issues, then she listens and sometimes she agrees. Then if you say to her, "Well that makes you a feminist Mum", she gets very put out by it' (318).

It was also the case that some women argued that through their own involvement in feminism, their mothers felt more comfortable with the label and more able to talk about the issues, though it is also possible that their daughters' involvement led some mothers to actually change or reassess their views. For example:

> Maybe ten years ago, my mother would have said, 'I'm not a feminist but this, this and this', and now she would be happy to call herself a feminist, she's got lots of feminist books. I think she's always had it there but she couldn't bring herself to call herself a feminist when we [respondent and sisters] kept saying, 'It's all right' (418).

'Oh yes dear, very nice'

The following three themes are rather more negative in their emphasis. The first expressed a perception that respondents' mothers are basically not very interested in the issues and certainly not prepared to engage in discussion or debate, even to express disagreement. This theme is illustrated most clearly by the following extract:

> Oh mothers! My mother says, 'Oh yes dear, very nice' and doesn't really understand the first thing about it. She doesn't interfere and she doesn't support. She just says, 'Oh yes, very nice', whatever it is I do. And if she likes it, then fine, and if she doesn't like it, she doesn't say anything. She might say, 'Well, perhaps you shouldn't be quite so forceful about this'. She doesn't really know what's best and she leaves it up to me to decide. She doesn't push her views on me at all. I've no idea what she thinks quite honestly (230).

Other respondents echoed this feeling of a lack of communication with their mothers and a perceived lack of interest in the issues on the part of their mothers. Respondents here emphasized a sense of difference and often a regret that they felt unable to talk to their mothers about the issues that concerned them.

'She just wants me in a relationship'

This theme also expresses a perceived lack of understanding on the part of mothers, this time specifically the idea that feminist groups are perceived by mothers as being anti-men and therefore as threatening the possibility of marriage and family. For example, one respondent explained:

> My mother is uncomfortable with the idea of women only environ-ments. It's not something she was brought up to feel good about and therefore she has a suspicion of it, the same way she has a suspicion about a lot of things that are alien to her. She's very heterosexist in outlook and she assumes that women only groups are some sort of

lesbian conspiracy. She's very concerned for me to be married or in a long-term relationship and every time I spend *not* in mixed company, she thinks is another wasted moment when I could be meeting this right person who I'm going to marry and settle down with. The fact that I'm not necessarily interested in marriage is beside the point (417).

Other respondents also felt that their mothers' main wish was to see them married and 'settled down' and that they found it impossible to understand that any woman could be happy being single and independent – 'she just doesn't understand that I can be happy without a bloke' (187).

Here mothers were seen not as disinterested but as rather anxious and worried about their daughters' involvement in feminism and the effect that it might have on their lives. Respondents here recognized that their mothers were motivated primarily by a concern for their daughters' welfare but felt that it was impossible to explain to their mothers that their concern was misplaced.

'She's like a cork on water. She just bobs around'

The final theme is the most negative where respondents expressed a clear hostility towards their mothers and their views. Respondents' own involvement in feminist groups was seen here partly as a *reaction* to mothers and was an important way in which women expressed a sense of difference. This hostility comes over most clearly in the following extract:

My god! My mother doesn't have any views. She is very simple. She agrees with the last person she's spoken to. She is very weak. She's like a cork on water. She just bobs around. We don't agree on anything really, we never really talk properly. I never talk to her about things that really matter. She always agrees with whatever I'm saying (614).

Other respondents were less hostile in their descriptions and mostly focused on inconsistencies in their mothers' views – 'she's not a consistent thinker, it's just off the top of her head all the time' (591).

Of course, without knowing more about our respondents' mothers it is impossible to judge the extent to which views of similarity or difference are justified. As elsewhere, the data is interesting for what it tells us about respondents' own constructions of relationships and events and their perceived impact on beliefs and action. It was certainly the case that many respondents saw elements of their family background as influential in leading them to political activism. Our sample is too small to draw conclusions regarding the differential impact of mothers and fathers, but we can speculate that where parents occupied traditional gender roles in the family, fathers may have provided positive role models to a greater extent than mothers.

Developing an Activist Identity

Finally, family experiences were also seen as influential in developing a sense of activist identity – seeing oneself as a 'doer', an 'action-oriented type person'. For example, discussing her turning away from the church and community groups with which her parents were involved, one respondent reflected that:

> There's a left-over element that you 'do things', a 'doer', you go out and do things. There's a philosophy that you're left with, a feeling about fighting inequality and about being aware of the inequalities and doing as much as you can to change it (422).

In explaining why *others* get involved, respondents also referred to the importance of being a 'doer':

> I would have said the women in the groups that I've been in are fairly concerned about other things as well. They are probably the type of people who would do things about other issues, apart from women as well. I think you either enjoy and want to carry on doing it or you think, 'I'm not really the kind of person for this' and stop doing it (002).

This feeling of being a 'doer' relates to factors found in Chapter 3 to be significantly related to participation, namely the desire to do something positive for women as a group and the perception of oneself as an activist. The sense of oneself as a 'doer', the desire to give behavioural expression to attitudes and values, seems to be an important aspect of participation. Indeed, the quantitative analysis presented in Chapter 3 suggested that this is one of the most significant characteristics of activists. From data presented in this chapter, it seems that this characteristic is engendered for many people in childhood and family experiences and it is no doubt reinforced by countless subsequent experiences.

This theme also emerged very clearly from Andrews' (1991) study of longstanding political activists. She argues that a sense of socialist identification on the part of her respondents comprised both a sense of *being* (indicating consciousness) and *doing* (carrying out actions consonant with beliefs). These two components go together in what Andrews calls a 'culture of responding', such that activists not only have an ability to *perceive* social problems, but also a desire to *respond* to such problems through action. The need to take action represents a feeling of responsibility, that one cannot simply see a problem and do nothing about it. Feeling responsible and taking action were essential components of these respondents' activist identities.

Others have suggested that feeling a need to take action may be a particular feature of women's midlife political consciousness. Stewart and Gold-Steinberg (1990) argue that for individuals with relatively strongly formed political identities of any sort (for example, as feminists), 'midlife may be experienced in terms of an urgent need to translate beliefs and values into effective action' (p. 547). Perhaps because time is seen as limited by such women, it is seen as important to do what can be done; they have established their own strengths and weaknesses and moreover, they have more time and freedom to pursue political activities. Pursuing these activities provides a way of reaffirming past political identities in new ways. As Fiske (1980) points out, the 'middle aged may have few eternal truths or treasure troves of values to bequeath, but we are old enough to know that there comes a time when one must stand up and be counted' (p. 261).

To sum up, aspects of personal background were drawn upon by the majority of our interviewees to provide a context within which personal characteristics and social beliefs developed.

Life Events, Discrimination and Social Support

The next set of factors drawn on to explain involvement concern particular life events experienced by the respondents. These events were of a number of different types, of which the most common was adult experience of discrimination.

Experiencing Discrimination

The shock of being at the receiving end of discrimination was particularly strong for those women who spoke of having been brought up to believe that men and women are equal and that gender relations are unproblematic. These women who had acquired a sense of confidence that they could achieve whatever they put their minds to were particularly hard hit by the experience of direct discrimination and this provided a strong trigger for involvement.

In fact, references to discrimination of some sort seemed to be such an important feature of respondents' accounts of involvement that we decided to obtain some more detailed information about the nature of discrimination that women encounter. In a second questionnaire sent to a sub-group of our main sample (see Chapter 3), respondents were asked whether they could recall any particular occasions when they had experienced discrimination as a woman and, if so, to give brief details. Of 383 returns to this second questionnaire, 292 women responded positively to this question, representing 76 per cent of participants. This total number comprised 253 activists, of whom 82 per cent responded positively, and 130 non-activists, of whom 65 per cent responded positively. Responses were coded into different types as in previous analyses and are shown in Table 4.2.

Over half of the responses related to discrimination encountered in an employment context. A number of these were general comments, concerning

Table 4.2: Types of discrimination experienced by women

Category	Frequency
Employment	166 (57%)
Interpersonal interaction	61 (21%)
Family/education	29 (10%)
Sexual harassment	25 (9%)
Other	11 (4%)
Total	292

women's feelings of being under-utilized and undervalued. Many women felt that their contributions and skills were being ignored. A particular case is the way in which men often appear to misidentify women as secretaries or assistants, as 'organizational tea lady':

> I have been asked many times to pour the tea at meetings. I'm constantly asked if I am my colleague's secretary. People assume because I'm Dr [ ] that I'm a man (287);

> Rather than particular occasions I've been aware of general attitudes: assumption I won't understand 'difficult' technical details, being invisible in meetings with predominantly male colleagues, facing same deadlines as male colleagues without the backup they receive from their wives (433).

Manifestations of the exclusion that many women feel were very varied. Many comments suggested that women feel that their individuality is undermined, being perceived as a 'woman' rather than as an equal colleague. One woman was told, 'I don't need you on interviewing panels. I already have a woman for that' (003).

Other comments focused particularly on issues of promotion, pay and the problems of combining children with careers. Many women talked of hitting the *glass ceiling*, a concept popularized in the 1980s to describe a barrier so subtle that it is transparent, yet so strong that it prevents women from moving up in the management hierarchy. By way of illustration, some of the women from our sample quoted examples of male colleagues achieving considerably faster promotion, despite no differences in qualifications or experience, or in some cases, that the woman was *more* qualified. Where women confronted their employers, they were sometimes told that men 'needed' promotion more or simply that higher management did not want women in the boardroom.

Many respondents felt that they were unfairly penalized when they took a career break to have children and felt uncomfortable about the consequences of exercising their maternity rights. Some referred to a change in colleagues' attitudes once they had had children and an inference that they would not be as capable as they had been before. Some women recounted experiences of selection interviews where they had been asked about their plans to have children and how they intended to combine their careers with looking after children – and, in one case, with looking after a husband! In addition, women were aware of discrepancies between their own level of pay and rewards and those of male colleagues and partners.

Other forms of discrimination related to perceived unfairness in the family or in educational contexts similar to experiences discussed earlier in this chapter, such as 'Being asked, "Developmental psychology – isn't that a very *difficult* subject for a housewife?"' (185); instances of sexual harassment, such as 'Working for a senior doctor who continually tries to put his arm around you' (060); and a number of varied contexts, such as discrimination on mortgage and other financial applications.

A further large proportion of the comments about discrimination were of the 'nothing in particular, everything in general' kind. Comments in this category focused on interpersonal interaction and included sexist remarks and feelings of being ignored, patronized, talked over and not listened to. Thus, one woman commented, 'Nothing specific – just "Oh you can't do that", "What a waste of an education. You'll only get married and have children", "You don't like football, do you?", "You don't know anything about computers, do you?"' (169). Women also described how they were troubled not so much by blatant forms of sexism, but by a more insidious and subtle form of discrimination, which reflects recent social psychological theorizing of *modern* or *symbolic* forms of prejudice. Here it is argued that in a cultural climate which stresses equal opportunities for all, people feel a pressure to maintain a liberal self-image – 'I'm not sexist/racist but . . .' – and that prejudice is driven underground only to emerge in more subtle forms, making it all the more difficult to combat.

Most of the research which has been conducted to date on this contemporary form of prejudice has focused on racism. Adopting the term 'aversive racism', Gaertner and Dovidio (1986) argue that this form of prejudice stems from the so-called *American dilemma* which combines an ideology of egalitarianism with a history of racism (see also Dovidio and Gaertner, 1986). The result is a conflict for American whites between the desire to be non-prejudiced and unacknowledged negative feelings towards blacks. Aversive racists are very concerned about their non-prejudiced self-images and, in inter-racial contexts with clear social norms, will be sure to avoid behaving in any way which could be interpreted as racist. However, these researchers present experimental evidence to show that in situations where social norms are ambiguous or conflicting, whites do discriminate and may seek to justify their behaviour by reference to some factor other than race. In this way they can protect their socially desirable non-prejudiced self-images.

It is easy to see how similar ideas may be applied to the context of gender (Benokraitis and Feagin, 1986). In this context also sweeping changes in political and social conditions mean that it is no longer acceptable in most situations to express openly sexist attitudes. Consequently, traditional measures of sexism appear to show a significant decrease in prejudice and indeed some bias in favour of women, though this bias is found predominantly when evaluating men and women in traditionally feminine arenas or occupational roles (Eagly and Mladinic, 1994). However, this change may again not represent a quantitative change in degree of prejudice as a qualitative shift in the form in which prejudice is expressed. In line with attempts to develop measures of modern racism (see McConahay, 1986), the expression of modern sexism reflects beliefs that 1) discrimination is a thing of the past because women now have equal educational and employment opportunities; 2) women are pushing themselves into places where they are not wanted; 3) these tactics and demands are unfair; and 4) recent gains are undeserved and women are now getting more attention and status than they deserve.

A scale to test these beliefs – described as *neosexism* – has recently been devised by Tougas, *et al.* (1995). In their study they found that old-fashioned sexism and neosexism were linked but only the latter had an impact in regression analyses on support given to affirmative action for women. It thus appears that the measure of neosexism is more sensitive to the contemporary expression of sexist beliefs. Similar findings come from research by Swim, *et al.* (1995). They also found evidence to support the distinction between old-fashioned sexism (obviously unequal treatment of women and the questioning of women's intelligence) and modern sexism (less sympathetic responses towards women's issues). Furthermore, they suggest that modern sexists may adhere more strongly to individualistic values and attribute sex segregation at work to individualistic causes rather than to discrimination or prejudice against women. This research suggests that there may be interesting connections between gender identity, individualism and the contemporary expression of sexism.

It has been argued that this more subtle form of sexism, while on the surface more socially acceptable, is actually more difficult to combat – 'like a virus that mutates into new forms' (Gaertner and Dovidio, 1986, p. 85). Whereas old-fashioned prejudice may be susceptible to conventional techniques of attitude change and to legal and social pressures, attempts to alleviate modern sexism are made more difficult by the fact that individuals already believe that they are non-prejudiced and work very hard to maintain an egalitarian self-image. Moreover, because of their adherence to individualistic values, such people would also resist any attempts to increase the salience of gender categorization.

This recent research confirms what we know already from employment statistics, for example, and from women's own perceptions; namely that prejudice has not gone away but new and subtle forms of prejudice have developed alongside the more traditional expressions of bias. Thus, the majority of women in our present sample, particularly the activists, were aware of discrimination towards women as a group in a range of contexts and moreover, felt that they *personally* had been on the receiving end of unfair treatment – in the family, in educational settings, at work and in a whole host of other contexts. This perception sets our sample apart from the participants in various other research studies, who have recognized a general problem of discrimination but denied – or at least downplayed – any personal effects (see for example, Birt and Dion, 1987; Briet, Klandermans and Kroon, 1987; Crosby, *et al.*, 1989; Hafer and Olson, 1993; Nagata and Crosby, 1991). Indeed, Crosby (1982) argues that women rarely perceive themselves as victims of discrimination and points to a phenomenon known as the denial of personal disadvantage (see also Crosby, Cordova and Jaskar, 1993), otherwise known as the personal/group discrimination discrepancy (Taylor, *et al.*, 1990). This refers specifically to the acknowledgement of discrimination at the group or societal level but denying or downplaying its occurrence at the personal level – the 'gap between group discontent and personal contentment' (Crosby, 1982: 165). For example, Crosby, *et al.* (1993) review a number of studies where employed women felt that they personally had been exempt from the obstacles of sex discrimination, although the objective data showed that they had not been as fortunate as they imagined (see also Clayton and Crosby, 1992; Crosby, 1984; Crosby, *et al.*, 1989; Nagata and Crosby, 1991; Taylor, *et al.*, 1994).

Crosby, *et al.*, (1993) suggest that there may be a number of reasons for this common finding. First of all, there may be cognitive reasons relating to the way in which information about self and others is presented and processed. For example, experimental studies show that subjects are more likely to perceive discrimination operating in an organization when they are presented with information in an aggregate form (for the organization as a whole) compared with a segmented form (department-by-department) (Crosby, *et al.*, 1986).

Second, there may be motivational factors which combine with information-processing to lead people to deny the extent to which they are personally harmed by systematic cultural biases. One such factor is the threat which would be posed to an individual's belief in a just world (Lerner, 1980). This is the hypothesized desire to live in a world in which abilities are rewarded and wrong-doings punished. It is interesting in this respect to note that Hafer and Olson (1989) have demonstrated that women with a strong need to believe in a just world are less likely than others to advocate either personal or collective actions to correct unfair employment situations. A further motivational reason for the denial of personal disadvantage is that it may be emotionally aversive to imagine that one's co-workers or supervisors wish one ill. Individuals may also have a need to see themselves as special, unaffected by general norms and as people to whom bad things do not happen. For all of these reasons, Crosby and her colleagues suggest that there will be a general tendency to deny that one has been personally affected by the discriminatory practices which are seen to affect the group as a whole, though as Mikula (1993) points out, for victims of injustice, interpreting an incident as unjust and attributing blame to the perpetrator may in some cases increase the likelihood of maintaining a positive self-image. Ruggiero and Taylor (1995) argue that the minimization of personal discrimination permits a sense of control, for which disadvantaged group members may be prepared to sacrifice the short-term protection of self-esteem. In their study, individuals only perceived discrimination when the probability for discrimination was relatively certain.

Other possible explanations for the personal/group discrimination discrepancy are suggested by Taylor, *et al.* (1994), including the tendency to evaluate one's personal situation through comparisons with fellow ingroup members (rather than outgroup members) or with dramatic examples of discrimination that are highlighted by the media. On the basis of their own analysis, these researchers also suggest that the discrepancy between perceived personal and group discrimination may arise as much from an *exaggeration* at the group level, as from a denial or minimization at the personal level.

In further research, Taylor, *et al.* address the issue of individual differences by focusing on the distinction between personal and social identity. They hypothesize that for women with a strong sense of gender identity, 'an attack on "me" is an attack on all women, and conversely, an attack on women is also an attack on "me" personally' (1994: 246). Consequently, these women should not show the usual personal/group discrimination discrepancy, or at least not to the same extent as women with a weaker sense of gender identity, for whom perceptions at one level may or may not implicate perceptions at the other.

However, their findings showed no support for this hypothesis and higher ratings for group discrimination compared to personal discrimination were found across the board – *especially* amongst the strong identifiers. To explain this unexpected finding, the authors refer to the model of identity proposed by Turner, *et al.* (1987), where the increased salience of social identity is at the expense of personal identity (and vice versa). Here, a salient social identity does not represent a state where the 'I' and the 'we' are *synonymous*, but a state where the 'we' has eclipsed the 'I' altogether. Consequently, 'The more social identity is salient leading to vigilance in the perception of group discrimination, the less salient is personal identity and thus the lower the perception of personal discrimination' (Taylor *et al.*, 1994: 252).

The present findings are not consistent with this interpretation. The majority of our respondents, who were characterized by relatively high levels of gender identity, were only too aware of how their lives had been affected by discrimination. These women, many of whom are involved in collective action, by and large *have* made the connections between the personal and the political and *do* recognize the many ways in which cultural biases intrude into their own lives at home and at work. This would seem to contradict the hydraulic model of the self discussed earlier and its emphasis on limited attentional processes and point instead to a model of the self where it is possible for personal and social identities (the personal and the political) to be seen as inextricably intertwined.

Discrimination, experienced personally and by the group, seems here to be a powerful trigger for participation in collective action, although other research suggests that this need not necessarily be the case. For example, Lykes (1983) analysed the oral histories obtained in open-ended interviews with 52 black women focusing on their responses in situations of discrimination. Responses were analysed according to types of situation (personal prejudice vs. institutional discrimination) and types of coping strategy (passive, indirect/non-confrontational or direct/directed at the source of the problem). She found that more direct strategies were employed when discrimination was of a personal nature than when it was institutional (see also Adams and Dressler, 1988; Louw-Potgieter, 1989).

In their review of research examining behavioural responses to discrimination, Lalonde and Cameron (1994) suggest that it may be helpful to classify different situations of discrimination according to the interpersonal–intergroup continuum (Tajfel, 1978; see Chapter 2). They suggest that in some situations, discrimination may be interpreted at the interpersonal end of the continuum, especially when indices of systemic discrimination are not readily available, whereas in other situations, discrimination may be more obviously directed at an entire group and promote collective action in response. Their own research directly testing this hypothesis proved inconclusive however, due to methodological problems with the role-playing methods used. There must also be a question about the extent to which discrimination can ever be viewed as *interpersonal* behaviour since, from an intergroup relations perspective, as Lalonde and Cameron themselves state, discrimination represents a situation 'where an individual is unjustly treated on the basis of membership in a disadvantaged group' (p. 261).

It may be more useful to examine the situations in which behaviour by a member of a powerful group is *interpreted* as discrimination in the first place. Here again, Lalonde and Cameron suggest that central to this interpretation is the requirement that individuals process information at an intergroup rather than an interpersonal level, but it is not clear that this analysis takes us much further in specifying the specific conditions in everyday situations (of employment, for example) under which these different perceptions might prevail. We should also take account of the fact that we live in a culture where the concept of *discrimination* is widely available and it is a theme that we can draw on to explain and make sense of various experiences. The issue is further complicated by the ways in which the theme of discrimination coexists alongside that of *equal opportunities* which can serve to obscure acts of discrimination and lead to a more personal attribution of causality (see Wetherell, Stiven and Potter, 1987; also Chapter 2). Interpretation of an event as discrimination thus depends on personal, group and ideological factors and further research employing a plurality of different approaches and methods is necessary to address this issue.

Isolation and a Sense of 'Difference'

If we return now to the main body of qualitative data as represented in Figure 4.1, we can see that, in addition to discrimination, the second main type of situation precipitating involvement in collective action is one where the respondent experienced a sense of 'difference' from others, a feeling of being an outsider, of being isolated. Here, the group provides an opportunity to meet similar others – 'people like me' (187) – and sometimes to bring together social identities which are seen to conflict. For example:

> One of the reasons I wanted to be part of that sort of thing was because I do often feel like an outsider generally. I feel like I'm living on my own island completely separate from anyone around me. From a Jewish perspective, I've been brought up with an orthodox perspective and have a very traditional orthodox upbringing and a lot of that stays with me. A lot of that is very important to me. And yet from a secular perspective, I'm very liberal, I'm a socialist, I'm a feminist and in that one camp, in the Jewish camp, I'm an outsider because of those things and in the secular world, I'm an outsider because of the other things. So to find somewhere where the two can be brought together is actually very difficult (417);

> [as an older woman], one doesn't fit it. If you look at soaps or ads, one doesn't fit any of the categories (433);

> When I was at school, I was a bit confused about my sexuality and lesbianism was completely taboo at school, you could never talk about it but I thought that that was what I was, so I felt very different to a lot of the other girls, so that was the main reason why I joined the women's group as soon as I got to college, just because I wanted to meet other lesbians (418);

> It's good to be with other women who have been brought up the way I have been brought up and who know the sort of things I've been through. I've got a lot of English friends and they don't know how I feel, you know. Having been brought up the way I've been brought up in my [Asian] culture, I like to meet other women who have been. You can think you're quite alone. I never used to have that many Asian friends because there were a lot of white people around where I lived, there weren't many Asian people there and I very rarely got to meet them. I used to think, "This is just me", but then I got to meet some other Asian women and I found it was not just me, they had the same sort of problems with their parents and the same sort of experiences (596).

Very commonly this sense of isolation was in a professional context and was expressed by members of the work-related groups. This is consistent with findings from other studies which have found that where women are in token positions in organizations, they experience particular strains and pressures not felt by dominant members of the same organizational status (for example, Freeman, 1990). The disadvantages which have been associated with being the token woman include increased performance pressure, visibility, being a test case for future women, isolation and lack of female role models, exclusion from male groups and distortion of women's behaviour by others in order to fit them into pre-existing sex stereotypes (see Kanter, 1977; Scase and Goffee, 1989).

It has sometimes been argued that these difficulties are purely a consequence of numerical minority status and that men in minority positions experience similar problems (see Kanter, 1977). However, Ott (1989) found that male nurses actually enjoy some advantages from being one of the few among female colleagues. The relative uniqueness that numerical minority status employees possess, although a disadvantage for many women, may actually be an advantage for men among female majorities. Ott argues that to be a token is to be put under a magnifying glass accentuating the differences between majority and minority. If one belongs to a low status group with a negative stereotype, then being in a minority in an organization will make those stereotypical properties more salient, thereby creating a more negative image. If the token person is a member of the majority group however, then this same stereotyping process will create a more positive image. The same hypothesis can be derived from a consideration of self-categorization theory (Turner, *et al.*, 1987) and indeed, experimental work in this area has found that increasing the salience of gender identity has positive effects on self-esteem amongst men and negative effects on self-esteem amongst women (Hogg and Turner, 1987). The salience of gender identity has different effects for men and women which has important consequences for their employment experience. A number of women in the present study described the pressures of numerical minority status and expressed the need for support at work.

However, a sense of isolation was also experienced by some women in the home, particularly by those who had given up full-time jobs to stay at home with children. Again these sentiments are reflected in other research findings which point to the difficulties which women may experience when they are at home with children and without paid employment (see Oakley, 1980; Parry, 1986, 1987; Pistrang, 1984), particularly where they have given up professional careers (see Hock, 1978). Reviewing this area, Baker (1989) suggests that positivity of social identity in the transition to motherhood depends on the extent to which motherhood is a chosen activity and the strength of links with other mothers at this time.

In addition to discrimination and isolation, the need for support also arose from a variety of other life events and the respondent turned to the group for specific expertise or help. These crises included relationship break-down, retirement, bereavement, menopause, job insecurity, moving house, mental ill health, sexual abuse and domestic violence. All of these situations acted as triggers for initial involvement in women's groups which provided much-needed support and help in times of trouble:

> I think it comes out of oppression and a certain amount of anger and wanting things to change, things like divorce, childbirth can all give you that nudge to start thinking about other things and want to do things and not just be a victim (614).

Meeting and Helping Others

A related response focused on the desire to meet similar others. Frequently, the descriptions of other group members revolved around the notion of similarity to self and many respondents referred to the other group members as 'like-minded' and said that this was what attracted them to the group. For example, '[it's] about finding other people with similar backgrounds and similar experiences and that understanding. You think, "I've been through that as well", and you think, "Oh, it's not just me"' (596). Clearly, this desire to meet similar others is linked in some cases with a sense of isolation.

Relatedly, a number of respondents referred to their desire to help and support other women as the driving force underlying their activism, for example, 'to improve things for my two daughters and their generation' (179) and others referred to the need to 'put back into society everything you've taken out' (309). The desire to help others was particularly common both in a work context, where respondents expressed the wish 'to help other women on the way up' (171) and, in the context of pregnancy and childbirth, where women wished to provide the support which they themselves had received.

To sum up, life events and personal crises of one sort or another seem to play an important part in stimulating people to seek support from similar others and get involved in group action.

Social Beliefs

The next set of explanations turns away from personal support needs and concerns a constellation of related social beliefs which relate most clearly to those factors discussed in the social psychological literature (see Chapter 2).

Collective Relative Deprivation

The first and most important social belief is a sense of collective relative deprivation, of injustice and unfairness experienced by women *as a group*. A number of respondents referred to their behaviour being 'fuelled by anger' (128) at the low status of women, suggesting the importance of the affective as well as the cognitive component of relative deprivation, for example, 'Fury. Just the idea that things are wrong and that you've got to do something about it' (612). Obviously this factor maps exactly onto the collective relative deprivation factor which emerged in Chapter 3 as being a significant characteristic of activists. The specific dimensions along which this deprivation is felt can be explored here.

In some cases, respondents referred to *general* inequalities, for example, 'the way in my view women are regarded as second class citizens by men' (329), whereas in many cases, respondents referred to women's disadvantaged position in a particular context (which generally related to the group or campaign in which she was involved). These included *health*: 'Belief that the health service does not enable a full and appropriate health provision for women' (195); *education*: 'Believe in educational opportunities for women' (175); *medicine*: 'Concern with the career outcome of the increasing number of women entering medical education' (307); *the media*: 'To see more women in top executive positions in broadcasting and other professions' (315); *manage-ment*: 'I feel strongly that women are under-represented in management throughout the UK in all sectors' (452); *politics*: 'the lack of female participants running our country' (001); and *motherhood*: 'A woman's low status when she becomes a mother' (434).

Development of a Feminist Consciousness

Linked to the theme of perceived collective relative deprivation, a number of women referred to their feelings of identification with women as a group, for example, 'I think that being a woman is central to my identity and all around me I see problems with being a woman' (328). This clearly illustrates the operation of the gender identity factor discussed in Chapter 3. Evidence discussed there showed that activists have a much stronger sense of identification with women as a social group than do less active individuals. In their explanations for involvement, many women referred to the development of a feminist consciousness, which was often through educational experiences. For example:

Originally became interested in women's issues through study. Changed my life! Became angry! Until then, although aware of inequalities, I had never really thought about it (034);

> I went to college as a mature student and when I started to read things there, it was like reading something I'd always known, but I hadn't had the categories to classify things (503).

An important aspect of this feminist consciousness was the realization that personal problems were shared by others involving a change in attributions for problems from internal to external (see Taylor and McKirnan, 1984; see Chapter 2):

> I had an interview with someone doing research on Jewish women in mid-life and it suddenly made me realize that I was the characteristic Jewish woman in mid-life. And I had always thought that the difficulties I had were personal and that it was my fault that I wasn't coping. I just didn't realize that it is quite difficult and that it's common to lots of people (434);

> I became involved because I have always from childhood felt girls did not have the opportunities of boys. It has helped me to come to terms with the unfairness and injustices knowing that I am not alone and that my resentments are experienced by others and that there are cultural/ historical reasons for the treating of women as second class and invisible (020).

Belief in Collective Action

The third related social belief to be identified, in addition to collective relative deprivation and feminist consciousness, was a general belief in the efficacy of collective action. As one woman commented, 'you can't achieve anything on your own, you have to be in a group' (231). This sense of *group* efficacy clearly relates to the feelings of personal efficacy which have already been discussed. Where efficacy was discussed here by activists, it clearly connected with other political beliefs as well. The three factors (sense of collective relative deprivation, feminist consciousness, belief in the efficacy of collective action) are clearly strongly interrelated. Indeed, it may be argued that a sense of feminist consciousness entails the other two beliefs and reinforces them.

Group Services

This factor concerns the contacts and services offered by the group and here the motivation is primarily a professional one. Activism here reflects an instrumental orientation for self-advancement and supports the view of participation espoused by Olson (1965) in his idea of 'selective incentives' (see

Chapter 1). The argument here is that the only way in which groups can encourage participation on the part of rational individuals who might otherwise be tempted to free-ride (and derive collective benefits without incurring any personal costs) is by making certain rewards available only to group members. Thus, for example, Beaumont and Elliott (1989) have argued that many nurses in Britain join the Royal College of Nursing (rather than the unions, NUPE or COHSE) because the former offers insurance and legal protection to its members.

In the present context, this type of explanation was overwhelmingly drawn on by members of the professional groups, who referred to the value of group membership for networking and making business contacts. In addition, many women referred to training courses, lectures and library facilities which were connected to the group. Membership was seen as a way to 'improve my chance of getting to the top' (171) and provided the opportunity 'to learn from women who have broken the glass ceiling' (296). Another commented, 'I needed a networking system. Some of my male colleagues have this handed to them automatically and I was aware that women needed the same sort of opportunity' (382). However, this type of explanation was a minority response overall in interviews, being mentioned by only eight of the 30 interviewees.

The Role of Chance

Whereas all the factors which have been discussed so far encouraged respondents to actively seek out a group or campaign, there was also an element of chance mentioned by a number of women in stumbling across the group at the right time in their lives, or that 'it happened to cross my path' (433). Sometimes this was a recommendation from a friend who encouraged the person to join. More often the chance element was in the form of an advertisement for a group or meeting which struck a chord with perceived needs or interests at the time. The first contact with the group seems to have been very important for many people in determining any subsequent involvement and several respondents commented that they had been favourably impressed with the group or the atmosphere or the speakers at the first meeting; one respondent described how she was 'carried along on the buzz of it' (187). The role of chance was mentioned by over half of the interviewees in conjunction with other factors. Similarly, in discussing the factors which determined 'first wave' feminist activism, Banks (1986) cites personal recruitment networks and the effect of a particular speaker on a member of the audience as important ways into feminism. The role of such elements of chance should not be forgotten in explaining how individuals get involved.

Concluding Comments

A number of factors have emerged from this analysis as important triggers for participation in women's groups. Of most interest from a social psychological point of view are those relating to personal background and personal characteristics, the experience and interpretation of some life event or crisis, such as discrimination, and social beliefs. These explanations are clearly interlinked. For example, the interpretation of any particular act *as discrimination* depends to a large extent on group identification and feminist consciousness. Family background and socialization experiences provide a context within which subsequent experiences will be interpreted and understood. Concerns about justice and injustice pervade all of these categories in some way. As emphasized elsewhere, the concern here is not to identify a single cause of activism, but to explore the ways in which different factors interrelate and are given meaning in this context.

One important theme which emerged was the importance of personal experiences. For many women, it was the experience of injustice in their own lives which prompted them to try to do something about the inequality which they perceived as existing in gender relations more generally. This finding is consistent with theorizing by Wright, *et al.* (1990), who argue that, 'it is the personal experience with the injustice of a closed high-status group that leads those who are near to entry to instigate collective action' (p. 997; see also Taylor, *et al.*, 1987; Chapter 2 for detailed discussion). The present findings concur on the important role played by personal experience of injustice.

Finally, what can be said about similarities and differences between different types of group in respect to initial joining, i.e., groups concerned with health as compared to party politics, for example? In fact, it is striking that despite the very different aims and structures of the groups included, responses concerning initial involvement showed a broad consistency. In particular, the need for support emerged across the board as an important factor whether the respondent was talking about support in bringing up children or in the workplace. Whatever the particular context, respondents stressed the desire to find and interact with others in a similar position. Likewise, personal characteristics, such as seeing oneself as a doer, emerged equally in all the different types of group, as did aspects of personal background, such as experiencing discrimination as a child.

There were some minor variations. For example, the role of collective relative deprivation figured less powerfully in involvement in health/children related groups, where personal support was more important. Collective relative deprivation was a more important motivator of involvement in political groups and in work-related groups (professional and trade union), and personal experience of discrimination also figured largely in a work context. As noted previously, the contacts and services offered by the group were particularly important for the members of the professional groups who valued training courses, library facilities and the opportunity to network.

One way of explaining these differences might be to refer to Hinkle and Brown's (1990) typology of group contexts which suggests that groups may be categorized according to the extent to which they espouse an individualist (or collectivist) ideology and the extent to which they engage in intergroup comparisons for evaluation (see Chapter 2). For example, respondents' descriptions of child-related groups suggested that they would score low in terms of intergroup comparison, as there was usually no obvious outgroup, whereas descriptions of political groups suggested a more comparative emphasis. Motivations for joining groups located in the different cells of this typology may differ accordingly so that, for example, collective relative deprivation, which entails intergroup comparison, is more important when considering group contexts with a comparative orientation.

To conclude, in Chapter 3 a number of social beliefs were identified which clearly distinguished more from less active individuals. In Chapter 4, we have seen how some of these factors work as *causes*, encouraging activist behaviour and the origins of some of these beliefs in family experiences. In addition, certain other factors have emerged as important triggers for activism, such as the impact of some life event or personal crisis. This suggests the important role of the group as a provider of personal support as well as a vehicle for promoting social change. In practice, it may be difficult to tell where the desire for personal support in the face of discrimination at work, for example, shades into the desire to bring about social change and equal opportunities in the workplace.

In the next chapter, we will turn to look in more detail at the role of the group as a provider of support and at the other perceived outcomes of group involvement.

Chapter 5

Outcomes of Participation

In the previous chapter, data was presented concerning the factors which were perceived as leading to initial involvement in collective action. Six clusters of responses were identified. These were: Personal background, personal characteristics, various life events and the need for social support, social beliefs, group services and chance. In this chapter, the focus turns to the perceived *outcomes* of participation in collective action for the individual in terms of personal benefits and effects on social beliefs and identity. The data presented here sheds light on the issues of why people *continue* in their involvement in collective action, what they get out of participation and how they are affected by it.

This is an area where there is very little previous social psychological research on which to draw. Because so much work has been based on short-lived *ad hoc* laboratory groups, we know very little about people's feelings towards the significant groups in their lives or the perceived benefits of group involvement. Moreover, the literature on group processes is dominated by consideration of the *negative* outcomes of group membership, the conflict, prejudice and stereotyping which are usually the focus of attention in research into real-life groups. This is particularly the case with research based on social identity theory, where the pessimistic outlook has been noted and commented on (see Caddick, 1982: 149). Reviewing this (mainly North American and European) research on group processes, one could be forgiven for reaching the conclusion that group membership is a rather unfortunate but inevitable aspect of social life, the consequences of which are wholly undesirable and that, as a society, we would be better off without groups altogether.

By contrast with this gloomy perspective, the present findings cast group membership in a much more positive light. The data shows the important role played by group membership in people's lives and the perceived benefits to be derived from participation in collective action. Before discussing these findings, we will briefly review the small amount of previous research and theorizing into relevant aspects of group processes, concentrating on two specific areas: First, social psychological research into group socialization, and second, research into consciousness-raising in the context of protests and conflicts.

Group Socialization

The most significant recent research initiative into this topic has been under-taken by Levine and Moreland, 1985; Moreland and Levine, 1982, who have proposed a model of group socialization, by which is meant, 'the affective, cognitive, and behavioural changes that groups and individuals produce in one another from the beginning to the end of their relationship' (Levine and Moreland, 1985; 145). The model is intended to apply mainly, though not exclusively, to small autonomous voluntary groups whose members interact regularly, share affective ties and a common frame of reference and are behaviourally interdependent. It should therefore be applicable to the sort of groups which are the focus here.

Three psychological processes are proposed: Evaluation, commitment and role transitions. With an important emphasis on the reciprocity of relations between individuals and groups, it is argued that both the individual *and* the group engage in an evaluation of the degree to which the relationship is rewarding, comparing the outcomes to other available alternatives. On the basis of these evaluations, feelings of commitment arise on the part of both parties. Commitment can be expected to have important behavioural consequences. For example, it is suggested that a committed individual will be likely to accept the group's goals and values, experience positive affective ties to other group members, exert effort on behalf of the group and try to maintain group membership. The nature of commitment is likely to change over time resulting in role transitions, for example when a *new* member attains *full* member status. The individual may pass through five phases of group membership – investigation, socialization, maintenance, resocialization, remembrance – separated by four role transitions – entry, acceptance, divergence and exit.

The original model (Moreland and Levine, 1982) was heavily influenced by social exchange theory, suggesting that the value of a relationship – with an individual or a group – depends on the number, strength and frequency of rewards and costs. For example, relationships are considered rewarding when they generate many strong and frequently occurring rewards. These perceived rewards are related to the expectations which the individual has developed regarding the needs which the group is expected to satisfy. If the group fails to meet expectations, individuals may try to change the group's behaviour, or change his or her expectations, or leave the group. At any one time, it is argued that individuals have a general sense of the degree to which their relationship with any particular group is rewarding.

In a study of college students, Moreland, *et al.* (1993) have begun to study some of the perceived rewards of membership in voluntary campus groups, such as sports and recreation groups, fraternities or sororities and fine arts or media groups. Respondents here were *anticipating* joining these groups rather than being current members. The most commonly cited expected rewards were social in nature (40 per cent), such as meeting people and making new friends, and this is perhaps not surprising given the nature of the groups here. The next most common response concerned expected personal rewards (17 per cent), such as enhancing self-esteem, developing self-discipline or becoming more sociable. Other expected rewards were intellectual, such as learning new skills; physical, such as improving personal fitness; professional, for example, networking; or simply having fun. Students also pointed to a number of perceived *costs* of group membership, such as lost time and financial expense. Some indication of the individual's commitment to the group was then computed by comparing the relative values of perceived costs and rewards (though the authors acknowledge that to be true to their theoretical model would actually entail incorporating in addition values for perceived costs and rewards relating to all the *other* groups to which the individual *might* belong).

These authors have recently considered the role of self-categorization in group socialization and commitment (Moreland, *et al.*, 1993). Thus it is suggested that commitment to the group might depend on how *prototypical* the person perceives him or herself to be, where a prototypical member is one who embodies whatever characteristics make that group distinctive. Where an individual feels that he or she matches the group prototype, a high degree of commitment would be expected. Some indirect support for this view comes from a study by Hogg and Hardie (1991) who found that perceived prototypicality amongst the members of a local sports team was associated with more positive evaluations of the team, greater popularity and longer tenure (see also Hogg, 1987; 1992; 1993). Any changes in levels of commitment over time would here be related to changes in perceived prototypicality rather than to changes in perceived costs and rewards.

In the process of group socialization, individuals may undergo change in terms of their identity and their peceptions of the costs and rewards of group membership. During this socialization process, the group 'attempts to change the individual in ways that will increase his or her contributions to the attainment of group goals' (Levine and Moreland, 1985: 150–1). To the extent that the group is successful, the individual undergoes *assimilation*, which 'involves attempts by the group to change the newcomer's thoughts, feelings and behaviour in ways that will make that person more similar to full group members' (Moreland, 1985: 1174). This may be restated as an attempt to promote the prototypicality of the individual group member (though it is also stressed that at the same time individuals exert social influence on groups necessitating group *accommodation*). The speed of assimilation depends amongst other things on the level of commitment of the individual and the group to the relationship, the extent of differences between newcomers and oldtimers and the number of newcomers joining the group at any single time. The socialization phase ends when the individual is seen by him/herself and by the group as a full member.

Others have suggested that the speed with which new members are assimilated into groups and voluntary organizations is influenced by the degree to which an organization's activities are understaffed (Wicker and Mehler, 1971; see also Cini, Moreland and Levine, 1993). In an understaffed and under-resourced group – such as many of the groups under study here – there are many jobs to be done relative to the available population and, as a consequence, the small number of activists must work harder, engage in a wider variety of tasks and assume more responsibility than would be the case if there were more willing volunteers. It is argued that greater responsibility for group activities leads members to show more behavioural support for these activities, to have more feelings of self-improvement, challenge, importance and concern about activities (Wicker, 1968; 1969), as well as facilitating the assimilation of newcomers (see also Arnold and Greenberg, 1980; Wicker and Kauma, 1974; Wicker, *et al.*, 1976). Relatedly, it has been found that people who belong to larger groups are less satisfied with group membership, participate less often in group activities and are less likely to cooperate with one another (Levine and Moreland, 1990).

Finally, a number of researchers have pointed to the positive outcomes associated with participation in small voluntary groups. Reviewing studies of neighbourhood and community organizations, Wandersman (1981) refers to an increase in satisfaction with the environment, more positive attitudes towards government, an increase in feelings of control and in positive interpersonal behaviour and a decrease in mistrust and apathy. The need to distinguish different types of effects – at individual, organizational and community levels – is stressed, as well as the need to investigate possible mediating variables between participation and effects. Other studies, such as Sullivan (1983), have concurred that one of the major outcomes of participation is an increased sense of involvement in work and community activities, as well as increased self-esteem and positive changes in interpersonal relations (see also Gidron, Chesler and Chesney, 1991; Hartman and Gidron, 1991; Yahne and Long, 1988).

We turn now to the more specific context of research and theorizing regarding participation in protest movements, trade unions and situations of intergroup conflict and to the small amount of attention which has been devoted to the effects of such involvement on individuals.

Consciousness Raising

The term *consciousness raising* is used here in the sense defined by Klandermans (1992) as, 'the restructuring of beliefs that occurs as a result of participation in collective action' (p. 82), rather than referring to its more specific meaning in the context of the women's movement. In his discussion of the social construction of protest, he argues that collective action should be considered both as a dependent and an independent variable, that social beliefs both lead to and are in turn shaped by participation in protest activities. 'On the one hand, the social construction of meaning precedes collective action and determines its direction; on the other, collective action in its turn determines the process of meaning construction' (Klandermans, 1992: 82).

In all the research which has been conducted into the processes of meaning construction by those interested in social movements, Klandermans argues that one area that has been neglected is that of consciousness raising *during* episodes of collective action. Basing his approach on theories which stress the shared nature of social beliefs (see Moscovici, 1984), he argues that beliefs about action are formed and transformed by the formal and informal communication which takes place between participants involved in collective action and also by the impact of direct confrontations with opponents and competitors. For example, he cites Heirich's (1968) study of the Berkeley free speech movement which showed how a reconstruction of social reality took place during the 'spiral of conflict' which occurred (see also Delgado, 1986; Lane and Roberts, 1971; Schennink, 1988; Walsh, 1988). Consequently, once individuals become involved in collective action, 'their view of the world may change dramatically' (p. 93).

Unfortunately as Klandermans notes, there is very little empirical research which has been conducted to examine these issues. An exception is Fantasia's (1988) American study of trade union action where he describes the process of consciousness raising during action. Discussing a successful wildcat strike, he argues that an important shift took place in workers' ability to engage in further successful collective action. This was due to the formation of a group of activists and the perception that solidarity amongst the workers was possible and could be maintained. A 'culture of solidarity' and an internal network developed amongst workers with a common identity as activists.

In a subsequent description of a dispute between hospital workers and management, Fantasia elaborates on these points. He argues that something new is created in the context of collective action:

> An emergent culture is created in which new values are incubated, new forms of activity generated, and an associational bond of a new type formed . . . By the end of their campaign, activists thought of themselves as a collective entity that embodied a certain vision distinguishing them from others and representing a new approach to authority, hierarchy and relations to one another (Fantasia, 1988: 174).

Although this emergent culture was, he reported, ultimately dissipated by subsequent events, it served to sustain workers during the campaign and brought about changes in social beliefs and identity:

> Through it, in the heat of conflict, they shed some old ideas about hierarchy in the workplace as well as in the family. The moments of confrontation allowed them to see that authority could be challenged, and the culture in which they were enveloped gave that challenge

direction, continuity, and support in the face of a formidable counter-mobilization (Fantasia, 1988: 175).

It is argued that through taking part in union action, workers developed a new way of considering their interests in class terms rather than in individual terms. Fantasia concludes that through participation in collective action, workers 'developed new-found values of mutual solidarity (a new sense of "us", a new sense of "them", and emergent moral sensibilities about the values associated with each)' (pp. 232–3). This interpretation accords well with a social identity approach to intergroup relations and the way in which social categorizations are reinforced and given meaning through intergroup conflict.

A similar analysis is provided by Hirsch (1990) who argues that groups create commitment to their goals by processes of consciousness raising, collective empowerment, polarization and collective decision-making during the course of the conflict. He argues that loosely structured, non-hierarchical, face-to-face groups can provide havens, where individuals can become aware of common problems and begin to question the legitimacy of present institutional arrangements. Commitment to group goals increases and individuals are more prepared to ignore personal costs in favour of the collective goal.

In Fantasia's (1988) study, it was also argued that the new identity which emerged from workplace action also had important implications for the (mainly female) activists' home lives as well. Involvement in the union campaign required a loosening of traditional roles in the family since in order to participate fully, other members of the family had to take some responsibility for childcare and domestic tasks. Through their involvement, many women became politicized and referred to the links between personal and political growth amongst the activists:

> It was an education in knowing ourselves too. I think a lot of us grew a lot through it. We did things that we never thought we were capable of before ... it really strengthened us. It broadened our ideas as far as general politics in the town, and state politics [are concerned] (quoted in Fantasia, 1988: 176–7).

A similar argument was put forward regarding the involvement of women in the 1984–85 British miners' strike. Many of these women were miners' wives whose lives had previously been defined very much by traditional gender roles. Seddon (1986) argues that there were many gains for the women who took an active part in the strike organization. These included a gain in confidence in themselves as organizers, speakers and activists, as well as a new-found right to organize in the community. In addition, she suggests that these women gained a new understanding of the network of institutions which control their lives: employers, police, the courts and the media. Women who had previously had confidence in the fairness and objectivity of these institutions now questioned that perception in relation to their own and other industrial disputes. Aided by links with women in other groups and communities, these women developed new beliefs about state power. Moreover, contact with other communities led to a greater awareness of the oppression of other social groups on the grounds of race or sexuality for example. Seddon concludes that, '[t]he ideological leaps that some of the women have made are stunning' (p. 13) and refers to a joke amongst women in the coalfield about a miner who says to the union after the strike is over, 'Please can I have my wife back? Not this one, the one I had before?'

According to other researchers, many miners had their wish granted, at least in some respects. Waddington, Wykes and Critcher (1991) conducted a detailed analysis of the process of social change within these mining communities and found that for the majority of women in households supporting the strike, any reversal of gender roles during the strike was a temporary necessity without long-term implications. In most households, once the strike was over, traditional roles were reasserted and women returned to their former domestic roles. They argue that, contrary to the optimistic view that these women had undergone a transformation of consciousness, the only discernible enduring effect in the majority of households was 'a softening of the rough edges of masculine behaviour' (p. 92) and an acknowledgement by men that they ought to contribute more to housework and childcare. The strike had provided a glimpse of alternative gender relations but few acted upon it. Nevertheless, they suggest that their findings show that there is some *potential* for change in gender relations in these communities which could come about through women engaging with everyday issues rather than through a 'wholesale takeover of a readymade feminist consciousness' (p. 92).

A similar conclusion is reached by Winterton and Winterton (1989) who also argue that the view that gender relations in the coalfields was irrevocably changed has proved over-optimistic. In the absence of a clear focus for activity after the strike, women's groups disintegrated and many women felt rejected by the national union once the strike was over. The more long-term effects of the strike remain to be seen, though it does appear from these analyses that involvement in a one-off dispute – albeit a bitter one which lasts for a year – has only limited long-term effects and that any changes in attitudes need to be sustained by further activity.

Moving away from gender relations to other effects of this strike, Waddington, *et al.* (1991) argue that the greatest political effect of the action – and its eventual defeat – was a greater awareness of the power of the state and the inability of any one group of workers to defeat it. This stands in marked contrast to the findings of Fantasia (1988) (discussed earlier), who pointed to the increase in solidarity and group efficacy which was the outcome of *successful* strike action. Thus, the outcome of collective action – and the interpretation of that outcome by participants – are clearly crucial to understanding the effects of participation in any particular campaign, although Hartley, *et al.* (1983) point out that determining the success or failure of strike action is not always straightforward.

In their own study of the 1980 British steel strike, workers were asked whether the experience of being on strike had made them more or less militant in their attitudes to industrial relations in the steel industry. In response, 77 per cent of respondents replied that they had become more militant, whereas 20 per cent replied that the strike had had no effect on their attitudes and 3 per cent replied that they had become less militant (total n=534). For these workers at least then, involvement in one situation of collective action had made subsequent involvement more likely. Further evidence comes from Stagner and Eflal (1982) who found that union members on strike became more militant against the employer and reported more willingness to participate in union activities. Incorporating a comparison group who did *not* strike allowed these researchers to establish that attitudinal differences between the groups were indeed *consequences* rather than causes of strike action.

A different approach to the whole issue of outcomes has been adopted by McAdam (1989) in his study of the biographical consequences of activism (see also McAdam, 1986). He argues that participation in the popular social movements of the 1960s had a powerful and enduring effect on individuals. His review of research suggests that whereas there were methodological short-comings in many of these studies, findings did suggest that activists continued to espouse left-wing political attitudes, remained active in various forms of political activity, were concentrated in the helping professions and continued to define themselves as liberal or radical in political orientation.

His own study of activists in a civil rights campaign suggests that participation served to radicalize individuals as well as putting them in contact with like-minded people. Consequently, participants emerged from the project 'not only more attitudinally disposed toward activism, but embedded in a set of relationships and an emerging activist subculture ideally suited to reinforce the process of personal change' (p. 752). There are thus both attitudinal and structural components involved in the effects of participation.

It is possible to examine some of the issues which have been raised regarding group socialization and consciousness raising using the present data concerning involvement in women's groups. First, we can examine interview data where 30 activists were asked to comment on the reasons why they continue to be involved in women's groups and what they get out of participation. A number of factors emerged from this data as perceived rewards and other outcomes of participation. Second, in order to further explore *changes* in attitudes and identity, quantitative and qualitative data will be presented concerning self-reported change. Third, we can explore socialization processes in groups by comparing the responses of individuals who have been involved for varying lengths of time – new recruits and longstanding members. Fourth and finally, we can examine any actual changes in beliefs over a period of one year focusing on individuals who are newly recruited to the groups with other more longstanding members acting as a comparison group. These different types of information will be discussed in turn.

Perceived Outcomes of Participation in Women's Groups

The data to be presented here derives from interviews with 30 activists in women's groups (see Chapter 4 for details of respondent characteristics and discussion of analysis). Respondents were asked to explain the benefits they derive from participation and why they continue to be involved in the group. Responses are illustrated in Figure 5.1.

The frequencies with which items comprising the various composite categories were mentioned (social, political, personal development and professional

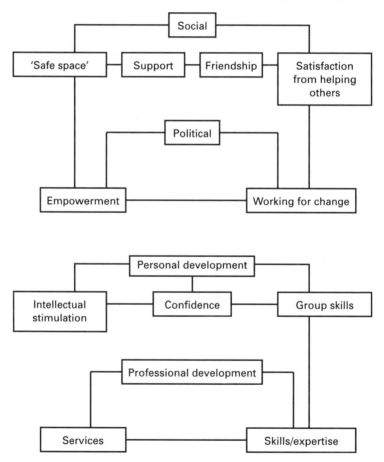

Figure 5.1: Perceived outcomes of participation in women's groups

Table 5.1: Perceived outcomes of participation: Frequencies

Category	Number of interview comments (n = 115)	Number of respondents (n = 30)
Social	57 (50%)	27
Political	23 (20%)	18
Personal development	23 (20%)	14
Professional development	12 (10%)	11

development) are displayed in Table 5.1. As in Chapter 4, this table shows both the number of times responses in each category arose and the number of respondents who drew on each category.

Table 5.1 shows that the benefits most commonly discussed were social in nature concerning notions of safe space, support, friendship and the satisfaction to be derived from helping others. It is to these factors that we turn first.

Social Outcomes

The first response of this type centred around the idea of the group as a *safe space*, a place where you can say what you like and not be judged, where the atmosphere is non-competitive and supportive, where individuals feel a sense of safety, solidarity, belonging and mutual understanding:

> It's a safe space, I can say what I want and it doesn't matter. I don't have to be 'all-knowing' and strong. To be in a space where it doesn't matter if you don't know what you think about something and you're still evolving your thoughts and you want to engage in a discussion in order to reach an opinion, to be in that sort of environment where you are being challenged but in a very non-hostile way is great (417).

A number of women commented on specific features of group structure and process which they perceived as unique to women's groups: 'Given that it is a women's group, it functions in a very "women way": It's non-hierarchical, very informal, we all sit round casually in a circular type environment and everybody participates' (417). One respondent described her reactions when she first attended a meeting:

> The first time I went to any kind of meeting, I just couldn't believe the atmosphere – there was no competitiveness and there was no hostility and it was just everyone listening to what she had to say and expressing

their views, but not in any sort of put-down type of way, they weren't trying to compete with the other people that were there (318).

The non-judgmental nature of the groups was commented on by a number of women as a key feature of the safe space idea. For example, one respondent referred to the value of:

> feeling accepted and being able to say what you need to say even though sometimes they're the most dreadfully negative things and actually being accepted for it, for example, my own negative feelings and my own very strong anger sometimes at my little baby. I remember bringing that up once – that once, when she was crying I was terrified of going to the top of the stairs in case I threw her down! It was nice to hear others saying how angry they felt also! (443).

Closely linked with the safe space idea is the *social support* provided by group membership for women who felt otherwise rather isolated – 'that wonderful solidarity of knowing and the laughter of recognition' (422). The importance of support was mentioned by a large proportion of the interviewees and by a large number of respondents in the questionnaire, particularly in the contexts of employment and bringing up children. Women referred to a feeling of reassurance of not being alone, that there are other women with similar views and who have experienced similar problems. In work contexts this was often linked to a lack of confidence, for example in situations where women had been on the receiving end of criticism of some sort. As one woman commented, 'When you share your experiences about work, you suddenly realize that a lot of women are experiencing the same thing' (237). In the context of bringing up children, the support was needed more around feelings of guilt over perceived inadequacy as a parent – 'the realization that your problems are shared and that just because you handle something badly, it doesn't mean you're a dreadful mother' (499). Some respondents commented that women's groups were providing a substitute extended family for them in the absence of grandparents and other relations living round the corner.

In all these cases, groups were seen as providing a sense of reinforcement and strengthening which comes from mixing with people with similar views, who have been through similar experiences and are fighting the same battles. Indeed, in a few cases, respondents referred to the reassurance which comes from finding that some other women have more extreme views, making their own views seem quite moderate by comparison and thereby ameliorating a view of oneself as a freak in the context of wider society. The importance of support is summed up by a respondent who commented:

> I think that with a lot of women I have talked to, it seems to be about finding other people with similar backgrounds and similar experiences.

Suddenly, you realize, 'I've been through that as well', and you think, 'Oh, it's not just me' (596).

There are clear connections here with the explanations which were given for initial involvement in terms of coping with a personal crisis, particularly a feeling of isolation, and the strength which comes from changing an attribution for personal problems from internal to external.

In addition to the safe space and support provided by group membership, a third social aspect is *friendship*. Nearly all of the interviewees referred to the close friends they had made in the group, 'friendships that were vital with people who really knew what I was going through' (422) and to the benefits of company with like-minded others – 'a close network of people who've got the same ideas as you and who you don't have to keep on arguing with or explaining things to' (418). Groups were seen as providing a context where women could meet others with interests and beliefs in common. Many respondents commented on the questionnaire that they enjoyed their group meetings and activities and the twin benefits of support and friendship were often mentioned together, for example, 'Out of the friendships came the moral support to do the campaigns, whatever they were' (437).

A final social aspect – less frequently mentioned – concerns the satisfaction to be gained from helping and supporting other group members. For example, respondents involved in groups concerned with childbirth and children, referred to the personal satisfaction of helping other mothers, particularly when they themselves subsequently get involved in the group.

Political Outcomes

The next set of factors concern more overtly political outcomes. Distinct from the feeling of helping other *individuals* in the group, the main factor here is the opportunity to help bring about wider social change for women as a whole. The group provides a structure for political activity and an opportunity for wider political involvement. Some women discussed the positive feelings which come from working towards a common goal and the sense of involvement which comes from organized political activity and participation in mass rallies and demonstrations:

> I like the meetings and I like discussing things. I like the activity. I like getting things together – banners, making up chants, getting the coaches. I like the activity and all the things that are going on and just thinking about it, the buzz of activity (431).

Others stressed the importance of maintaining a certain level of activity even in a political climate perceived to be unsympathetic:

> There's also this question of bearing witness which I think is quite impor-
> tant even if an issue is dead for the moment, or if something is unfashion-
> able, you still need to bear witness to those ideas and that kind of way of
> being, to show that it might well be quiet at the moment but don't forget it.
> It hasn't gone away and it does still matter to some people (433).

An important aspect of these political outcomes was a sense of empowerment which goes with working as part of a group. Respondents described 'a
feeling that it's quite possible, maybe not tomorrow, but it is possible to change
women's roles and to challenge the sort of relationships they have with men'
(503); and 'a very invigorating and uplifting sense that things can change and
happen' (464). Alone, many women commented that they feel isolated and
powerless; as part of a group, they feel empowered and part of a larger
movement for social change.

Personal Development Outcomes

The next set of factors refer to personal development of various sorts. First and
most important, a number of women referred to *intellectual stimulation and
personal growth* through group activities. For example, one respondent argued
that the group fulfilled a need for intellectual stimulation which was experienced after leaving higher education:

> While you are at university or polytechnic there is so much there, all
> organized for you or so it seems, to dip into, you just have to take what
> you feel like at any given moment and when you go out into what I hate
> to call *the real world* in the workplace, etc., immediately that goes ...
> After a little while, you really miss that and you really want it from
> somewhere and there isn't a ready community to go to find it. You have
> to create those sorts of environments (417).

Similarly, other respondents who had retired from paid employment argued
that they get a feeling of participating in something that's meaningful, a feeling
of still being involved in things (see Andrews, 1991 for a similar finding):

> If I weren't doing all this, I wouldn't have any real incentive to get up
> in the morning, dress myself up and that to me is important because I
> think so many people when they retire feel that they are useless, that
> they've nothing else to contribute (356).

For a few respondents the personal growth came from reanalysing their
own experiences and comparing them with those of other group members. The
group provides:

a chance to reprocess what I've been through. I really feel very proud of it. I don't feel proud about lots of my life but I do feel proud of the way I've been a mother. So when I hear other people saying things, it gives me a chance to re-value what I did and even what I didn't do. It also gives me a chance to hear the issues facing people, women in the 1990s and what it is people are really up against. So it's a kind of intellectual experience really – I give a lot of support, at least I think I do, but what I'm personally getting out of it is a mental thing (434).

An even more common point was the importance of getting other people's perspectives and that this provided a route to personal growth. Many felt that talking to other women about their experiences is the only way to really understand problems and issues facing them.

A second related personal benefit is that of *increased confidence*. One respondent argued that:

I've always been a feminist, for example, but it's made me more willing to talk about my beliefs and if somebody challenged them to actually argue, because they're valid, they're my beliefs. I might not be right, but they're what I actually believe and it's given me the confidence to actually say, 'Well, this is what I believe' (187).

A further element of this confidence comes from the opportunity to make comparisons with others in the group:

a kind of 'Well, she's done it, so could I' feeling. It's difficult to pin down but that's the kind of feeling. After I've been to group meetings, no matter what it's on, I'll go out feeling 'I can do that, I can succeed', you know, 'I've done better than her and I've not done as good as her', so it's a comparison thing, so it's strengthening (230).

A third aspect of personal development mentioned by some people concerned the development of *group skills*. Some women referred to the general skills of coping with groups, speaking in group meetings, dealing with different viewpoints. Others referred to more specific skills, such as training on chairing meetings and running groups successfully.

Professional Development Outcomes

The final set of perceived benefits were those to do with professional development, though Table 5.1 shows that this category was discussed less frequently. These outcomes were either the development of particular *professional skills or expertise*, such as training or professional contacts or alternatively, referred to the particular *services* offered by the group, such as information, courses, seminars and library facilities. Respondents referred to the value of being able to draw on the experience and expertise of other women – by sitting on committees and talking about matters of common concern and hearing different perspectives. In addition, many respondents discussed the professional value of networking and the opportunity to talk shop and get to know people in the same line of work. This factor relates clearly to the motivation for joining groups in the first place, which was discussed in Chapter 4 and concerned the contacts and services offered by some groups particularly those in a work context.

The Personal and the Political

The perceived outcomes of participation which have been described are very clearly intertwined and relate to wider issues in the women's movement and particularly to connections made between the personal and the political. One of the main themes in the development of the women's movement has been the process whereby personal experience is explored among women in a support-ive context. In many instances this has formed the base on which theory and political strategy have been built. Whether or not women use the term *consciousness raising* to describe the function of these groups, the process remains an important political activity. Coote and Campbell (1987) describe how consciousness raising was

> a means of challenging and transforming women's constructed sense of femininity. It named and endorsed individual feelings and experiences and discovered how far they were common to women in general. It affirmed differences as well as similarities. It enabled women to go on working out their politics for themselves (p. 256).

This relates very closely to the kind of personal empowerment described by the women in our sample.

The notion of a safe space so often mentioned is a vital component in this process. According to Jardim (1993), self-empowering processes are more likely to take place in a group characterized by a flat structure with relationships of greater equality and where status positions are not important (see also Hirsch, 1990). An expressed goal of many feminists is to 'flatten the hierarchy' (Konek and Kitch, 1994: 218) and, where women here talked about the notion of a safe space, they described non-hierarchical group structures which on the whole rejected the concept of leaders and led. Many of the women's groups included here were small in size, thereby giving all members an opportunity to contribute and to provide and receive support. For many women the opportunity to share experiences in such an environment was often the first stage of empowerment which was subsequently transformed into a more overt kind of political action. Drawing clear distinctions between personal and political outcomes is not always easy.

Similar themes emerged from Andrews' (1991) study of political activists. Here again respondents described the sense of belonging and the strong friendships which developed as a result of political involvement, as well as the feeling of being part of a larger whole and the enthusiasm and empowerment which derives from that feeling. Belonging to political parties had personal and political significance for these respondents in the same way as for the present sample of activists.

In concluding our review of this interview data, we can say that our respondents were overwhelmingly positive in their feelings towards the groups to which they belonged and stressed the benefits to be had from membership. One respondent commented, 'Everything is positive about it. I haven't had anything negative from it at all, it's all been hugely positive and I feel sorry for people who don't realize that they can gain that sort of thing themselves, it's very easily done' (192).

Moreover, the perceived benefits were similar across the different types of group, in particular the importance of social support and friendship. The role of political factors was mentioned mainly (but by no means exclusively) by the members of political and work-related groups and professional development outcomes were discussed almost entirely by the members of professional/ management groups. Overall however, it was striking once again how similar sentiments and the connections between personal and political factors were expressed across the very different types of group.

Exploring Perceived Personal and Political Changes

We move away now from the perceived benefits of group involvement to examine perceptions of changes in social beliefs. The extent to which these changes may be attributed to the effects of participation as opposed to other influences is obviously an issue to be addressed here. The data to be discussed here is both quantitative and qualitative.

On the basis of themes emerging from interviews, eight statements were devised for use in a questionnaire completed by 383 women of varying levels of activism (see Chapter 4). Respondents were invited to report on ways in which they felt they had changed in their beliefs over the previous ten years. Each item was scored from 'Strongly disagree' to 'Strongly agree'. The items are shown in Table 5.2 and intercorrelations in Table 5.3.

Responses on these items were highly intercorrelated (see Table 5.3) and factor analysis extracted two factors. The first comprised items 1, 2, 4, 8 and 3 and may be broadly interpreted as referring to change in *political attitudes*. The second factor comprised items 5, 6 and 7 and may be interpreted as referring to

Table 5.2: Items concerning self-reported change

1	I have become more aware of different forms of discrimination, such as racism.
2	I have become more aware of women's oppression.
3	My beliefs about feminism have become more complex.
4	I have become more angry about women's oppression.
5	I have learned how to deal with groups more effectively.
6	I have gained self-confidence.
7	I enjoy the company of other women more.
8	I have a stronger belief in collective action by women.

Table 5.3: Intercorrelations between self-reported change items

Item	1	2	3	4	5	6	7
1							
2	62						
3	22	33					
4	38	62	29				
5	27	19	20	10			
6	14	15	16	03	57		
7	34	35	22	30	33	33	
8	39	51	20	48	28	16	57

For key to items, see Table 5.2
Decimal points have been omitted from correlation coefficients
Coefficients > 10, $p < 0.01$; of 10, $p < 0.05$; under 10, n.s.
n = 366

personal change, though given the comments which have been made about the close connections between the personal and the political in this context, we must be cautious about maintaining too clear a distinction between these factors now.

Of course, simply examining the responses of the activists on these items will not enable us to draw any conclusions about the effects of participation in collective action since agreement with any or all of these statements may simply result from changes over the life-cycle. All we can do here is to compare the responses of more and less active individuals and, should differences emerge, make use of the qualitative data to explore the extent to which those differences are perceived as resulting from participation as opposed to other influences. Accordingly, the sample was split (at the median) according to women's subjective perception of themselves as 'actively involved in women's groups and campaigns'. This provided a more active group (n = 182) and a less active group (n = 184). Results of analysis comparing the responses of the two groups are presented in Table 5.4.

Examining the mean scores shows that all respondents tended to agree with the statements possibly reflecting general life-cycle changes but it is interesting

Table 5.4: Reported changes in beliefs by less and more active groups: Mean scores, standard deviations and F statistics

Item	Less active group (n = 184)	More active group (n = 182)	Error MS	F
1	4.06 (.80)	4.26 (.84)	.67	7.04
2	3.83 (.94)	4.04 (.90)	.85	6.04
3	3.78 (.91)	4.07 (.89)	.78	14.39
4	3.30 (1.04)	3.65 (1.05)	1.09	10.12
5	3.76 (.79)	4.14 (.77)	.59	29.54
6	4.05 (.85)	4.34 (.71)	.60	15.96
7	3.46 (.88)	3.86 (.84)	.74	19.10
8	3.41 (.85)	3.91 (.91)	.77	26.17

For key to items, see Table 5.2
All F values significant at $p < 0.01$, except item (2) where $p < 0.05$
Multivariate F-test: $F(8,356) = 6.85$, $p < 0.01$, age as covariate

that the more active group expressed significantly more agreement on all eight items. The least significant differences were on those items 1) and 2) relating to a growth in the *awareness* of oppression, whereas the strongest differences were on the item relating to dealing with groups effectively 5) and on the final item 8) relating to support for collective action by women.

To explore some of these perceived changes in more detail and to try to tease out the causes of these changes, we can also present qualitative findings from an open-ended question on the same questionnaire where respondents were invited to comment on any perceived changes in their attitudes, again over the previous ten years. Of the 383 total returns, responses to this particular question were received from 209 women currently actively involved in women's groups and campaigns and from 102 women not currently active.

Analysis of the responses from the more active women showed that five main categories of response could be distinguished which accounted for nearly three-quarters of the total number of responses given. These are displayed in Table 5.5.

Table 5.5: Perceived changes: Percentage of total responses from qualitative data

Category	Less active group	More active group
Greater awareness of women's oppression	17.6	21.5
Views become more complex	10.8	12.9
Greater belief in collective action by women	1.0	7.1
More pessimistic about achieving social change	3.9	20.1
More pragmatic about achieving social change	5.9	8.6
Total percentage	39.2	70.2

Three of these categories map onto the questions where respondents provided quantitative data: A greater awareness of women's oppression; the development of more complex views concerning gender issues; and a stronger belief in collective action by women as the means of achieving social change. In addition, two further categories of response emerged, which were also concerned with the prospects of achieving social change for women: The first was a general sense of pessimism about the prevailing social climate, and the second was the development of a more pragmatic view which was reconciled to the slow pace of change.

When these responses were compared with responses from the less active women, some interesting differences emerged. Less active women also commented that they had become more aware of women's oppression, that their views had become more complex and (to a lesser extent) that they had developed a more pragmatic approach to social change. This suggests that changes in these respects may reflect changes in life-cycle and social roles. However, hardly any of these women commented that they had developed a stronger belief in collective action by women (mirroring the very significant difference found here in the quantitative data) and the pessimism which featured amongst responses from more active women was also not reflected amongst the less active group. Indeed, the responses from the less active group were much more varied and difficult to categorize: Responses to these five categories made up only just over a third of the total number of responses and no other main categories could be distinguished.

The biggest single category from more and less active women was the development of greater awareness of women's oppression. Some women linked this explicitly to the effects of group involvement, for example, 'the group has opened my eyes to women's oppression which I hadn't really taken seriously before' (434). More commonly however, this was seen as a response to experiences in some new social context or role, such as experiences at work or becoming a mother – or both and having to deal with the children/career dilemma. For example:

As I have got older I have realized that there are structural obstacles to women's progression which I knew nothing of when I was younger. Because of more exposure to the issues and due to having been thwarted on occasions, either professionally or personally, by structural obstacles in the workplace or in life (067);

I have realized how male-oriented and influenced are the legal-social set up, as regards pregnancy, birth, breastfeeding, working, living with small children, etc. I think it's because I've actually had experience dealing with these situations, whereas before I had children my life was relatively unaffected (097).

Life-cycle changes, in particular having children, was seen as a major influence on attitudes and identity as women had first-hand experience of problems of childcare and other people's attitudes to working women and to mothers. Having children was not the only life-cycle change mentioned however. Some respondents referred to retirement and an accompanying awareness that older women can become 'more and more invisible and undervalued' (577). In some cases, women linked their greater awareness to a change in attributions made for women's success and failure, such that having once believed that lack of success amongst women was due to internal factors, such as lack of ability, they had now come to appreciate the social and structural barriers to women's advancement.

Perhaps also in response to taking on new roles at home and at work, many women described how their views had become more complex in various ways. Very commonly, this took the form of a recognition of differences *between* different women, as a result of sexuality, race, culture, religion, physical and mental ability and so on. Respondents therefore felt less inclined to talk about women's issues or women's oppression in general without qualifying which women and how different women can be affected. Respondents argued the need to take seriously the diversity of women's lives, values and views and not to write off women with different views as unreconstructed, falsely conscious or deluded.

As problems between different groups of women become more obvious, the task of building solidarity between women *as women* is transformed into building solidarity between groups of women who share similar problems or experiences. Many women had come to recognize different varieties of feminism, some very different from others, which makes the task of presenting a united front against patriarchy that much more difficult. Relatedly, many women expressed the view that they had become increasingly critical of some women (not supporting others, not taking action, or conversely, being too aggressive) and increasingly understanding of men's situation. In this sense, intergroup relations have become less clear-cut.

Many women put these changes down to life-cycle events and social roles, again becoming a mother – and having sons in particular – were seen as influential. Others referred to the increased contact which they had had with different women in women's groups which allowed them to find out about differing perspectives and experiences. Underlying a number of explanations was the view that the initial discovery of feminism as a way of thinking and explaining experiences had transformed into a solid underpinning for beliefs on which acknowledgement of difference could be built.

Related to the development of more complex views about gender relations, many women – both more and less active respondents – felt that they had become more pragmatic and less radical in their approach to achieving social change. Women felt that they had become less impatient with society, more sympathetic to a 'drip drip' approach to social change and to a view that gender relations won't change overnight. Many described their current views as softer, calmer, more long-term, philosophic, mellower, more pragmatic, less uptight and some said that, as a consequence, they now feel able to discuss gender issues less emotively and do not get so upset about sexism. This change of outlook was generally put down simply to getting older – some added 'wiser'.

Finally, there were two categories of rather contradictory response which were drawn upon almost exclusively by the more active women. One – in some contrast to the growth of pragmatism described above – was a stronger belief in the need for women to take collective action and to work together to achieve change. Respondents here said that they had come to believe even more strongly that women must take an active role in changing their circumstances and that talking must be translated into action.

However, with regard to the possibility of actually *achieving* social change in the present social and political context, many of the more active women expressed a deep sense of pessimism. This was commonly linked to the perceived enduring effects of Thatcherism and the long years of Conservative government. Women expressed views that the women's movement has become very fragmented, that fewer and fewer women seem prepared to identify themselves as feminists and that progress seems as far off as ever. Consequently, some activists felt 'increasingly depressed and demoralized' and had a 'deep sense of hopelessness and despair'.

It is interesting that this sense of pessimism did not feature so clearly amongst the less active women. It is possible that for longstanding activists, whose participation dates back to the 1960s and 1970s, a sense of expectation was built up that collective action would bring results. Subsequent changes in the political climate were consequently felt all the more keenly, together with a sense of disappointment that gender equality appeared as far off as ever despite all the hard work and campaigning.

In summary, a number of perceived changes in attitudes have been identified by the respondents in this sample relating to their views of gender relations and the possibilities for achieving social change. Some of these comments may be related to a developmental model of feminism developed by Downing and Roush (1985). This suggests that some variations in feminist positions may be related to stages in women's feminist identity formation. According to this model, women move from non-identification to a stage at which women are 'sensitized to women's oppression' and feel anger and guilt. The third stage concerns the discovery of sisterhood and immersion in women's culture, often preferring to socialize with women to the exclusion of men. Feminists in the fourth stage have transcended traditional sex roles, recognized the positive aspects of being a woman and have learned to 'evaluate men on an individual basis'. Stage five feminists are committed to social change and have learned to translate their feminist identity into 'meaningful and effective action' (see also Bargad and Hyde, 1991).

Identifying the causes of these changes in identity and beliefs is difficult if not impossible. In some cases, women themselves pointed to life-cycle changes and the adoption of new social roles, particularly motherhood, and to their experiences in women's groups and more generally to the impact of age and experience. Although differences were found in the quantitative data between the responses of more and less active women, it is impossible to put these differences down to the effects of participation since it is just as likely that experiences of discrimination (for example), which were found to be important in motivating participation in women's groups (see Chapter 4) were also important in influencing the beliefs discussed here. Once again, we must point to the constant interaction between attitudes, identity, behaviour and the interpretation of life experiences.

Comparing New Recruits and Longstanding Members

A further way of exploring the outcomes of participation in collective action is by comparing the responses of individuals who have been involved for varying lengths of time. The present sample of individuals who were actively involved in groups may be divided into three sub-groups: Those who had been involved for less than a year (n=65); those whose involvement had lasted between one and three years (n=98); and those who had been involved for over three years (n=184). By comparing their levels of participation and social beliefs, we can explore whether any significant differences emerge which could be attributed to socialization effects in groups.

With regard to participation levels, very clear and significant differences emerged across the three groups with regard to self-perception as an activist $(F(2,339) = 7.41, p < 0.01)$, participation in women's groups $(F(2,339) = 8.47, p < 0.01)$ and individual protest activities $(F(2,339) = 3.23, p < 0.05)$. There were no significant differences with regard to collective protest or informal participation. Where there were significant differences, these arose from the fact in all cases that the longstanding activists (over three years) differed significantly from the other groups being much more active. (Age was entered as a covariate in these analyses though it proved to be non-significant in all cases.) Mean scores are displayed in Figure 5.2.

When we turn to social beliefs however, we find only one significant difference, which was for efficacy $(F(2,247) = 5.68, p < 0.01, \text{age n.s.})$, where longstanding activists scored significantly higher than the other two groups, possibly supporting the idea that involvement in political activity over a period of time does feed back into feelings of political efficacy.

There was one other variable which also showed a significant difference between the three groups and that related to identification with the activist group $(F(2,339) = 3.54, p < 0.01)$. Here there was a steady increase in scores across the three groups and the longstanding activists registered a significantly higher score (mean 3.91, SD=.59) than the new recruits (mean 3.66, SD=.73).

131

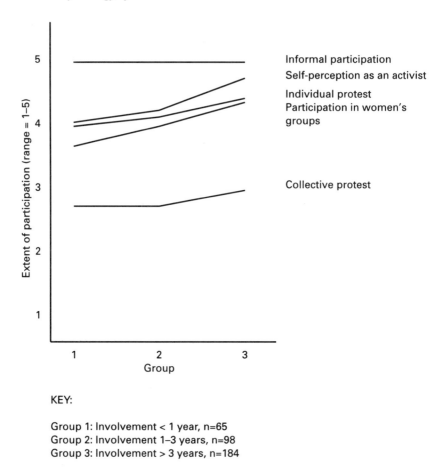

Figure 5.2: Participation in a gender context: A comparison according to length of involvement

Identification with the group was computed as the aggregate score derived from the following items: 1) 'I identify strongly with other members of the group/campaign'; 2) 'I often feel critical of other members of the group/campaign' (reverse scoring); 3) 'I feel strong ties with other members of the group/campaign'; and 4) 'I feel I do not fit in with other members of the group/campaign' (reverse scoring) (see Brown, *et al.*, 1986). Correlations computed between these four individual items and duration of group membership showed significant positive correlations in the cases of items 1), 3) and 4), though not item 2).

Mean scores on these four items showed that the lowest score was found on item 2); in other words, a number of activists who felt very committed to the group in many ways were also prepared to voice some criticism (see Kelly, 1988 for a similar finding). As the correlational analysis showed, this criticism was as likely to come from longstanding members as from new recruits.

In an open-ended question inviting respondents to describe their feelings towards the group, a number of women expressed this criticism which focused on many different aspects of group structure, process and strategy. In a number of cases it resulted from a perception that other members were insufficiently active or that the group as a whole was more concerned with *talking* than *doing*. For example, some women referred to a sense of despair at the apathy of other members, who were only too happy to criticize yet less willing to do anything. Poor organization was often the subject of criticism and it was often felt that too much time was spent planning and talking and not enough time spent on getting things done and taking action. In some cases, it was felt that other members were too sectarian towards other groups and campaigns or too strident. Other criticism focused on disagreements over strategy, for example, 'trying to be too many things to too wide a range of women' (240), whilst others focused on lack of unity in the group: 'squabbling between committees on getting their cause to the top of the agenda' (358); or structural problems: 'a low and almost unacceptable level of communication between the national organization and its branches and its individual members' (134).

However, a number of women took the opportunity to describe positive feelings towards the group (such as those described earlier in the chapter) and it was the case that mild and stronger criticism was often stated within the context of the respondent's broad sense of affinity with the group and its aims and members.

In conclusion, findings comparing the responses of new recruits and longstanding activists suggest that over time, individuals participate more, develop a greater sense of their own identity as activists and a stronger sense of identification with the group, as well as a greater sense of political efficacy. As one respondent put it, 'Our ties have become closer due to the passage of time and further sharing of experience. I now feel that I belong and feel more comfortable in their company' (409).

In other ways, new recruits and longstanding activists were similar in their beliefs, and a possible explanation for this finding will be suggested in the next section.

Comparing Participation and Social Beliefs Over Time

The final way in which we can examine the outcomes of participation in collective action here is to test actual changes in social beliefs across a year's time span, focusing on those individuals who are relatively new to the group and comparing them with the more longstanding activists. Our sub-groups were somewhat smaller here than in the previous analysis owing to attrition in the sample by the follow-up stage. Consequently, the sub-groups were now as follows: Individuals involved for less than two years (n = 80) compared with individuals who had been involved for over three years (n = 142).

However, analysis here showed no significant differences in patterns of change relating to participation or social beliefs between the two sub-groups. In addition, and rather more surprisingly, patterns of identification with the activist group also showed no differences, in both cases showing a slight decrease over the course of the year, despite the fact that we might have expected new recruits to show increases in identification in the early stages of their group membership by comparison with longstanding members.

One possible explanation for this finding – and for the broad similarity in beliefs discussed in the previous section – is that whereas our new recruits reported that they had been members of their group for a relatively short time, it is quite likely that they had been involved in *other* women's groups or campaigns for much longer. There is considerable overlap between the membership of different women's groups, and many of our activists were members of more than one group. Many interviewees described how the most dramatic changes in attitudes and identity occurred on joining a *first* group or campaign. It is this first experience which is crucial, and one might not expect such clear changes to occur on joining other groups subsequently. Future research on this question should target people getting involved in their *first* political group or campaign.

Concluding Comments

What can we conclude about the outcomes of participation in collective action? In accordance with the theorizing into group socialization which was discussed at the beginning of this chapter, respondents in the present study had a clear sense of the rewards to be gained from group membership. Amongst our respondents, the most frequently described outcomes related to social benefits, in common with Moreland, *et al.*'s (1993) study. Whereas in that study the social benefits mainly revolved around friendship, in the present study – because of the very different nature of the groups involved – a large element of the social outcomes concerned support and solidarity with like-minded others (as well as friendship).

The links between outcomes defined here as social, personal and political were an important feature of the findings and perhaps this is to be expected in the context of women's groups, where connections between personal lives and group status have always been stressed. Social support provided in a safe space allows women to explore similarities and differences in their experiences and may provide a stepping-stone to more explicit forms of political action. As described earlier in this chapter, Hirsch (1990) has suggested that small groups may provide havens in which members develop an awareness of common problems and question the legitimacy of current intergroup relations. Experiences of perceived injustice may be compared promoting an awareness of both personal and group discrimination (see Chapter 4).

Consistent with some of these perceived outcomes, respondents described a number of changes in their social beliefs over time. More active women expressed significantly more agreement with items concerning the awareness of women's low status, feelings of anger about that status and the need to take collective action, as well as items relating to personal benefits, such as increased self-confidence and the ability to deal with groups effectively. Of course, attributing these perceived changes to the effects of group participation was not possible. However, findings from the qualitative data suggested that certain changes may be particularly connected with participation (endorsement of collective action by women, learning to deal with groups effectively, enjoying other women's company more), whereas others were attributed to a greater extent – at least by respondents themselves – to life-cycle changes and the adoption of new social roles (development of more complex views about gender relations and feminism, a greater pragmatism about achieving social change).

Whereas previous research described at the beginning of this chapter into consciousness raising mainly concerned single episodes of conflict, the present findings allow some insight into longstanding group involvement. Comparisons of the participation levels and social beliefs of longstanding activists and more recent recruits showed that the former group reported higher levels of participation, a greater perception of themselves as activists, a stronger sense of identification with the activist group and a stronger sense of political efficacy. In accordance with the suggestions made in Chapter 3, this suggests that attitudes and behaviour become mutually reinforcing over a period of time promoting a sense of activist identity.

If we consider the relationships between the findings presented in this chapter and those presented in Chapters 3 and 4, we can reflect on the links between attitudes and behaviour. For example, relative deprivation emerged in Chapter 3 as related to intentions to participate in certain forms of action and in Chapter 4 as a perceived *cause* of activist behaviour. Here we see a heightened sense of relative deprivation emerging as a possible *outcome* of participation. In addition, greater awareness of *women's* oppression may spill over to promote a growth in awareness of *other* forms of discrimination as well. It may well be that interaction with other activists and involvement in campaigns serves to fuel both awareness and anger at women's low status *and* the low status of other social groups. Similarly, other factors, such as gender identity, political efficacy and collectivist orientation, may be seen as both causes and outcomes of participation in women's groups.

The data presented in this chapter emphasizes the positive outcomes associated with group membership. Given the tremendous sense of personal satisfaction and political empowerment which our respondents described, why is involvement in collective action such a minority pursuit? This question is the focus of the next chapter.

Chapter 6

Explaining Non-activism

Involvement in collective action is a minority pursuit. The great majority of people do not *join* political groups at all, let alone get actively involved. The focus in the present chapter turns to the majority response: Why is it that so many people do not wish to get involved? How can our understanding of this response be informed by social psychological theory?

Once again, there is no existing body of social psychological literature on which we can draw but a number of different strands of work which can be pulled together to provide some theoretical background. Of particular relevance is the small amount of research which has been conducted into the cultural value of individualism and the negative way in which group membership *per se* may be viewed by the members of an individualistic culture. Relatedly, in the context of political participation, it has been argued that the electorate in Britain has become increasingly apathetic and disaffected with political systems and institutions in general and consequently less likely to get involved in any political activity. Within this broad cultural context, a large body of social psychological research has been conducted around the issue of minority influence, on which we can draw to examine the ways in which minorities, such as political groups and the activists who comprise them, are viewed by majorities and the obstacles which stand in the way of their influence. This research suggests that minorities are frequently perceived as cranky and dogmatic and that members of the majority group are consequently reluctant to become associated with the minority because of the negative implications for their own social identities.

In this chapter, a review of these areas will be followed by consideration of issues which are specific to trade union and gender contexts and presentation of data from these contexts where individuals explain their own lack of involvement.

Culture, Individualism and Group Membership

An important consideration in understanding non-activism relates to cultural context and in particular to a dimension of cultural variation which has attracted much recent attention, namely individualism–collectivism. An influential study

136

was conducted by Hofstede (1980), who investigated cross-cultural variations in a questionnaire study carried out between 1967 and 1973 (see Chapter 1). Questionnaires were distributed to samples of IBM employees in 65 countries and were returned by approximately 88,000 respondents. Countries were then classified as high or low on a dimension of individualism–collectivism. The countries ranked as highest on individualism were the United States, Australia and Britain. Using a variety of different measures and working with a number of different theoretical orientations, others have concurred on the relatively high scoring of most European and North American countries on individualism however it is defined (see Chinese Culture Connection, 1987; Schwartz, 1992; Schwartz and Bilsky, 1987; 1990; see Smith and Bond, 1993 for a review).

In recent social psychological analysis, Triandis, *et al.*, relate the construct of individualism–collectivism specifically to group membership:

> The major themes of collectivism are self-definition as part of group(s), subordination of personal goals to ingroup goals, concern for the integrity of the ingroup, and intense emotional attachment to the group. The major themes of individualism are a self-definition as an entity that is distinct and separate from group(s), emphasis on personal goals even if pursuit of such goals inconveniences the ingroup, and less concern and emotional attachment to the ingroups (1988: 335).

The broad characterization of cultural difference which is described in this analysis suggests that in collectivist cultures people's lives and identities are dominated by a small number – possibly a single – ingroup to which they are more or less permanently attached (where an ingroup is defined as a set of people with whom one shares some attribute that contributes to a positive social identity). Preserving ingroup harmony by conformity to group norms is very important since leaving the group is difficult, if not impossible. Personal goals are subordinated to the greater collective good even where this entails high personal cost. By contrast, it is argued that in individualist cultures there are many more ingroups. People's relationships with these groups tend to be more superficial, groups make fewer demands on individuals and if the costs of group membership are perceived as too high, the individual will simply quit the group and possibly join an alternative group. Consequently, people develop greater skills in entering and leaving social groups. Individual attachment to any one group is less strong and a person has considerable freedom to act independently of others – to 'do one's own thing'. Within an individualist culture, each individual accumulates a diverse and to some extent unique collection of group memberships, and the importance of any one group rises and falls with changing personal needs.

Of course, this is a very crude characterization of a highly complex topic. Triandis and his coworkers acknowledge important differences between different types of individualist and collectivist culture as well as highlighting individual differences within cultures. Nevertheless, their research provides a useful starting-point for a *social psychological* analysis of individualism–collectivism which is grounded in a consideration of the relationship between individuals and groups. For our present purposes in considering non-involvement in collective action, the analysis suggests that involvement will be less likely in individualist cultures because of an individual's relatively weak sense of attachment to any particular social group. Consequently, if a group fails to make a positive contribution to social identity, a person is more likely to pursue a strategy of individual mobility – quitting the group and possibly finding an alternative – than a strategy of collective action to improve the status of the whole group. Because of the greater importance of personal goals over group goals in individualist cultures and the personal costs entailed in participation in collective action, an individual response must be more likely. This is consistent with the analysis of collective action developed by Taylor and McKirnan (1984; see Chapter 2) and, in common with that analysis, neglects the feelings of group loyalty which people may have even in individualist cultures. In a collectivist culture, where identity is bound up more or less permanently with a particular ingroup, improving the status of that group as a whole would be the only viable route to improving personal status. Moreover, as Taylor and McKirnan (1984) point out in their analysis, the tendency to make internal attributions for individual outcomes, which is so dominant in individualist cultures, would also lead people to individual rather than collective strategies (see Chapter 2).

Given the primacy of the individual over the group in individualist cultures, we might expect that people's attitudes to group membership *per se* would be more negative than in collectivist cultures, at least in situations where this membership is perceived to entail any personal costs. Here we can only draw inferences from related areas of study in group processes. For example, in research examining perceptions of homogeneity within groups (stereotypes), a frequent observation has been the tendency to perceive 'them' as all alike, at the same time perceiving 'us' as individuals. So common has this observation been, that it has gained the name, the 'outgroup homogeneity effect' (though research based on self-categorization theory has recently highlighted some situations in which the perception may be reversed, indicating greater perceived *ingroup* homogeneity. See Simon 1992; Simon and Pettigrew, 1990).

Why should the outgroup homogeneity effect be so prevalent? A number of explanations have been put forward, including different amounts of contact with and information about outgroups (see Quattrone, 1986 for a review), but one possibility concerns the intrinsic positive value which may be attached to heterogeneity and uniqueness in individualist cultures. For example, Snyder and Fromkin (1980) argue that, '[t]he need to see oneself as unique is a potent and continuous force in our society' (p. 3). Consequently, being part of a group where everybody is unique or different in some sense may make a positive contribution to social identity, whereas seeing oneself as more or less interchangeable with fellow ingroup members may threaten this sense of personal uniqueness (Kelly, 1989). Group membership here entails some personal cost in terms of identity. This highlights a tension in identity between maintaining personal uniqueness and a sense of difference on the one hand, and seeing oneself as a member of social groups and categories on the other.

This tension is examined by Brewer (1991; 1993a; b) in her theory of group identification as the product of a search for 'optimal distinctiveness'. This assumes that social identity is activated in order to meet powerful competing needs for *differentiation* of the self from others and *inclusion* of the self into larger social collectives. An optimal level of social identity can be seen as a compromise between differentiation and inclusion. At either extreme, the person's identity is threatened; being highly individuated leaves one feeling isolated, while immersion in highly inclusive groupings is a threat to one's sense of personal uniqueness. Discussing the role of optimal distinctiveness in mobilizing group identification (and possibly collective action), Brewer (1993b) suggests that in contexts where demographic subgroups constitute distinct minorities, depersonalization will enhance group consciousness and politicization, whereas in contexts that are demographically homogeneous, the search for optimal distinctiveness will lead to intracategory differentiation in the form of sects and factions. These optimally distinctive subgroupings may engage social identification to the possible detriment of the superordinate collective.

Finally, in discussing the negative value attached to group membership in our culture, we might note again the emphasis in social psychological study which was commented on in Chapter 5, namely the almost exclusive focus on *negative* outcomes associated with group membership – conflict, prejudice, stereotyping – and lack of research into the positive outcomes of group membership – solidarity, support, loyalty and cooperation. This academic agenda can be understood once it is appreciated that European social psychology has been dominated for much of its existence by an ideology of North American individualism (Sampson, 1977).

If we turn to Britain itself which is the setting for the present research, it is uncontroversial to state that Britain is an individualist culture when considered in a world context. One way in which this individualism might manifest itself is a relative lack of concern with society, community and political institutions. Consistent with this view, some have argued that compared with other industrialized countries, levels of interest in politics are substantially lower in Britain and cynicism about politicians is widespread (for example Kavanagh, 1971; 1989; Marsh, 1977). Marsh (1990) reports that less than a tenth of the British adults surveyed said that they were 'very interested' in politics, and Heath and Topf (1987) showed that up to two-thirds of British adults endorsed opinions reflecting a general cynicism with politics and politicians.

The extent to which levels of political cynicism and disaffection may have increased in recent years has been the subject of some debate. For example, Beer (1982) has argued on the basis of survey data, that there has been an increase in distrust of government and politics which represents a collapse in deference and civic culture (see also Almond and Verba, 1980; Marsh, 1977). Some have argued that political cynicism is particularly marked amongst young people and have expressed fears that youth unemployment will nurture political disaffection and reaction (Unesco, 1981; see also Cochrane and Billig, 1982a; b).

However, Heath and Topf (1987) argue that cynicism about politics and politicians is a longstanding feature of British political culture. Moreover, Parry, *et al.*, present data suggesting that strongly negative outlooks do not necessarily lead to apathy and disengagement anyway. These researchers argue that 'it is the sense of efficacy, of confidence in the capacity to act, which makes a greater impact than a person's broad attitude to the authorities who are the targets of that action' (1992: 188). Bhavnani (1991) also argues that cynicism amongst young people is not necessarily an indication of political apathy and may even act as an impetus for political activity in protest movements.

Moving away from the specific issue of political cynicism, there has been some recent debate as to whether or not Britain has become more individualist in general under successive Conservative governments in the period since 1979 (see Chapter 1). Some have argued that a new type of individualism – *Thatcherism* (moulded by Prime Minister Margaret Thatcher) – has reshaped people's attitudes, identities and consciousness. 'Thatcherite individualism' is the belief 'that it is generally better for people to look after themselves (and their families) than for them to combine as a society to provide for themselves collectively' (Rentoul, 1990: 168). This argument has been put most cogently by Hall (1992), who has argued that people's identities, which were once stable, coherent and firmly rooted in communities and social class relations, have become transformed and segmented so that individuals are now characterized to a greater extent by a myriad of intersecting and cross-cutting identities, making collective action (at least in class terms) less likely (see also Jenkins, 1987; Marquand, 1988). This analysis actually fits in well with the analysis of individualism developed by Triandis and his coworkers which, as discussed, also connects individualism with a large number of ingroups, any one of which has only weak significance for the individual.

Others have disputed the idea that British culture has been transformed in the 1980s and that new times make collective action less likely. In a detailed study of young people's attitudes and identities, Banks, *et al.* (1992) found that whereas their respondents showed little interest in party politics and even less activity, this did not necessarily mean that they considered politics unimportant. In interviews, it was common for individuals to explain that they regarded their present lack of interest as a temporary phase (see also Bhavnani, 1991; Bynner and Ashford, 1994). These researchers conclude that there is no evidence of any general 'sea change' in political culture and that their respondents were not 'Thatcher's children' in an ideological sense of having internalized the dominant values of an enterprise culture.

Similarly, in an analysis of data from the British Social Attitudes Survey, Rentoul (1990) concludes that there is no evidence for an increase in individualism and, if anything, the growing importance attached – particularly by young people – to environmental problems and green issues, which involve the curtailment of individual freedoms, will make the growth of individualism even less likely over time (see also Inglehart, 1990; Rentoul, 1989). Thus, rather than argue that young people have lost all interest in politics, it seems rather that the form which their interest takes has shifted away from mainstream party politics towards single issues, such as anti-racism, sexuality, homelessness, human rights and the environment.

Finally, Kelly and Kelly (1991) adopted a social psychological analysis to argue that 'them and us' attitudes at work remain largely unchanged, contrary to the idea that new management practices adopted in the 1980s have brought about a new spirit of cooperation between workers and managers (see also MacInnes, 1987). Thus, we can conclude that whereas Britain can undoubtedly be characterized as individualist within the context of the world's cultures, there is little evidence that it has become significantly *more* so under the influence of successive Conservative governments in the 1980s.

To sum up, the non-involvement of the majority in collective action must be understood within a cultural context which favours individualism. Such an ideology asserts the primacy of the individual and the achievement of personal goals over group goals and may lead people to have a negative view of groups and group membership in general which makes collective activities less likely. In her discussion of political activism and inactivism, Brunt comments that:

> It is not after all obvious why anyone, particularly in such an apolitical culture as Britain, should ever choose to define themselves as political. When politics is such a marginalised and minority activity, 'admitting' to being a 'political animal' of any sort, let alone a left one, is distinctly odd. For the common sense opinion of politics is that, like religion, it spells trouble (1989: 152).

Given a cultural context in which political activity in groups is unusual, how are the people who *are* active viewed by the majority?

Perceptions of Political Minorities and Activists

Of particular relevance here is a body of research which has developed into the topic of minority influence, i.e., that which is exerted by a minority over a majority. This topic was developed partly with a view to understanding how certain ideas, espoused initially by small groups can develop into significant and influential social movements, examples being the women's movement and the environmental movement. The development of this academic interest can be contrasted with a previous concern with the opposite scenario, namely the power of majorities to induce conformity in a subordinate party. On the strength of this early research, it was assumed for a long time that minorities could never be more than the powerless targets of influence, soaking up attitudes and beliefs from the larger group on whom they were dependent for information and social approval. More recently however it has been shown beyond doubt that there are situations in which a relatively small minority *can* induce change in the attitudes of majority group members, and the focus has turned to examining the specific conditions which facilitate or hinder this type of influence.

Of particular importance is perception of the minority's behavioural style and the interpretation which is placed upon that behaviour. Moscovici and his co-workers (see Moscovici, *et al.*, 1969) have argued that a crucial element of the behavioural style displayed by successful minorities is *consistency*, both over time (diachronic consistency) and between minority group members (synchronic consistency) (see Moscovici, 1985). Such consistency promotes social conflict whose resolution may entail some influence, not least because of an attributional process whereby consistency will be interpreted as indicating confidence and conviction on the part of the minority that they are indeed presenting a real alternative to the status quo. As Turner explains:

> A consistent minority is distinctive and visible, creates conflict, doubt and uncertainty about established norms, signals that it will not compromise or budge, that it is confident, committed, certain (it must feel strongly to stand out) and provides an alternative norm, a new way of looking at things, which would resolve the conflict if the majority will move (1991: 87).

Papastamou and Mugny (1985) have pointed out, however, that it is possible to think of many minorities which are undoubtedly consistent, such as certain extreme left-wing political groups, but which fail to exert influence. They suggest that consistency carried to extremes may be perceived as *rigidity*, a clear and blatant refusal to consider any negotiation or compromise with the majority. Such a perception will only serve to alienate members of the majority group who will strongly resist any attempted influence. Again one possible explanation for the impact of behavioural style – this time the negative impact of perceived rigidity – rests on attributional processes and interpretation that the message expressed does not constitute a real alternative but simply reflects a characteristic of the minority itself, namely its dogmatism.

In further analysis, Papastamou and Mugny (1985) argue that the majority actually comprises two separate social entities: First, the *power*, by which is meant the dominant group which dictates the social norms and rules; and second, the *population*, comprising the people who are dominated by this power and who have internalized the dominant ideology. To the extent that the power wishes to preserve the status quo and resist social change, it will be in its interests to prevent the diffusion of oppositional minority ideas. One means of doing this is by making widely available systems of representation which ensure that minority behaviour is *interpreted* as rigidity (since the degree to which behaviour is seen as rigid as opposed to consistent is inevitably a matter of judgment to some extent). Encouraging the population to perceive minority behaviour as rigidity should serve to counteract any possible influence. If it is successful, the power thereby deprives the minority of the only weapon at its disposal, namely its advocacy of a coherent alternative to the dominant ideology and the social conflict which that entails.

To illustrate these processes, a number of experimental studies have been conducted to demonstrate the ways in which minority influence may be diminished by the so-called *psychologization* or *naturalization* of minority behaviour. This refers to the interpretation of behaviour as deriving from natural, intrinsic characteristics of the minority, such as psychological traits (see Papastamou, 1986). For example, Mugny and Papastamou (1980) found that the same argument expressed by several (rigid) minorities was more influential than when expressed by a single (rigid) minority, for whom a process of psychologization was more likely. Even more clearly, Papastamou, Mugny and Kaiser (1980) instructed subjects to read a text expressing a minority viewpoint (attributed to a single minority). Half of the subjects were led to believe that they would later have to describe the author's personality (psychologization condition) and the other half were told that they would have to summarize the main ideas in the text (non-psychologization condition). Findings showed that concentrating on the psychological traits of the author was sufficient to reduce the influence of the text (though this was particularly the case with a flexible rather than a rigid minority for whom the process of psychologization was possibly already underway. See Papastamou and Mugny, 1985, for a review). Finally, Papastamou (1986) showed that psychologization constitutes a barrier to *minority* influence (but not majority influence) and that this effect is particularly strong where subjects' own opinions are close to those of the influence source. These subjects run the highest risk of being identified with the deviant minority.

An additional consideration in determining the success of minority influence relates to the wider group membership of the source and the target of influence (see Abrams and Hogg, 1990). A number of studies have pointed to the greater effectiveness of fellow ingroup members as opposed to outgroup members in promoting influence (see Clark and Maass, 1988a;b; Kelly, 1990b; Maass, Clark and Haberkorn, 1982; Martin, 1988a;b;c; Mugny, Kaiser and Papastamou, 1983; Turner, 1991 for a review). This difference may be explained by self-categorization theory (Turner, *et al.*, 1987). According to this approach, the acceptance of influence is mediated by its implications for identity. Influence from a source perceived as an outgroup may be resisted because acceptance may imply a change of social identity as perceived negative outgroup characteristics are attributed to the self (Mugny, 1982; Mugny, *et al.*, 1984). Thus, if a minority is perceived as an outgroup – and moreover if powerful groups can promote this perception – influence will be diminished. Approaching the minority will risk attribution to the self of all the negative connotations associated with the minority position and this entails a psychological cost which individuals will be reluctant to pay. As Paicheler (1988: 151) argues, one reason for the rejection of minority influence arises from a fear of being different, of being categorized as deviant.

Thus, minorities have to confront the twin obstacles of group membership on the one hand and psychologization on the other. Examining the interaction between these factors, Mugny, *et al.* (1983) found that the effect of psychologization was greater when the minority shared the subject's group membership. Reviewing these findings, Papastamou and Mugny argue that:

> Confronted with a minority categorized as an outgroup, the existence of a stereotype is sufficient to undermine minority influence. Psychologisation mitigates the unavailability of this alternative within one's own group. To psychologise is to exclude those who are not already excluded by virtue of their existing social characteristics. It is the social creation of stigma (1985: 128).

Thus there are a number of obstacles facing minorities which go some way to explaining the reluctance of many majority group members to approach them. Minorities may be seen as rigid or dogmatic, driven by idiosyncratic psychological characteristics rather than by belief in a genuine alternative to the status quo. This is a representation of minority behaviour which is made widely available by powerful groups who have an interest in preserving the status quo. Furthermore, acceptance of influence from a minority perceived as an outgroup entails a large psychological cost as stereotypical outgroup characteristics are attributed to the self and social identity redefined. Again, powerful groups may seek to exploit this factor by reinforcing perceived group boundaries which divide *us* in the population from *them* in the minority. According to this research then, the problem for minority groups is to present their arguments in such a way as to maximize perceived flexibility and common group membership while maintaining a consistent style of argument.

To summarize the arguments which have been made, there are a number of strands of social psychological work on which we can draw to provide some theoretical background for explaining non-activism. At a cultural level, research into cultural values, particularly individualism–collectivism, suggests that in an individualistic culture, such as Britain, personal goals are given primacy over collective goals and group membership itself may be seen in a rather negative light in terms of its implications for identity. In such an ideological climate, the active minority is given a bad press. Activists' behaviour may be interpreted as dogmatic and extreme, and, in an attempt to preserve the status quo and defend their superior position, powerful groups in society will seek to exploit this perception. Minorities will be *psychologized*, whereby behaviour is interpreted as resulting from psychological characteristics – 'crankiness' – rather than from belief in a genuine alternative to the status quo and their status as an outgroup will be reinforced. Both of these strategies will lead members of the majority to be reluctant to associate with the minority because of the negative implications for social identity and a fear of being labelled as deviant.

In addition to these factors which may deter individuals from involvement in collective action of any sort, there are also factors which are specific to particular contexts, and these will be discussed as we turn to consider non-activism in trade union and gender contexts.

Non-activism in a Trade Union Context

The number of people who are *members* of trade unions greatly exceeds the number who are actively involved. Most people are content to pay their subscriptions and leave others to carry out the day-to-day running of the local union branch, rarely if ever even attending general meetings. The inactivity of the majority, though a topic of frequent speculation amongst activists, has not been the subject of detailed academic study. What social psychological work there has been in this area (see Klandermans, 1986a; see Chapter 2) has focused on reasons for *participation* and the assumption is made that non-participation is the opposite side of the coin. Thus, Klandermans (1986a) identifies three main theoretical approaches in the psychology of union participation: Frustration–aggression theory; rational choice theory; and interactionist theory. Accordingly, we can suggest that people do *not* get involved because they are generally satisfied with their work situation, or because the perceived costs outweigh the benefits or because they belong to cultures and communities outside work which are unsympathetic to trade unions. The precise way in which these factors may act to deter involvement is not known, since there is a lack of research conducted at an individual level. For example, Klandermans (1986a) points out that within rational choice theory – arguably the most popular of these approaches in recent years – the nature of *individual* choices themselves are not studied. They are simply assumed and then used to explain collective processes.

Lawrence (1994) argues that whereas it is the case that theories of union participation in general – or of *men's* union participation – have indeed focused on reasons for involvement, most influential explanations of *women's* union participation have focused on barriers to involvement. Thus, Wertheimer and Nelson's (1975) study of women trade unionists identified three types of barrier to participation which may help to explain women's underrepresentation in unions. These are: *Union-related*, suggesting that unions are perceived as unresponsive to women's interests and concerns; *work-related*, suggesting that women are underrepresented because they tend to be concentrated in low status, low-paid, part-time jobs (factors which are generally associated with low levels of activism); and *cultural–societal–personal* reasons which, despite the all-encompassing title, has tended to mean the practical obstacles presented by combining employment with domestic and childcare responsibilities.

Other studies have concurred on the significance of these factors. For example, Purcell (1979) notes that most active female shop stewards in her study were single or did not have children, that many women workers may be put off by the male club aspect of trade unionism and that women may appear to be less militant because they tend to work in industries where workers are in a weaker bargaining position and so have less opportunity to exercise industrial militancy.

Where unions have tried to increase levels of participation amongst women, initiatives have included examination of union structure, such as collection of membership statistics; special appointments/ committees, such as equal opportunities officers; additional activities at conferences, such as reserved seats for women; activity at workplace level, such as worktime meetings, childcare provision, transport provision after late meetings; education and training, such as women-only schools/training, positive discrimination in selection of students, childcare provision at courses (see, for example, EPIC Industrial Communications/IRSF, 1987; also Ledwith, *et al.*, 1985). A number of these initiatives assume that the main barrier to women's participation is a practical one concerning lack of opportunity to participate. As Lawrence (1994) points out however, the removal of practical obstacles to participation (such as greater childcare provision) does not of itself provide a positive reason for participation. As such, tackling such barriers is necessary but not sufficient, since individuals may choose to use their new-found time and flexibility to engage in other activities.

Low participation levels by women must be seen within an overall context where non-activism is the norm. For example, Harrison (1979) conducted a comparative study of men's and women's participation and found that 63 per cent of men and 75 per cent of women never attended branch meetings. Perhaps the most striking aspect of findings such as this is actually not the difference between men and women, but the low levels of participation by employees as a whole, though it is important to recognize that *reasons* for non-participation may differ somewhat between men and women.

Findings from Lawrence's (1994) study identified a number of factors which inhibit participation. Work-related factors included working in jobs which lacked the relevant skills for union work, for example, lack of familiarity with the conduct of formal meetings and negotiating skills, inflexibility of work routines and lack of union facilities agreements which make union work more difficult. Other inhibiting factors emerged from interviews with male and female shop stewards who pointed to the considerable personal costs and stresses of union activism, such as working in the evenings and weekends, the pressures put on personal relationships with partners and the problem of taking union work home mentally. Whereas these factors are generally applicable to men and women, they may affect women more strongly. For example, Lawrence reports that women seemed to be less willing to let job performance be affected by union activities and felt more guilty about taking time off for union activities. Similarly, women in traditional relationships may receive less support from their partners for their union involvement than men might expect from their partners. All of these factors might be expected to depress overall levels of participation, particularly amongst women.

The assumption of a steady and low level of participation by employees as a whole has not gone unchallenged, however. For example, emphasizing informal aspects of participation, Fosh (1993) argues that there is more workplace participation than is commonly thought, that there are surges and troughs in levels of participation and that surges in participation may be accompanied by a shift in attitudes from a more individualistic attitude of leaving union activities to others to a more solidaristic attitude, where individuals assume their share of group action. In social psychological terms, this would be interpreted as a shift from personal to social identity.

In support of this argument, Fosh found evidence from observation and interviews showing that although union members might be disillusioned to some extent and without a strong ideological belief in unionism, they did share an underlying view of the union as a collectivity, where unity amongst members was seen as a counterveiling power against that of management:

> They had an underlying commitment to solidaristic action that came to the fore when they felt the occasion merited it. In times of difficulty, they turned to their union as the natural guardian for their interests (1993: 585; see also Nicholson, *et al.*, 1981).

This suggests that non-involvement in formal types of participation, such as meeting attendance and office-holding, does not give the full picture, and that many people do feel an underlying attachment to the union which is only translated into behaviour at certain times, particularly times of personal need. Non-activism here then – at least in formal activities – should not be taken to indicate any deeper disillusionment with collective action as a strategy when the situation demands.

To sum up, a number of explanations for non-activism in trade unions have been suggested, relating to the job, the union and the individual's personal circumstances. The aim of the present research was to examine people's own explanations for their non-activism in the light of this previous theorizing into union participation, as well as the social psychological research into group membership and influence which was discussed at the beginning of this chapter.

The data which follows was derived from a questionnaire study of 350 members of a trade union (NALGO) (see Chapter 3).[1] In an open-ended question, 126 people provided explanations for their non-involvement and these are displayed in Table 6.1.

Table 6.1: Explaining non-involvement in trade unions

Category	Number of comments	Per cent	Rank
Lack of time	29	23.0	1
Too political	27	21.4	2
Unrepresentative	15	11.9	3
Lack of communication, information	14	11.1	4
Intimidating meetings	11	8.7	5
Role conflict	11	8.7	5
Miscellaneous	19	15.1	
Total	126		

A cluster of responses can be distinguished which combine the social psychological factors of group membership and social influence with perceptions of the union. These are that: The union was perceived as too political; union activists as unrepresentative of the majority; that there was insufficient communication between the activists and the ordinary members; and that union meetings were intimidating because of the otherness of the activists which was manifest in unfriendly interpersonal relations and their use of jargon. Obviously there are clear connections between these factors. The differences between them will hopefully become clear with further illustration.

The most common of these responses emphasized that the union was too political and too much time and energy was spent on issues which were seen as irrelevant to employees' immediate employment concerns. It was stressed that unions should devote their energies to improving terms and conditions – 'nuts and bolts issues' as one respondent put it – and not to broader political – and especially international – issues. For example, 'Union activity generally is too political. Such outside issues as supporting foreign problems is not a task for unions which should concern themselves with pay, conditions and the support of individual *members'* rights only' (197).

The implication of this charge, which was made explicit by some respondents, was that the union was not doing enough to look after their own personal interests and this sentiment represents what has been referred to in the union participation literature as an instrumental as opposed to an ideological orientation to unionism (van de Vall, 1970). For example, 'Often find that my previous participation in union activity – usually strike action – is for somebody else. I don't often see the benefit that the union is doing for me!' (009).

The charge of being too political was also associated for many people with being too *militant* and a perception that the union takes action 'at the drop of a hat'. In the words of respondents:

The union has a tendency to militant action in favour of strikes without logical collaboration. They seem hell bent on confrontation with employers (042);

I do not participate too much in union activities because it is too politically biased. Myself and a lot of others feel that the union is too militant. The first sign of unrest and it's 'tools down'. They are always slagging off the government and I think these people are basically frustrated and just need something through which to vent their aggression (086).

In this latter excerpt connections between the perceived militancy of the union and the psychological characteristics of its activists are made explicit. It is a good example of the way in which activist behaviour may be psychologized and influence counteracted.

The perception that union activists are unrepresentative in some way comprises the second major category. Activists were variously described as 'people who see things in very "black and white" terms' (177); 'left-wing activists who alienate people by taking on too many silly causes' (140); and 'not in tune with the vast majority of the membership' (306). Respondents commonly referred to a divide between the political, extreme, militant active minority and the moderate, responsible and silent majority:

At present only the active 'minority' govern the union. If more ballots were held, then the 'silent majority' would be heard and a democratic union would be achieved (008);

I don't participate fully because I'm not the type of assertive person that likes to BUT that is a fundamental problem with unions. Ultimately they don't really represent everybody because the 'type' of person that generally pushes forward in union activism is on the other side of the same coin as the 'type' of person who tramples up the management ladder! (025).

A number of respondents expressed anger at the way in which they felt that the union was being run by a small clique of people 'in the know' who took decisions which affected the whole membership. Few acknowledged the logical solution to this perceived problem – namely greater participation by the majority. In some cases, the issue of important decisions being taken by a relatively small number of activists was related to communication problems in the union; this more structural criticism forms the third category.

A number of respondents stated that they were unable to get involved in union activities because they were simply not informed about them in time to be able to plan their attendance. Some added that union activists had been very unhelpful when approached for information about activities. One respondent commented, 'This questionnaire is the first communication I have had from the union in two years of membership!' (007).

When respondents *did* hear about meetings in time to attend, many people found them intimidating and off-putting. The atmosphere was perceived as aggressive, the background and context of matters being discussed was rarely explained to newcomers and consequently not understood. Jargon was frequently used and activists were not introduced to others. Many people said that they found it difficult to speak at such meetings, particularly with the expectation that the content would not be popular with activists. As a result of these factors, one respondent stated that having attended a meeting once, she would never do so again. Another commented:

> At meetings it feels like only those 'in the know' can participate because they know the rules. I have witnessed people being intimidated by those with greater experience and most of my colleagues have had the same experience. There is no real encouragement for most members to participate. I believe this is the single biggest obstacle to the problem of lack of involvement of most members (054).

Of all the explanations given for non-involvement, accounts stressing the unfriendly and intimidating nature of meetings seemed to be the most strongly felt. The combined picture built up by the factors which have been discussed is a sense of alienation from the union and a perceived sharp divide between the minority of activists and the rest of the union membership, where the activists were seen as more political, more militant, unhelpful and unfriendly. It is clear that such a view – accurate or otherwise – provides an enormous deterrent to greater involvement.

In addition to these factors two other major categories emerged from the data. The first explained non-activism as due to role conflict where respondents occupied some type of managerial position in the organization. Here respondents were often keen to stress that their views were very much in line with the union but they felt constrained in their behaviour. For example, 'I used to be active but find I can't do this now as a "manager". My ideas though haven't changed' (066). Finally, respondents drew on the most common explanation for non-activism of all – lack of time.

In addition to these factors a number of comments were made which comprised the *miscellaneous* category. These included disapproval from colleagues, lack of personal confidence and feelings of powerlessness, a perception of unions as white, male-dominated, old-fashioned, large, remote and ineffective. With respect to this last factor, respondents referred to a political climate which they felt had stripped unions of most of their bargaining power.

Findings here illustrate the way in which social psychological issues of identity and group membership combine with specific perceptions of the union and its activists. Many non-activists saw themselves as part of the silent majority, whose interests and concerns were very different from the active minority. Thus, although practical obstacles, such as lack of time and opportunity, did figure as an important part of people's explanations, as did union-related factors, such as the perceived inappropriateness of political issues, these were frequently framed within a broader perception of *them* and *us* in the union, where becoming one of the activists would entail a considerable redefinition of identity. Of course, this does not rule out the possibility that, were the situation to change, for example, in the form of a new threat from management, categories may be redefined to make collective action by the whole member-ship more likely.

We turn now to consideration of some of these same issues in a gender context where a more extensive study was conducted.

Non-activism in a Gender Context

In the context of gender relations, there has been some discussion about women's reluctance to identify themselves as feminists despite their endorse-ment of ideas which could be interpreted as feminist in content, such as complaints about male privilege. For example, Griffin suggests a number of reasons for the common disclaimer, 'I'm not a women's libber . . .' including the predominantly negative representation of feminism in the media, male intimida-tion and the threat of lesbianism associated with the label 'feminist'. Griffin argues that collective resistance to patriarchy by women is defined as unfemi-nine and consequently that feminists are seen as unattractive to men: 'Once such a negative category is in place, feminism can be used as an accusation, and a means of silencing insubordinate women. "You're not a women's libber, are you?" becomes an insult, a threat with overwhelmingly negative connotations' (1989: 186).

Analysis of the way in which women's collective political activity is represented in the media is provided by Young (1990) who examined reporting of the Greenham Common peace camp (a protest by women outside a cruise missile base in England). Young argues that the media created a mythology around the peace camp which centred on the fact that the protesters were women and provided an elaborate account of the protesters' deviance, where the protest was variously represented as a criminal activity, a witches' coven and a threat to the state, the family and the democratic order. Politically active women were represented as unattractive, masculine and aggressive and Young argues that such images go beyond the Greenham Common context to characterize and censure women's political activity in general.

Dominant images of feminists as aggressive and unattractive help to explain why so many women are reluctant to identify themselves with this label. Rowland (1984) reports the findings from interviews with feminists and anti-feminists which showed that feminists were often depicted as hating men and being opposed to marriage (see also Rowland, 1986). Goldberg, Gottesdiener and Abramson (1975) found that men and women saw feminists as less physically attractive than non-feminists (see also Jacobson and Koch, 1978), though Johnson, *et al.* (1983) later found that it was only *outspoken* supporters of the women's movement who were perceived in a negative way. Since outspoken critics of the feminist movement were also perceived negatively in this study, this suggests that the negative representation was associated more with militancy and activism than with feminism as such. More recently, Percy and Kremer (1995) used repertory grids and interviews to explore the meanings of feminism with self-identified feminists and non-feminists. They found that many women who supported feminist ideals did not identify as feminists because of a negative stereotype of feminists as outspoken and hostile, especially towards men. Feminists were seen as individuals whose views take priority over all other aspects of their lives, notably heterosexual relationships and families. Percy and Kremer conclude that 'the negative value attached to the "feminist" stereotype in a heterosexist society enables its use to justify the patriarchal status quo, to derogate individuals attempting to bring about social change, and to deny the legitimacy of their claims' (1995: 218–19).

Discussion earlier on in this chapter regarding the psychological cost entailed in accepting minority influence is highly relevant to this context. Given the unfavourable stereotypes surrounding feminism, redefinition of identity as a feminist could be costly. However, while reluctant to adopt the label *feminist*, many women are happy to endorse feminist ideas. Renzetti (1987) found American college students reluctant to identify themselves as feminists although they were broadly supportive of the women's movement. She suggests two possible explanations. The first suggests that the lack of identification these women have with feminism is just one manifestation of a new conservatism and wider retreat from liberalism characteristic of American life in general. She suggests as a second explanation that the attitudes of younger women may signal the start of a second stage of feminism; that most college women are not reacting against feminism, but rather that they would like to see the women's movement redirected to better meet their current needs. This is consistent with Komorovsky's (1985) findings which suggest that whereas many college women embrace feminist ideals, they do not accept the collective efforts of the women's movement as the most appropriate means to achieve their own goals. Younger women are more likely to believe that women can succeed as individuals and without collective action. In line with this reasoning, Renzetti (1987) hypothesizes that support for feminism may increase during their college careers as their attitudes in general become more liberal and as they personally experience discrimination in their everyday lives. Data presented in Chapter 4 would support this view.

The perceived inappropriateness of collective action as a means of achieving feminist goals is also commented on by Condor. She argues that there is a pervasive view of time as linear and irreversible, 'an historical trajectory directing human life slowly but inevitably towards a utopian end-point of gender equality' (1989: 15). The danger of subscribing to this idea of progress as inevitable is that the need to take action to bring about change is no longer seen as necessary or appropriate. So much has been achieved that feminism as a movement becomes seen as irrelevant and old-fashioned (in the same way that the trade union movement is seen by some people as out of place in contemporary employment relations).

In the present research we were interested in how these ideas might emerge in women's own accounts of their non-involvement. Our discussion here is based on findings from three sources. The first is in-depth interviews with ten women who were not at the time involved in any formal groups or campaigns. Five of these women had in the past been members of groups but had taken the decision to leave the group and did not wish to be involved in any further activities. The advantage of talking to these women was that they had given a good deal of thought to the issue of involvement and had clear ideas about the factors which put them off any further activity of this sort. For this reason, they had more to say about some of the issues although the *types* of explanation they provided did not differ. The other five women had never been involved in any groups or campaigns. (Appendix 7 provides background information about the interviewees.)

The second source for this discussion is qualitative data taken from a questionnaire (see Chapter 3) on which many non-active women responded to an open-ended question with accounts of the reasons for their non-involvement. In total, there were 138 of these accounts ranging from a couple of sentences to several pages in length. Twenty-six of these women had previously been involved in women's groups.

The third source is interviews with 30 activist women who were asked why they thought *other* women did not wish to get involved. (Background information about these women is provided in Appendix 6.) As these types of explanation reflected almost exactly the types given by the non-activists themselves, they will be discussed together and comparisons made between the frequencies of explanations given by the two groups. Data from interviews and from questionnaires was analysed to extract common themes and arguments and the discussion which follows is based on this analysis.

It should be remembered that the sample of respondents in this study was limited to women who had in common a broad sympathy with the idea that women as a group are disadvantaged (see Chapter 3). Consequently, one major reason why women may not get involved, namely that they endorse an entirely different view of gender relations, is not covered here. Instead, the issue here is, given a broad belief that women are disadvantaged in society, why do so many women choose not to get involved in collective action to try to bring about some change in status relations?

The reasons which were given in this context have been categorized into three different levels of explanation: Societal, group and individual, though

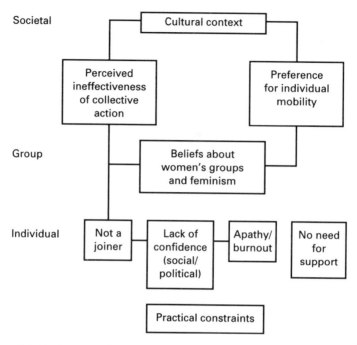

Figure 6.1: Explanations for non-involvement in women's groups: Overview

obviously there are important connections between these different levels. These are illustrated in Figure 6.1.

The frequencies with which each explanation was given by non-activists in the questionnaire, by non-activists in interviews and by activists in interviews is shown in Table 6.2.

Analysis of the frequencies with which non-activists' explanations occurred in the questionnaire showed a similar picture to the interview data, with the main differences being the lower frequency in the questionnaire of explanations based

Table 6.2: Explaining non-involvement in women's groups: Percentage of total explanations

Explanation	Non-activists interview (n = 59)	Non-activists questionnaire (n = 212)	Activists interview (n = 109)
Cultural context	6.8	9.9	3.7
Beliefs about women's groups	40.7	28.3	39.5
Individual factors	40.6	24.5	34.8
Practical constraints	11.9	37.3	22.0

(n refers to coding units)

on individual factors and beliefs about women's groups and the greater frequency of practical constraints as an explanation. As was discussed in Chapter 4, these differences may be explained by the different research contexts – the greater focus on individual experiences in interview and the ease of drawing on time constraints in particular as an explanation on the questionnaire.

Cultural Context

At the societal level, a number of respondents pointed to the cultural context of Britain in the 1990s and contrasted the prevailing political climate with earlier times (1960s, 1970s) when women's groups and campaigns were at their most popular. Respondents discussed the excitement of those earlier days and some expressed regret at how times have changed:

> After five years of very heavy involvement in the women's movement in the 1970s, the movement sort of petered out ... The years I spent in the movement were some of the best in my life and I regret it isn't still going in the way it used to be (251).

A feeling of hopelessness was expressed as people felt unsure how to develop a radical politics in the current political climate.

Specific aspects of this cultural-level response concern the perception that collective action is ineffective in the present political climate and an emphasis on individual mobility instead as the way forward personally and for women in general which echoes the analysis previously discussed by Renzetti (1987). A number of respondents commented that groups in the 1990s are limited in terms of what they can achieve and felt that people working in groups are naive if they think that they can achieve any real social change by this means. Others commented:

> My firm belief is that any major changes should be effected by using personal contacts and networking. It may not work but the days of Mrs Pankhurst and the 'votes for women's issues' are inappropriate in this day and age (376);

> I am unsure any campaign would be listened to ... I also feel powerless in the face of the climate of continuing Conservative government agendas in the country and industry (284).

These extracts illustrate the very clear connections between cultural, group and individual levels of explanation. A particular cultural and ideological context is associated with beliefs about the inefficacy of collective action and a feeling of individual powerlessness. This pattern of beliefs was evident in the trade union as well as the gender context. Collective action was compared to grasping at straws and seen as pointless because, 'Who will listen?'

In addition to these comments referring to an unsympathetic political context and the consequent ineffectiveness of collective action, others were sceptical of the value of collective means in any political context as a way of bringing about social change:

> Change is an evolutionary process, which cannot always be hurried (524);

> I feel that women's rights are often viewed as bolshy, lefty if brought to the attention of the media in the light of large public demonstrations attended by all women and consequently they are often dismissed. I feel therefore that quieter, more 'acceptable' and 'educated' methods such as writing to your MP are more effective (527).

A related argument concerned the importance of individual mobility as a way of improving the position of women and puts the case that it is now up to individual women to make the most of the new opportunities which are open to them. For example, 'I believe women will only be accepted as equals when they stop thinking of themselves primarily as "women" and rather as individuals and get on with life to the best of their ability' (515). For these women, collective action is not seen as an appropriate way of bringing about social change.

It is this inappropriateness of collective action which was stressed by activists in their explanations for the non-activism of others, particularly young women. These people linked it explicitly to an ideology of individualism which they felt had been developed and reinforced by a conservative political climate, for example, 'We are entering a very selfish era, a whole "me" culture, Thatcherism' (422); 'I think perhaps they grow up thinking "Well, I can become anything", you know, they're Thatcher's children' (499). One woman elaborated on her view of the younger generation and what she saw as their reluctance to get involved in any group activities:

> It is a difficult question but it's also a very important question because mostly women don't join. Why don't they join? . . . I'm forced to say I think it's a kind of conventionality, a kind of implicit attitude that I see in the young women that I know, where it's very important not to be seen to get excited about things . . . it seems important not to get embarrassingly, old fashionably, passionate about things, that everything can be thought through in a sensible and rational manner, which is true, of course, I acknowledge that. There isn't an instinct for looking for wrongs and sorting them out. You see I went to university in the late 50s, 60s so it was all campaigns for this and that – the big thing was the nuclear thing – we had an instinct to go out and protest. Now I see that people don't have that

instinct – and of course I don't actually think running out in huge excited rabbles is particularly useful! So I'm not saying that I would like to see that back, not at all, far from it – I had doubts about that even then. But it seems to me to have swung tremendously the other way. There's a blandness and unwillingness to get excited which I find quite fascinating . . . they have this coolness and not wanting to get excited about issues which I see as a generation thing (437).

Thus, despite the evidence discussed earlier which does not support the ideas of a new individualism and 'Thatcher's children' (Banks, *et al.*, 1992; Rentoul, 1990), it was a *perception* and *interpretation* for non-activism which was widely shared amongst our older respondents.

Beliefs about Women's Groups and Feminism

A number of different points were made about women's groups and feminism and these are illustrated in Figure 6.2.

Of all these explanations at the group level, the most frequently cited (in questionnaire responses) was the feeling that gender issues are treated too simplistically in women's groups (40.0 per cent of the total number of explanations), followed by group style and image (28.3 per cent) and lack of identification with women activists (18.3 per cent). Explanations to do with structure and process in women's groups comprised less than 10 per cent of the total number of explanations from questionnaires (see Table 6.3). It was interesting that the treatment of gender issues in women's groups was not perceived as problematic by activists who preferred to cite style and image as the main deterrents to involvement by others.

Closely linked to cultural context, it was certainly the case that a powerful reason for not getting involved related to the perceived style and image of women's groups and feminism in general. The single description which

Table 6.3: Beliefs about women's groups: Percentage of total explanations

Explanation	Non-activists interview (n = 24)	Non-activists questionnaire (n = 60)	Activists interview (n = 43)
Style and image	4.2	28.3	74.4
Issues	54.2	40.0	–
Membership	4.2	18.3	16.3
Structure	12.5	5.0	4.7
Process	25.0	8.3	4.7

(n refers to coding units)

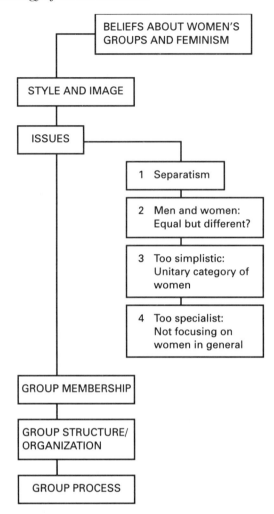

Figure 6.2: Explanations for non-involvement in women's groups: Focus on group level

occurred most frequently was 'aggressive', others being 'strident', 'dogmatic', 'emotional', 'militant', 'intolerant'. Even women who considered themselves to be quite sympathetic to a feminist ideology, often said that they found the style of women's groups to be off-putting. It was argued that feminists did their cause more harm than good by being aggressive and some women referred to the issue of non-sexist language as an example of where they felt feminism had gone too far: 'If women want to be taken seriously, they should not indulge in what are often verbal/linguistic quibbles such as "herstory" instead of "history"' (600). It is striking how an issue such as this seems to have penetrated public consciousness and is vividly remembered as an example of 'feminist extremism' and it is an example of the way in which aspects of minority influence may be subverted by the dominant ideology. As discussed previously, the influence of the minority is thereby counteracted.

These aspects of group style were voiced very commonly by non-activist women who argued the need to present views without being harsh or brutal. Women's groups were perceived as too extreme and lacking in common sense or wisdom. In a discussion of the anger expressed in women's groups, one respondent argued that this anger can take over your life to the point where you start to almost enjoy discrimination because it provides some confirmation for your feminist views. Summing up much of the sentiment expressed here, one respondent explained, 'I think it's because of the picture that's painted of feminism in the mainstream media . . . they seem to be kind of like the stereotypical man-hating loud-mouthed woman who basically wants to be a man' (613).

Amongst *activists*, the perceived style and image of feminism and feminist groups was overwhelmingly the single largest category of explanation for others' non-involvement. Activists referred to 'the slight fear of lesbians' (236) and 'the screaming witch' (230) image. Elaborating on this issue, one activist commented:

> I think because in many ways [feminism] gets tangled up with recognition of a different sort of sexuality that perhaps people feel nervous about it . . . I think a lot of women don't want to be branded as bra-burning feminists and I think that's a lot to do with the image created in the press . . . I think the fear of being thought different, or ridiculed for being different tends to keep people on a central broad path within the mainstream of opinion (093).

One particular aspect of the feminist image which was seen to be off-putting was that feminist groups were seen to be *anti-men* and this was seen by activists as problematic for many women. In particular it was felt that if women are experiencing good relationships with the men in their lives, then there would appear to be a mismatch between their personal experiences and the (anti-men) messages which they perceived to be coming from women's groups. They would consequently be deterred from involvement in groups which they felt had got it all wrong about men.

In associating oneself with an anti-men image, there is a consequent danger of losing femininity. Activists recognized that the dominant representation is that being feminine and being a feminist are mutually exclusive. Some argued that this was not necessarily the case; others that there is a type of femininity and feminine power which feminists *do* have to relinquish in order to gain a different – and more equal – type of power with men. In some senses it was argued by these latter women that joining a women's group *does* entail 'losing' men in the sense that women are keeping a distance from them and saying that they don't really need them all the time – not living life completely through the male world. Thus becoming active in a women's group was seen by some as definitely entailing a change in identity:

> They think that feminists want women to be lesbians or men or something. They feel they want to be women and like being women and maybe by joining a women's group, they won't be any longer ... they are more worried about what they might turn out like rather than the fact that someone else might not approve (418);

> Some women do think that it detracts from their femininity and that their femininity must be preserved at all costs because they define themselves very much as something that men like and approve of and men only like and approve of feminine women (521).

To conclude, the sentiment expressed by many activists is summed up in the following extract: 'They [non-activists] associate feminism with the radical, fringe, lunacy lesbian type view and they don't see it as something that normal, sensible, educated, rational women would be doing' (318).

The second perceived problem noted by non-activists with women's groups concerned the treatment of particular issues. Four issues were identified as the focus of criticism and it is interesting to note that these issues were not mentioned at all by the activists who instead placed far more emphasis on style and image as inhibiting factors (see Table 6.3).

The first issue relates to the points about style which have just been made and is the issue of separatism. Separatism – commonly associated with 'man-bashing' – was described by many as 'wrong, counter-productive' (591). Many respondents argued the need to work problems through with men rather than excluding them. Closely related, the second issue was the perception that women's groups are trying to make women either *the same* as men or *superior* to men, both of which were seen to be wrong and to be counter-productive. Thus some women referred to the way in which they felt that feminist groups try to deny biological differences between men and women and to treat people in a more androgenous way; others referred to feminists fighting for superiority over men. Women, it was argued, should be seen as equal but different.

The third and fourth issues stand in some contradiction to one another and were voiced by different groups of respondents. On the one hand is the criticism that women's groups adopt an oversimplistic and monolithic idea of the category *women*, one which focuses on white, middle-class women and ignores important differences between different women based on race, class or sexuality. In contrast to this belief, other respondents saw women's groups as too much targeted towards specific categories of women, such as lesbians, women from ethnic minorities or with disabilities, and not sufficiently focused on the experiences of all women. As a result, they felt they could not identify with the concerns of the group.

These rather contradictory themes touch on current debates within the women's movement itself. On the one hand, feminists have raised concerns regarding the way that the category *women* has functioned to obscure the heterogeneity which exists within the category. It is argued that the experience of white middle-class women is too often taken to be representative of the experience of all women and that there is a need to challenge the narrowness of this focus, particularly with regards to race, class and sexuality. On the other hand, there are those who express concern over what they see as the disjointed and fragmented nature of the women's movement. They argue that if feminism has any hope of being heard, or of achieving a significant political impact, then there is a requirement that it speaks in a single voice. Differences between women and between types of feminism are seen to be threatening to the possibility of a coherent women's movement. Spelman (1988) argues that this dilemma

> leads us to the paradox at the heart of feminism: Any attempt to talk about all women in terms of something we have in common under-mines attempts to talk about the differences between us, and vice versa ... Is it possible to give the things women have in common their full significance without thereby implying that the differences among us are less important? How can we describe those things that differentiate women without eclipsing what we share in common? (p. 3).

These issues are central to current feminist thought and evidently impact quite strongly on non-activists' decisions to remain uninvolved in collective political activity (see Chapter 7).

Closely related to these issues surrounding feminism and the style and image of feminist groups, a number of non-activists referred to their feeling a lack of identification with the members of such groups which deterred them from joining. A number of non-activists noted that they felt a sense of difference between themselves and the members of women's groups, though the social categorization which denoted the difference varied. Frequently it referred to sexuality, sometimes to political differences, sometimes to perceived differences in aspirations and ambitions. The following extracts sum up a common sentiment: 'I always presume that the type of women who are part of groups are too "right on" and "no make-up" for me to get on with' (562); and 'I'm not one of those women with the dungarees and cropped hair, honest' (591).

Amongst *activists*, the most frequently noted factor relating to group membership as a possible deterrent for others was that the group members tend to be white and middle-class and that women who do not fit this profile might feel excluded, that the language of women's groups is 'in some ways quite alien to working-class women and nothing to do with their concerns' (236). It was suggested that for working-class women, the substance of a political meeting may seem less relevant or useful given the demands imposed by everyday pressures of work and childcare. One activist argued. 'I think maybe working-class women don't have the time – they're doing real things, sorting real things out' (431).

A number of points were made about the structure and organization of women's groups. Again some contradictory themes emerged. On the one hand were respondents who disliked what they perceived as an *unstructured* situation with no clear chairperson or agenda or ground rules. On the other hand and in complete contrast to this, other respondents argued that they disliked *too much structure* in group contexts. For example, one respondent referred to the hierarchical structure which she felt inevitably emerges:

> There is always going to be a leader of the group and whether or not they put huge amounts of effort into making you feel like they don't know any more than you or aren't any better than you, they are still the teacher if you like so they do hold a bit of power over you. Anybody that portrays themselves as being knowledgeable or as being able to help you, they are setting themselves up in a power relationship to you and in a hierarchical relationship and I don't take kindly to that (504).

Relatedly, a number of respondents referred critically to aspects of group process. It was felt by the non-activists that too much attention was paid to process and emotion and not enough to politics and action. This may be rather draining personally and may detract from getting things done. Thus one respondent admitted to

> a deep suspicion of all those words that are exchanged, all those anecdotes, all those stories and it raises a dilemma for me because on the one hand, I feel that women should have support if they need it . . . but I also think that a lot of that talking dispels radical energy, that you talk things out and you talk all your problems out and you go home and you feel better and you still put up with stuff at home because you've got an outlet, you can talk away from home. You don't have to talk to your partner or to your mother or to your boss, because you've got this place that you go after work or after home or for coffee where you can say those things that you actually want to say at home (519).

The argument here then is that the groups are not constructive or radical enough in their actions, that they are essentially discussion groups which can be dominated by feelings of resentment, where people talk about their problems but don't do anything about them. For some women then their non-involvement was because they felt that the groups were not radical or political enough for them and they preferred more direct forms of action. This type of criticism was accurately perceived by the activists who also felt that it was important for groups to be seen to be positive and dealing with the issues.

Finally, discussing personal problems in groups was seen by both activists and non-activists as an inhibiting factor since it was thought that it might lead some women to feel that they were being disloyal to their families if they joined and discussed their personal problems and relationships with others outside the family:

> Maybe women don't want to show that they are not coping because that is quite a big deal to say 'I don't think I can cope – with this marriage, with this relationship, I don't think I can cope with the children, I don't think I love my husband any more'. It's a private battle in many ways and it is not always something you want to make public. I think it is quite a big step for quite a lot of women to be able to discuss their inner most feelings and fears even with other women (504).

A different sort of disloyalty may be felt by women who have enjoyed happy family relationships:

> They've not expressed [a sense of injustice] before because it seems wrong to express it. It seems ungrateful when you've got a nice relationship and children ... I think also that older women who have spent half their lifetime bringing up children and looking after male partners, in a way there's a risk of saying, 'What you've done up to now is not much, it's not worth very much'. And I think people can't think like that. So I think that's probably why a lot of us have become involved in small steps. It's too much, it throws your past and part of yourself into the rubbish bin and I think that's something that puts people off (503).

In sum, a large part of the explanation for women's non-activism revolves around perceptions of feminism and feminists. An overriding perception of feminists as *too aggressive* came through in a number of different ways and was linked to a feeling that militant feminist action is no longer appropriate – and may indeed be counterproductive – in today's circumstances.

Of course, the views of feminism which came across in a number of these accounts were at great odds with views from our activists (see Percy and Kremer, 1995 for a similar finding). When activists were asked in interview how they would define feminism, a number of definitions emerged, all of which were largely positive. The most common theme was a recognition of gender inequality and a feeling that women's rights need protection and advancement. *Equality* between the sexes was viewed as the primary feminist value, in terms of social, political and economic rights as well as in interpersonal relations. Many women stressed that they were not asserting women's superiority. Also included in many definitions was a notion of *action*, that to be considered a feminist one has to be working for change in some way, though this could be practical or intellectual. A third common thread which ran through a number of different definitions was that being a feminist is also about *identity*, both being conscious of yourself as a woman and feeling good about this knowledge. In social psychological terms, it is about having a positive social identity as a woman.

This combination of factors – perceived inequality in gender relations, the need to do something to bring about change and a positive gender identity – are well summarized in the following interview excerpt:

> To me being a feminist is about liking myself as a woman and being happy. At a base level, it's about feeling good about being a woman and wanting to share that feeling with other women, it's about talking to women, it's about women's voices being heard, it's about understanding that things that happen to you are not accidental and are not haphazard, that there are systems that operate and that part of the system that operates is patriarchy. That therefore means that women have been allotted a particular role to play or a particular position to take and it's about challenging that and seeking to overturn that, throw it out on the dustbin heap of history (417).

Finally, a number of women were keen to stress what feminism is *not* and this generally consisted of a distancing from the stereotype of bra-burning, man-hating extremists which came through in various forms in some of the accounts which have been discussed from non-activists.

Individual-level Explanations

We turn now to explanations for non-involvement which focus on the individual. Five distinct factors can be distinguished. The first is the individual's feeling that she is not 'a joiner' of groups. Typical of this feeling are the following extracts:

> I never join anything if I can avoid it . . . I'm not a groupy person. I don't join things (591);

> I regard myself as a person and I do not want to be identified by a group. I would like to stand for myself and on my own and get my rights as a person (516).

These sentiments clearly relate to points made in the discussion of individualism and group membership at the beginning of this chapter. There it was argued that a certain tension in identity is created in individualist cultures between maintaining a sense of personal uniqueness on the one hand and seeing oneself as a member of social groups and categories on the other (see Brewer, 1991;

1993a; b). This may lead to a certain ambivalence in attitudes to group membership which was also evident amongst our sample of activists. It is well illustrated by an excerpt from an interview with one such respondent who is discussing her involvement in women's groups:

> I'm a really anti-group person – not in a conceptual sense at all – I mean I'm very much into collective action. I do think that's the only way to get things done in many instances although individual action cannot be underestimated. I think it is too often underestimated. But I am a believer in collective action and collective responsibility and collectivism. Having said that, I'm not a group person at all and I don't aspire to be part of groups at all. But I think it's a very natural human process to want to be part of a group. I think it's very unnatural not to and I think for lots of these women the motivating force within them is that they want to be part of a group as such (417).

Indeed, it was also the case that many people who had been actively involved in a number of groups over the years maintained that they did not see themselves as joiners of groups or even as group members. One such activist stated, 'I don't think of myself as a member of a group. I just have certain ideas in concert with [the group] as a whole' (318). These excerpts are indicative of a general feeling of ambivalence towards group membership which was evident in a number of interviews with activists and non-activists alike. In an individualist culture, such as Britain, being a member of a political group which seeks to promote collective interests and, even more so being an *activist* in such a group, is not in keeping with dominant cultural norms.

Other individual-level explanations for non-activism focused on lack of confidence, either socially or politically. Non-activists themselves emphasized the social side and the feeling that others in the group would know more and that they would feel insufficiently politically correct, for example, 'I would feel uncomfortable as a new girl, daren't open my mouth because I'm bound to say something that's crass and wildly out of date or out of touch' (592). Lack of confidence socially also refers to shyness and the effort involved in walking into a room of strangers and getting to know them. By contrast, activists emphasized lack of confidence in a more political sense as meaning a feeling of powerlessness and inability to bring about any change – 'they don't see themselves out there in the wider world actually influencing things' (325). These feelings of personal inefficacy clearly connect with factors discussed at a cultural level concerning the perceived ineffectiveness of collective action.

The next individual aspect mentioned by non-activists was that of apathy or laziness, a feeling of not being bothered, being too passive or – for some ex-activists – a feeling of burnout – having been involved in women's groups in the past. Again this burnout sentiment is connected to the cultural level and the rise and fall in activity amongst women's groups.

A further set of comments come from women who said that they felt no personal need for the social or emotional support provided by a group. A number of respondents commented that they had a group of female friends who provided support, and others said they had a supportive partner or husband. Elaborating on this theme, one respondent said that she didn't need a specific time and place in which to discuss her feelings since this was 'very much part of my everyday existence. It's the way I talk about life, it's not something I have to join a group to go and do' (504). Another argued that women in general have less need of formal groups than men since they have been socialized to feel that they can discuss their feelings more easily than men: 'Women are just more natural in terms of their social life. We talk to people we're with, we just gather anyway and that's what we do and we don't need to have a structure for it in the way that men seem to' (591).

One important reason why women may feel that they have no need for the support of a women's group is that they feel that they have never personally been the victim of discrimination and therefore involvement is seen as unnecessary. For example:

I have not been faced with any sexism in my life yet so I don't feel I should or need to join any women's groups (554);

I think if I were discriminated against at work I would try and find a group to help fight it ... I think if someone discriminated against me in a particular way and I felt strongly enough about something or other, I'd get involved with trying to change things, but up till now I've not really had any experience like that or known anyone who has been discriminated against (354).

These comments provide a clear mirror image of the comments which were made by activists (discussed in Chapter 4) regarding how they came to be first involved in the group, where there was a great deal of emphasis on how experiences of discrimination triggered involvement.

Of course it is possible that non-activists here were displaying the common tendency to deny personal disadvantage (see for example, Crosby, *et al.*, 1993; Chapter 4 for discussion). Related evidence is reported by Briet, *et al.* (1987) in a study of how women become involved (or not) in the women's movement in Holland. Although more than half of the women sampled shared a positive attitude towards the movement itself, when asked whether the issues affected the respondent personally, an entirely different picture emerged. Seventy-eight per cent regarded the women's movement as unnecessary as far as they were concerned; 88 per cent were satisfied with their own position. These researchers conclude that:

Three-fourths of the women evidently saw the women's movement as something from another world. Of course, there are a lot of women who are very badly off, they admitted, and they thought it a good thing that the women's movement stand up for these women, but they did not consider themselves members of this group (p. 56).

In the light of this perception, it is not surprising that mobilization attempts amongst such women are ineffective.

Finally, a set of factors could be distinguished in the present data relating to practical constraints which prevented involvement in collective action. As in the trade union context, the most frequently mentioned constraint was lack of time. This was mentioned by over a third of the non-activists who provided explanations for non-activism on the questionnaire and it was often mentioned in the context of other commitments, such as bringing up a family, a demanding job or study. A number of respondents referred to being 'frightened of over-committing myself' (304) and felt that once involved, they would get pushed into taking on too much: 'You've only got to be a little more articulate, a little more confident and you've got yourself labelled the spokesperson and it just becomes all-pervasive, all-encompassing' (592). Other practical constraints were lack of money, lack of transport to far-away meetings, lack of knowledge of local groups or lack of personal contacts with existing members and various personal circumstances which made involvement difficult, such as lack of childminding facilities, physical disability, age. Women giving these responses had no objection in principle to involvement but felt that they lacked the opportunity.

Activists also perceived the importance of practical constraints limiting others' involvement, particularly shortage of time and problems of organizing around work and childcare. As one put it:

I think for a lot of women, particularly who've got young kids and who don't have enough money, time is so much taken up with the frustration, the grind of getting your daily life together, you can't actually see beyond that (311).

Other Ways of Promoting Social Change

Although the accounts have been categorized into discrete types, there is of course considerable overlap between some of the types and here, as elsewhere, many respondents drew on more than one explanation. It was notable that one of the most frequent comments made, in addition to those which have been discussed, was to argue that there are other ways of being political and promoting social change for women as well as joining women's groups. Respondents referred particularly to bringing about change in work situations and trade unions, in mainstream politics, in bringing up children (especially sons) in certain ways and in arguing things out with people in the course of everyday life.

The particular importance of work-related activities was confirmed by responses to an open-ended question in the questionnaire which asked about the ways in which respondents would be promoting women's issues. Responses are shown in Table 6.4.

Clearly then our 'non-activist' sample were interested in women's issues and keen to help bring about social change for women but did not find the type of collective action offered by women's groups to be attractive to them personally.

Concluding Comments

Comparing findings from the trade union and gender contexts shows that a number of factors emerge in common as explanations for non-activism. In both cases, respondents pointed to a cultural context in which collective action was perceived as ineffective in actually bringing about any social change. In the union context, respondents argued that the strength of unions has been considerably reduced by Conservative legislation in the 1980s and the defeat of the 1984–85 miners' strike still figured largely in people's memories. In the gender context, it was argued that *collective* action by women is now less effective than individual action, such as using personal contacts, networking and providing role models for other women.

It was striking that in both contexts there was a perception voiced by some respondents that collective action, as represented by the feminist movement or the trade union movement, is in some sense old fashioned and inappropriate for today's circumstances. Individual action was seen as more effective and more in keeping with the political climate. The fact that this was a common perception does provide some evidence for a new individualism, as discussed at the

Table 6.4: Ways of promoting women's issues: Responses from activists and non-activists

Behaviour	Frequency	Per cent	Rank
Work-related	172	49.0	1
Women's group-related	63	17.9	2
Informal discussion	32	9.1	3
Local community involvement for example, local politics	28	8.0	4
Writing articles	24	6.8	5
Miscellaneous	32	9.1	
Total	351		

beginning of this chapter. People may be just as committed to the *goals* of the feminist and trade union movements, while feeling that different strategies are needed to achieve them. Of course, we cannot tell from the present data whether the same feeling extends to other more recent social movements, such as campaigns around issues of sexuality, human rights and the environment.

Linked with the perceived inappropriateness of collective action was a negative perception of activists in both contexts which centred around a view of such individuals as too aggressive. Thus, collective action, represented most crudely as consisting of marches and demonstrations, was seen as too militant; and individuals who are active were seen as aggressive, strident and unreasonable. Quieter, individual approaches were seen as preferable. The way in which activist behaviour is commonly interpreted as aggressive also emerged from Lawrence's (1994) study of union activists, where respondents argued that one of the problems facing female union office-holders is that assertive behaviour is seen as aggressive and not feminine. The interpretation of activist behaviour as aggressive may be a particular problem for women since it conflicts with prevailing notions of femininity. Some of our respondents commented on the perceived conflict between femininity and feminism.

These negative perceptions of activists, common to both contexts, provide some evidence of the way in which minority behaviour may be psychologized and its impact thereby reduced. Widely available representations of political activists, particularly women, present an image of aggression and stridency, of behaving in a dogmatic fashion and not responding with any flexibility to current social and political conditions. The idea that political activists have the status of outgroup members is reinforced by the idea that they are unrepresentative of the silent majority with a sense of otherness which is manifest in behaviour such as using jargon in meetings which renders majority group members unable to participate. In the gender context, the otherness of feminist activists is even supported by a physical stereotype – the dungarees, cropped hair and no make-up – to which some respondents referred. As research discussed at the beginning of this chapter has showed, representing minority behaviour as deriving from the psychological characteristics of outgroup members is a very effective way of increasing the psychological cost of accepting minority influence.

In addition, certain other individual-level factors emerged in both contexts, such as not perceiving oneself as the *type* of person who gets involved in action and practical constraints, mainly lack of time.

Other factors were specific to the different contexts. For example, at the group level, a number of explanations for non-activism in a gender context revolved around the way in which women's groups were perceived to represent gender relations as too simplistic and the issue of separatism. Factors concerning the style and image of women's groups, their membership and, to a lesser extent, group structure and group process also figured in people's explanations. In the union context, it was argued that unions should spend more time on 'nuts and bolts' issues of members' terms and conditions and less time on issues perceived as too political, particularly international issues, and this criticism perhaps reflects the rather more instrumental orientation to membership which people may have in this group context. Respondents here also referred to structural problems to do with organization and communication (or lack of it) with the union.

In conclusion, we can say that a number of the explanations given for non-activism clearly relate to the social psychological issues discussed at the beginning of this chapter, such as a cultural context of individualism linked with a negative representation of group membership in general and active political minorities in particular. Collective action in the trade union and feminist movements is seen by some as old-fashioned and inappropriate to today's circumstances, consequently involvement may pose a considerable psychological threat to social identity.

Note

1   This study was conducted by Caroline Kelly and John Kelly and is also described in: Kelly, C. and Kelly, J. (1994) Who gets involved in collective action?: Social psychological determinants of individual participation in trade unions. *Human Relations*, **47**, 63–88.

Chapter 7

Conclusions

In this concluding chapter, we have two aims: First, to bring together some main themes from the empirical findings; and second, to explore some links between social identity and social movements.

Main Themes

Evidence from both trade union and gender contexts suggests that collective action is commonly seen as inappropriate in 1990s Britain. Despite previous research discussed in Chapter 6 which suggests that people may not actually be any more individualistic in their general outlooks than previously, the present research shows that there is a common perception that collective means of achieving change are no longer effective. In the trade union context, respondents referred to the defeat of the 1984–85 miners' strike, which continues even ten years on to symbolize the perceived weakness of the trade union movement and the power of the State. In the gender context, many respondents argued that women's groups and campaigns seem powerless in the present political climate. In both contexts, many argued that individual mobility is currently a more effective and appropriate way of bringing about social change and, in the gender context in particular, respondents referred to the value of role models and networking.

Given this preference for individual action, it is not surprising that common perceptions of political activists are unfavourable. Central to this unfavourable representation is the idea that activists are too aggressive (by contrast with the 'quieter', more 'reasonable' approach of individual action). Many respondents in the union context described their attendance at union meetings where they felt intimidated by the perceived stridency of the union activists. A picture was built up of a perceived sharp divide between the minority of activists and the rest of the union membership, often described as the silent majority.

In the gender context, unfavourable images of activists are overlaid by representations of feminism and feminists (see Griffin, 1989; Percy and Kremer,

1995). One of the most common explanations for lack of involvement in women's groups centred around reluctance to become associated with the feminist stereotype. As one woman put it, 'I'm not one of those women with the dungarees and cropped hair, honest'. Women's groups were commonly perceived as aggressive and anti-men and associating with this image entailed a danger of losing femininity. Being feminine and being a feminist were perceived by many women as mutually exclusive.

These perceptions of activists and feminists were discussed with reference to theories of social identity and social influence. In this literature, it has been argued that accepting influence from a minority source may entail a high psychological cost as perceived minority characteristics are assigned to the self (see for example, Mugny, 1982). This is because in accepting influence, one moves closer psychologically to the source of that influence. In a cultural context where political activists are represented as a minority outgroup with negative characteristics, acceptance of influence may pose a considerable threat to social identity.

If collective action is widely seen as inappropriate and activists as too aggressive, what leads some people to involvement? The present data concerning participation in a gender context allows us to address a number of related questions. In Chapter 4, we explored women's reasons for *initial* involvement in collective action. Here, one of the most important factors which emerged in a number of different ways was the personal experience of injustice or unfairness. For some women, this occurred in the family where they felt they were unfairly treated by comparison with brothers or other male relations; for other women, injustice took the form of perceived discrimination in later life, often in employment or educational contexts. Many women referred to the glass ceiling which prevents women from moving up the employment hierarchy. For women who had been brought up in the family to believe that gender is *not* an issue, this experience was particularly shattering and often led them to feel that they had to do something about it.

It was notable that our more active respondents were acutely aware both of discrimination towards women as a group *and* of personal disadvantage. This sets our sample apart from participants in many other studies who have recognized a general problem of discrimination, but downplayed any personal effects, and a number of cognitive and motivational reasons have been suggested for this discrepancy (see for example, Crosby, *et al.*, 1993). Activists here were only too aware of the many ways in which cultural biases intruded into their personal lives at home and at work. These findings support Taylor, *et al.*'s suggestion that for women with a strong sense of gender identity, 'an attack on "me" is an attack on all women, and conversely, an attack on women is also an attack on "me" personally' (1994: 246). On this basis, it was suggested (Chapter 4) that a model of the self is implied where the personal and the political are inextricably intertwined for these activists.

At this point in particular we can see the intricate ways in which identity and injustice interact: The interpretation of an event *as discrimination* depends to a large extent on a sense of gender identity and consciousness and entails an attribution for problems encountered which is external rather than internal, placing the burden of responsibility for change with ideology, structures and institutions rather than with individual characteristics. Consequently, it is difficult to pin-point experiences of discrimination *per se* as the starting-point for involvement in action. Many respondents described the initial trigger as a feeling of unfairness or injustice which was then *interpreted* as discriminatory with the development of a feminist consciousness and the realization that such experiences are shared by other women.

Once involved in collective action, self-perception as an activist becomes an important factor in promoting further activity. Analyses presented in Chapter 3 showed that the strongest correlate of subsequent behaviour was the extent to which the respondent saw herself as an activist. This sense of activist identity also emerged as important in women's own accounts of their involvement and non-involvement presented in Chapter 4. Many of the more active women explained their involvement by referring to a sense of themselves as *a doer* or an *action-oriented type person* and argued for the importance of doing *something* rather than nothing. Some activists felt that this orientation had its roots in socialization in the family, where involvement in local community or church groups resulted in a left-over feeling that one has a moral duty to speak out against injustice. Arguments about the *effectiveness* of collective action in terms of actually bringing about social change were secondary here, particularly given a political context which has been described where collective action is commonly seen as ineffective anyway.

This theme is reminiscent of research by Oliver (1984) into participation in neighbourhood collective action, where she found that activists expressed the sentiment, 'If you don't do it, nobody else will' and that it was this sombre thought which motivated involvement. Contrary to expectancy-value theory (see Chapter 2), activists were more pessimistic than non-activists about the chances of their neighbours getting involved in action. Similarly, in the context of anti-nuclear campaigning, Tyler and McGraw (1983) found that activist behaviour was unrelated to judgments of perceived effectiveness and rather reflected a sense of moral responsibility. Activists felt that they had an obligation to try to prevent nuclear war whatever their chances of success. In an industrial relations context, other research reviewed in Chapter 2 also found that workers provided moral defences of their participation in strike action based on the perceived justness of the cause.

In all these cases, and in the present research as well, activism does not revolve around considerations of perceived effectiveness but reflects a feeling of moral duty or responsibility to 'stand up and be counted', to register a protest about injustice even if one cannot hope to bring about change, at least in the short-term. *Not* to do so, would be contrary to an important aspect of self. As in Andrews' (1991) study of longstanding political activists, identification here comprises both a sense of *being* and *doing* and both components are necessary to sustain and promote a valued identity.

By contrast with our activists, several of the less active women expressed a great reluctance to become identified as a political activist for reasons which have been discussed and also argued that they did not see themselves as the type of person who gets involved or joins groups at all. In fact, there was a general ambivalence towards the notion of group membership *per se* which was detectable in many accounts. This was related to Brewer's (1991) theory of group identification as the product of a search for 'optimal distinctiveness' which recognizes a tension in identity between seeing oneself as a member of social groups and categories on the one hand and maintaining a sense of personal uniqueness on the other. In an individualistic culture, such as Britain, this latter pressure may be particularly strongly felt.

Our more active respondents not only had a clear sense of themselves as activists; they also expressed a strong sense of gender identity which in the current context went hand-in-hand with a feminist ideology (though other researchers have argued that this need not necessarily be the case, see Condor, 1986). Analysis of the questionnaire data in Chapter 3 showed strong associations between level of gender identity and levels of participation in all forms of activity, both formal and informal. Also of great importance in these analyses was a variable relating to the perceived importance of 'doing something positive for women' and it was argued that this represented the behavioural expression of gender identity. Again, what was important here was doing something, rather than nothing, even in an unresponsive political climate.

Group identification not only showed a very strong direct relationship with participation in both trade union and gender contexts; there was also evidence that this variable had a moderating effect on relationships between participation and other social beliefs. This effect was more obvious in the gender context, where a number of differences emerged between the correlates of participation for relatively weak and strong group identifiers. Most strikingly, a sense of collective relative deprivation was a much more powerful correlate of participation for strong identifiers than for weak identifiers (whose participation was more strongly associated with political efficacy and collectivist orientation) and this finding points once again to important connections between identity and perceived injustice. Identification with a social group and a sense of collective injustice go hand-in-hand in this context.

Not only were the variables of political efficacy and collectivist orientation more important as predictors of action for weak identifiers; so too were the expectancy-value variables, in particular attitudinal factors derived from Ajzen and Madden's (1986) theory of planned behaviour (see Chapter 2). The calculation of costs and benefits associated with action seems to be more important for those individuals who identify relatively weakly with the group in question. For strong identifiers, participation in collective action – doing something positive – is central to their social identity, as activists and as women, and calculations of costs and benefits are of less significance (see Kelly and Kelly, 1992).

As noted in Chapter 3, however, the specific pattern of variables predicting participation is likely to vary according to the context. For example, in the present research, considerations of the effectiveness of action (as measured by Klandermans' notion of *goal motives*) proved to be important in the context of trade union involvement and this may be because individuals have a fairly instrumental orientation to group membership in this context. By contrast, as we have discussed already, involvement in collective activities in a gender context is partly a way of expressing support and solidarity with other women, giving a behavioural expression to gender identity, as well as bringing about social change. Indeed, the whole question of what is meant by *effectiveness* is raised in the context of the women's movement which has always stressed the importance of *personal* consciousness and change anyway.

The support and solidarity aspects of involvement in women's groups and campaigns came across clearly in Chapter 5. Some respondents discussed the importance of maintaining a certain level of activity even in an unresponsive political climate – the need to 'bear witness' and show that the issues still matter. As was noted in Chapter 5, the present data on the positive outcomes of group membership is in stark contrast to the usual emphasis in the social psychological literature on group processes, particularly that concerned with social identity theory, which is dominated by consideration of the negative outcomes, such as conflict, stereotyping and prejudice, which may be associated with group membership and identification.

By contrast here, respondents pointed to a number of very positive outcomes of participation in groups. Foremost amongst these were those social outcomes to do with support and solidarity. A number of women argued that the group provided a safe space, where you can say what you feel and not be judged, where the atmosphere is non-competitive and individuals feel a sense of safety, belonging and mutual understanding. For many women the groups provided the opportunity to make friends with like-minded others who shared their experiences. In common with Hirsch's (1990) analysis, it appears that these loosely structured, non-hierarchical, face-to-face groups provide havens, where individuals can become aware of common problems and question the legiti-macy of present institutional arrangements. Through sustained contact of this sort, women may become politicized and increasingly see the links between the personal and the political.

Many respondents discussed the political outcomes of involvement which referred to the opportunity to help bring about social change for women as a whole, as well as helping other individuals in the group. Involvement gave many of these women a sense of empowerment and a feeling that it is possible to challenge and change the *status quo*, which refers simultaneously to women's relationships with men as a whole and these women's personal relationships with men at home and at work. Here there were very clear links between personal and political outcomes of group involvement. Other outcomes concerned personal development and intellectual stimulation, which often came from the opportunity to compare experiences with others, and the development of group skills.

Chapter 5 also contained data concerning perceived personal and political *changes*. The more active women in the sample felt that they had become more aware of, and more angry about women's disadvantage; more aware of other forms of discrimination; had developed a stronger belief in collective action by women as well as more complex views about feminism; and also learned how to deal with groups more effectively, gained self-confidence and gained more enjoyment from the company of other women. Less active women also agreed with a number of these sentiments (though to a lesser extent) and pin-pointing the extent to which involvement or non-involvement is responsible for the differences is of course impossible. However, qualitative data discussed in Chapter 5 allows us to speculate that certain changes may be particularly connected with participation (endorsement of collective action by women, learning to deal with groups effectively, enjoying other women's company more), whereas others were attributed to a greater extent – at least by respondents themselves – to life-cycle changes and the adoption of new social roles, particularly motherhood. Here then, as elsewhere, specifying precise causes and effects is difficult since social beliefs, identity and action are continually negotiated and re-negotiated in everyday experience.

Social Identity and Social Movements

We turn now to a consideration of some of the links which can be made between social identity and social movements.

The last decade has seen an increase in the number and diversity of social movements reflecting a range of different issues. Within the women's movement alone, there is an incredible range of different groups and campaigns which is at least partly reflected in the groups covered in the present research (see Appendix 2). At the same time, some have argued that there has been a corresponding decline in class-based social movements and a fragmentation of identity in a post-modern society (see Hall, 1992). Instead of building on the common interests of large categories of people on the basis of class, community or union, there is an emphasis on creating smaller scale, local interest groups which reflect particular needs and identities. An individual may belong to several different groups each meeting different and specific needs.

Some personal benefits from this proliferation of women's groups were discussed by our respondents. For example, women were pleased to have the opportunity to meet with others who share their particular identities and the issues and problems which accompany them. Finding a space where different and sometimes conflicting identities, based on sexuality, religion, politics or age, could be expressed in a supportive atmosphere was obviously important to many women. Many were sympathetic to the criticism that the women's movement has for too long equated women's experience with that of white, middle-class women and expressed the still pressing need to address the concerns of women from different classes and ethnic groups in particular.

The idea that it is problematic to treat women as a homogeneous social group has been made in an academic context as well. In the application of social identity theory to gender relations, it has been argued that early work mistakenly treated women as a unified group with a negative social identity *vis-à-vis* men (see Skevington and Baker, 1989; also Chapter 1 here) and that there is a need to recognize diversity amongst different women (see Billig, 1985, for a more general discussion of this theme). Indeed, where McDowell and Pringle (1992) ask what is the significance for the future of feminism of the recognition of diversity among women, we might substitute 'social psychological theory' for 'feminism'. In both cases, the attempt to summarize and conceptualize people's experiences is undermined by the idea that everybody's experiences are different.

In the context of academic theory, dissatisfaction with traditional approaches has led some researchers to abandon altogether theories which emphasize coherence and consistency in cognition and behaviour and move instead towards alternative approaches which emphasize inconsistencies and contradictions (see Potter and Wetherell, 1987). In the case of social movements and feminism in particular, McDowell and Pringle (1992) argue that for some women, the recognition of differences has led to a denial of the possibility of a feminist politics which assumes the unitary interests of women:

> The strength of the post-modern critique of a unitary conception of 'woman', itself, and the recognition of the fractured and contradictory nature of subjectivity has also led to despair about the possibilities for feminist political action and change. Indeed, the term 'post-feminism' has been coined as the corollary of post-modernism (p. 251).

While other feminists are not so pessimistic and suggest that diversity should be seen as a sign of strength, effective mobilization of a large number of diverse groups is difficult. Fragmentation may be associated with a reduction in political power as large-scale social movements are replaced by a proliferation of small local groups which must all compete with each other for resources. Many of our respondents commented that such groups can turn into 'talking shops', where personal problems are discussed and support is given but there is little political action taken. It is also relevant that researchers interested in individualism and collectivism have suggested that where people belong to several different groups, collective action on behalf of any one of them is less likely (see Chapter 1). In social identity terms, reducing the salience of any particular category would be expected to reduce the chances of collective action on its behalf. In order to be an effective political force (by which we mean here, one which successfully campaigns for changes in structures and institutions), there is a need to also remember common interests and not to be swamped by difference and diversity. In the context of academic theory, recognizing some commonalities in people's experience and attempting to theorize them need not preclude a recognition of difference, but provides a structure for understanding the social world and a route for changing it.

In the case of gender, if we were in any doubt about the common problems which many women share, we need look no further than statistics regarding employment. In 1993 the average earnings of full-time working women were only 77 per cent of the average earnings of men (McIlroy, 1995). Although women constitute an estimated 52 per cent of the British population, they are under-represented in many areas of life. Britain's record in giving women senior positions in public life is particularly poor. For example, a survey carried out by the European Commission in 1986 in its campaign against inequality (quoted in Ashworth, 1992) showed that Britain has a lower proportion of female MPs and members of the upper house of Parliament than most EU member states, a lower proportion of ministers and senior civil servants and minimal representation for women in employers' organizations. In the health service, the largest employer of women in Europe, women make up 90 per cent of nurses and midwives, 75 per cent of the ancillary workers but only 1 per cent of consultants. Maternity rights are poor by comparison with other EU countries and there is a lack of good, reliable and affordable childcare facilities. An Institute of Management study published in 1994 (quoted in *The Times*, 3rd May 1994) found a decreasing number of women in managerial positions in large companies, which was attributed both to discrepancies in salary between men and women and to the particular problems which women face in working in a predominantly male culture with little flexibility for the needs of women to combine work and home responsibilities.

From our research alone, a number of themes emerged which seemed to unite women, albeit from a predominantly middle-class sample. Indeed, it was striking that despite the tremendous range of different groups with diverse aims and structures, women talked overwhelmingly about similar issues and problems – dealing with discrimination and isolation at home or at work, juggling home and work responsibilities, looking after dependent relatives, lack of available and affordable childcare provision, people's changing attitudes when you become a mother. A sense of disadvantage *as a woman* emerged in all these contexts along with the need for support from other women.

Thus, while we should be alert to diversity and difference, we should also remember those issues which can be used to unite women. Too great an emphasis on diversity and difference may threaten political power in the same way that political parties which are seen to be divided lose power since this is widely perceived (rightly or wrongly) to be a sign of weakness. This issue is addressed by Spelman in the context of the women's movement, who argues that 'the possibility of a coherent feminist politics seems to require a singleness of voice and purpose' (1988: 161). In fact, there is a large body of social psychological evidence which attests to the importance of maintaining a united front in order to exert social influence (see Chapter 6).

The central challenge for the women's movement then, as for other social movements, is how to reach all women and present a united front, while at the same time, recognizing diversity amongst women. A similar challenge exists for contemporary social psychological theories of categorization and identity, namely how to conceptualize the experiences of large numbers of people in a way which recognizes both common and diverse aspects of identity and experience.

Appendixes

Appendix 1

Union Participation Items: Factor Analysis

		Factor loading
Factor 1	*'Easy' forms of participation* *(46.6 per cent of variance)* *(internal reliability .84)*	
	Discussing union affairs	.78
	Taking part in union action	.75
	Attending union rallies	.74
	Attending union meetings	.68
	Reading union journals	.68
	Voting in union elections	.65
Factor 2	*'Difficult' forms of participation* *(14.3 per cent of variance)* *(internal reliability .81)*	
	Standing as an elected official	.86
	Being a union delegate	.80
	Speaking at branch meetings	.76
	Helping with union campaigns	.60

Appendix 2

Women's Groups

Women in the present sample belonged to the following groups. Group names are as provided by respondents and in some cases refer to women's sections of larger organizations.

Work/management
Association of Management Development; UK Federation of Business and Professional Women; Soroptimist International; Women in Management.

Work/other professional
Association of Radical Midwives; Association of Women Barristers; British Federation of University Women; Industrial Society; LBS Women's Network; National Committee of Working Women's Organizations; Medical Women's Federation; Royal College of Midwives; Women's Engineering Society; Women in Engineering; Women in Dentistry; Women in Fundraising Development; Women in Geography; Women in Media; Women in Medicine; Women in Medical Practice; Women in the Public Sector; Women in Publishing; Women in Theology; Women into Business.

Health/childbirth/children
Abortion Rights; Abortion Law Reform Assocation; Birth Control Trust; Campaign for Information and Choice; DES Action Group; Family Planning Association; La Leche League; Maternity Alliance; Maternity Services Liaison Centre; National Abortion Campaign; Mothers Apart From Their Children; National Childbirth Trust; Women and Cancer Group; Women's Health and Education Group of the Terence Higgins Trust; Working for Childcare; Wimbledon Working Mothers Group.

Party political
Campaign for Gender Balance in the Scottish Parliament; Change; Charter 88 Trust; Conservative Women's National Committee; European Forum of Socialist Feminists; European Women's Lobby; European Union of Women; International

Women's Forum; Labour Briefing; Labour Campaign for Electoral Reform; Labour Party; Labour Women's Network; Socialist Feminist Group; The 300 Group; Women for Socialism; Women Liberal Democrats.

Work/trade union
Women's groups from the following trade unions: AUT, BECTU, USDAW, UCATT, CPSA, MSF, NATFHE, NUT.

General
Fawcett Society; National Association of Women's Organizations; National Women's Network.

Other
African Women Solidarity Group; Akina Mama Wa Afrika; All About Eve; Black Women and Europe Network; Campaign Against Pornography; European Women's Study Network; Elizabeth Stonehouse Working Party; Feminist Review; Feminist Library; Feminists Against Censorship; Hackney Women Miners' Support Group; Harrow Women's Group; Hull Centre for Gender Studies; Irish Women's Perspective; Josephine Butler Society; Justice for Women; Lewisham Women's Workspace; Movement for the Ordination of Women; Midlife Experience Centre; National Pay Equity Campaign; Older Feminist Network; Rights of Women; Saga Centre; Southwark Women's Aid; Threshold; Tunbridge Wells Women's Group; UK Women Nuclear Network; Unitarian Women's Group; Women Against Fundamentalism; Women's Environmental Network; Women's Education and Training Network; Women's Education Steering Group; Women for Peace; Women's Media Resource Project; Women's Peace Group; Women's Safe Transport; Young Asian Women's Group.

Appendix 3

**Readiness to Participate in Different Types of Action in a
Gender Context: Factor Analysis**

		Factor loading
Factor 1	*Participation in women's groups* *(44.2 per cent of variance)* *(internal reliability .86)*	
	Acting as a spokeswoman for a particular women's issue (PR)	.85
	Spending time working for a women's campaign, e.g. fundraising (PR)	.78
	Attending women's meetings, or workshops (PR)	.73
	Raising women's issues in groups or organizations (PO)	.64
Factor 2	*Collective protest* *(12.6 per cent of variance)* *(internal reliability .88)*	
	Breaking the law, e.g. blocking the road with a street demonstration (PO)	.86
	Taking part in a rally or demonstration (PO)	.86
	Attending demonstrations, protests or rallies about women's issues (PR)	.78
Factor 3	*Informal participation* *(9.6 per cent of variance)* *(internal reliability .82)*	
	Discussing women's issues with friends or colleagues (PR)	.86

| | Reading articles, journals or watching films about women's issues (PR) | .85 |

Factor 4 *Individual protest*
(8.7 per cent of variance)
(internal reliability .65)

Contacting your MP (PO)	.85
Contacting the media, e.g. radio, TV, newspapers (PO)	.68
Signing a petition (PO)	.58

Key:
PR = prospective participation items
PO = potential participation items

Appendix 4

Reported Behaviours in a Gender Context: Factor Analysis

Factor loading

Overall participation
(59.7 per cent of variance)
(internal reliability .86)

Attending women's meetings, conferences or workshops	.83
Spending time working for a women's campaign, e.g. fundraising	.80
Acting as a spokeswoman for a particular women's issue	.80
Discussing women's issues with friends or colleagues	.78
Reading articles, journals or watching films about women's issues	.74
Attending demonstrations, protests or rallies about women's issues	.68

Appendix 5

Social Beliefs and Gender: Factor Analysis

		Factor loading
Factor 1	*Collective relative deprivation* *(30.2 per cent of variance)* *(internal reliability .81)*	
	In terms of power and status in society, women get a bad deal compared to men	.76
	Women as a group deserve a better deal in society	.75
	In terms of conditions and opportunities at work, women get a bad deal compared to men	.73
	It makes me feel angry that women in general have a lower status than men	.69
Factor 2	*Gender identity* *(10.8 per cent of variance)* *(internal reliability .84)*	
	I feel strong ties with other women	.79
	I identify strongly with other women	.74
	Being female is central to the way I think of myself	.73
	I rarely think about women as a group (R)	.60
	I am a feminist	.58

Factor 3	*Political efficacy*	
	(7.3 per cent of variance)	
	(internal reliability .55)	
	Every individual can have an impact on the political process	.78
	People working together can change government policy	.72
	There's not much point in participating in political campaigns: one person's participation won't make any difference (R)	.63
	I don't think politicians care very much what people like me think (R)	.43
Factor 4	*Collectivist orientation (gender)*	
	(6.0 per cent of variance)	
	(internal reliability .68)	
	Women must act as a group rather than as individuals	.72
	Improvements in conditions and opportunities for women will only be achieved through collective action	.69
Factor 5	*Collectivist orientation (general)*	
	(5.8 per cent of variance)	
	(internal reliability .52)	
	People should not be expected to do anything for the community unless they are paid for it (R)	.70
	Working with others is usually more trouble than it's worth (R)	.67
	In the long run, the only person you can count on is yourself (R)	.65
	I work better in a group than on my own	.23

Key:
(R) indicates reverse scoring on this item

Appendix 6

Appendix 6: Description of Activist Interviewees

Subject No:	Type of Group	Membership	Other Women's Groups	Ethnicity/ Nationality	Age	Occupation	Children
002	Work/professional	Over 3 years	4	British	25–34	Doctor	yes
093	Work/professional	2–3 years	/	White–UK	45–54	Fundraiser	yes
128	Work/professional	Over 3 years	/	White	35–44	Editor	yes
187	Party political	1–2 years	/	/	35–44	Civil Servant	no
188	Party political	Over 3 years	5	Turkish	45–54	Political Activist	yes
192	Work/management	6 months–1 year	1	British White	25–34	Chartered Surveyor	yes
203	Party political	Less than 6 months	/	East Asian	25–34	Researcher	no
203	Work/management	Over 3 years	/	British	35–44	Graphic Designer	no
231	Local women's group	6 months–1 year	4	Irish–British	25–34	Women's Officer	no
236	Ethnicity	Over 3 years	3	Irish	45–54	Trainer	yes
237	Work/management	Less than 6 months	1	Scottish	25–34	Financial Consultant	no
264	Work/management	/	/	British	35–44	Self-Employed	no

296	Work/management	1–2 years	/	British	35–44	Self-Employed	yes
309	Work/professional	Over 3 years	2	Russian	Over 55	Dental Surgeon	yes
311	Work/professional	Over 3 years	1	Jewish–Central European	45–54	Doctor	yes
318	General/umbrella organization	2–3 years	1	White–British	25–34	Copywriter	no
325	Party political	Over 3 years	/	White–British	Over 55	Lecturer	yes
356	General/umbrella organization	Over 3 years	1	British	Over 55	Retired	yes
417	Ethnicity	1–2 years	2	Jewish	25–34	Political activist	yes
418	Party political	Over 3 years	/	/	25–34	Teacher	no
422	Health/children	Over 3 years	/	/	35–44	Midwife	yes
431	Health/children	2–3 years	/	White	25–34	Researcher	no
433	Age related	Less than 6 months	1	White–British	Over 55	Retired	no
434	Health/children	Over 3 years	3	Jewish–British	45–54	Mother and writer	yes
437	General/umbrella organization	Over 3 years	3	Scottish–British	45–54	Editor	yes
443	Health/children	2–3 years	2	White–British	25–34	Mother and part-time librarian	yes
499	Health/children	2–3 years	1	English	35–44	Mother and editor	yes

Appendix 6 (continued): Description of Activist Interviewees

Subject No:	Type of Group	Membership	Other Women's Groups	Ethnicity/ Nationality	Age	Occupation	Children
503	Local women's group	Over 3 years	/	White–British	Over 55	University tutor	yes
595	Health/children	1–2 years	/	White	25–34	Community worker	yes
596	Ethnicity	6 months–1 year	/	Bangladeshi	18–24	Student	no

Notes:
Details are exactly as provided by respondents
/ indicates no information given

Appendix 7

Description of Non-activist Interviewees

Subject No:	Ethnicity/ Nationality	Age	Occupation	Children
354	British	25–34	Knitwear designer	yes
504	British	18–24	Community worker	no
519	British–Jewish	25–34	Journalist	no
521	Czech	35–44	Psychologist	yes
591	British	35–44	Commercial analyst	no
592	British	45–54	Careers information worker	yes
593	British	18–24	Postgraduate student	no
612	British	25–34	Postgraduate student	no
613	British	18–24	Student	no
614	Asian	35–44	Mother	yes

Notes:
Details are exactly as provided by respondents

References

ABELES, R.D. (1976) Relative deprivation, rising expectations and black militancy, *Journal of Social Issues*, **32**, pp. 119–37.

ABRAMS, D. and HOGG, M.A. (1990) Social identification, self-categorization and social influence, *European Review of Social Psychology*, **1**, pp. 195–228.

ADAMS, J.P.JR and DRESSLER, W.W. (1988) Perceptions of injustice in a black community: Dimensions and variations, *Human Relations*, **41**, pp. 753–67.

AJZEN, I. (1988) *Attitudes, Personality and Behaviour*, Milton Keynes: Open University Press.

AJZEN, I. and FISHBEIN, M. (1977) Attitude–behavior relations: A theoretical analysis and review of empirical research, *Psychological Bulletin*, **84**, pp. 888–918.

AJZEN, I. and FISHBEIN, M. (1980) *Understanding Attitudes and Predicting Social Behaviour*, Englewood Cliffs, NJ: Prentice-Hall.

AJZEN, I. and MADDEN, T.J. (1986) Prediction of goal-directed behavior: Attitudes, intentions and perceived behavioral control, *Journal of Experimental Social Psychology*, **22**, pp. 453–74.

ALLEN, P.T. and STEPHENSON, G.M. (1983) Inter-group understanding and size of organization, *British Journal of Industrial Relations*, **21**, pp. 312–29.

ALMOND, G.A. and VERBA, S. (1980) (Eds) *The Civic Culture Revisited*, Boston, MA: Little, Brown & Co.

AL-ZAHRANI, S.S. and KAPLOWITZ, S.A. (1993) Attributional biases in individualist and collectivist cultures: A comparison of Americans with Saudis, *Social Psychology Quarterly*, **56**, pp. 223–33.

ANDREWS, M. (1991) *Lifetimes of Commitment: Aging, Politics, Psychology*, Cambridge: Cambridge University Press.

APPELGRY, A.E. and NIEWOUDT, J.M. (1988) Relative deprivation and the ethnic attitudes of blacks and Afrikaans-speaking whites in South Africa, *Journal of Social Psychology*, **128**, pp. 311–23.

ARCHER, J. (1984) Gender roles as developmental pathways, *British Journal of Social Psychology*, **23**, pp. 245–56.

ARNOLD, D. and GREENBERG, C. (1980) Deviate rejection within differentially manned groups, *Social Psychology Quarterly*, **43**, pp. 419–24.

ASHWORTH, G. (1992) *When Will Democracy Include Women?* London: Change Thinkbook VII, Calverts Press.

Bagozzi, R.P. (1981) Attitudes, intentions and behavior: A test of some key hypotheses, *Journal of Personality and Social Psychology*, **41**, pp. 607–27.

Bagozzi, R.P. (1982) A field investigation of causal relations among cognitions, affect, intentions and behavior, *Journal of Marketing Research*, **19**, pp. 562–83.

Bagozzi, R.P. and Yi, Y. (1989) The degree of intention formation as a moderator of the attitude–behavior relationship, *Social Psychology Quarterly*, **52**, pp. 266–79.

Bagozzi, R.P., Yi, Y. and Baumgartner, J. (1990) The level of effort required for behaviour as a moderator of the attitude–behaviour relation, *European Journal of Social Psychology*, **20**, pp. 45–59.

Baker, D. (1989) Social identity in the transition to motherhood, in Skevington, S. and Baker, D. (Eds) *The Social Identity of Women*, London: Sage, pp. 84–105.

Banister, P., Burman, E., Parker, I., Taylor, M. and Tindall, C. (1994) *Qualitative Methods in Psychology: A research guide*, Buckingham: Open University Press.

Banks, M., Bates, I., Breakwell, G., Bynner, J., Emler, N., Jamieson, L. and Roberts, K. (1992) *Careers and Identities*, Milton Keynes: Open University Press.

Banks, O. (1986) *Becoming a Feminist: The Social Origins of 'First Wave' Feminism*, London: Wheatsheaf Books.

Bargad, A. and Hyde, J.S. (1991) Women's studies: A study of feminist identity development in women, *Psychology of Women Quarterly*, **15**, pp. 181–201.

Barling, J., Kelloway, E.K. and Fullager, C. (1992) *The Union and its Members: A Psychological Approach*, New York: Oxford University Press.

Barnes, S., Kaase, M. *et al.* (1979) *Political Action: Mass Participation in Five Western Democracies*, London: Sage.

Baruch, G. and Barnett, R.C. (1983) Adult daughters' relationships with their mothers, *Journal of Marriage and the Family*, **45**, pp. 601–6.

Bassett, P. and Cave, A. (1993) *All for One: The Future of the Unions*, London: Fabian Pamphlet 559.

Beaumont, P.B. and Elliott, J. (1989) Individual employees' choice between unions: Some public sector evidence from Britain, *Industrial Relations Journal*, **20**, pp. 119–27.

Becker, H.S. and Geer, B. (1979) Participant observation and interviewing: A comparison, in Filstead, W.J. (Ed.) *Qualitative Methodology: Firsthand Involvement with the Social World*, Chicago: Markham Publishing Co., pp. 133–42.

Beckwith, K. (1986) *American Women and Political Participation: The Impacts of Work, Generation and Feminism*, Westport, CT: Greenwood Press.

Beer, S.H. (1982) *Britain Against Itself: The Political Contradictions of Collectivism*, London: Faber & Faber.

Benokraitis, N.V. and Feagin, J.R. (1986) *Modern Sexism: Blatant, subtle and covert discrimination*, Englewood Cliffs, NJ: Prentice-Hall.

Berkowitz, L. (1972) Frustrations, comparisons and other sources of emotion arousal as contributors to social unrest, *Journal of Social Issues*, **28**, pp. 77–91.

Beynon, H. (1984) *Working for Ford*, Harmondsworth: Penguin.

BHAVNANI, K.K. (1991) *Talking Politics: A Psychological Framing for Views from Youth in Britain*, Cambridge: Cambridge University Press and Paris: Editions de la Maison des Sciences de l'Homme.

BIDDLE, B.J., BANK, B.J. and SLAVINGS, R.L. (1987) Norms, preferences, identities and retention decisions, *Social Psychology Quarterly*, **50**, pp. 322–27.

BILLIG, M. (1985) Prejudice, categorization and particularization: From a perceptual to a rhetorical approach, *European Journal of Social Psychology*, **15**, pp. 79–103.

BIRT, C. and DION, K.L. (1987) Relative deprivation theory and responses to discrimination in a gay male and lesbian sample, *British Journal of Social Psychology*, **26**, pp. 139–45.

BLUMER, H. (1969) *Symbolic Interactionism*, Englewood Cliffs, NJ: Prentice-Hall.

BOUCHIER, D. (1983) *The Feminist Challenge*, London: Macmillan.

BOYD, C.J. (1989) Mothers and daughters: A discussion of theory and research, *Journal of Marriage and the Family*, **51**, pp. 291–301.

BREAKWELL, G.M. (1979) Women: Group and identity?, *Women's Studies International Quarterly*, **2**, pp. 9–17.

BREAKWELL, G.M. (1990) Social beliefs about gender differences, in FRASER, C. and GASKELL, G. (Eds) *The Social Psychological Study of Widespread Beliefs*, New York: Oxford University Press, pp. 210–25.

BREINLINGER, S. and KELLY, C. (1994) Women's responses to status inequality: A test of social identity theory, *Psychology of Women Quarterly*, **18**, pp. 1–16.

BRETT, J.M. and GOLDBERG, S.B. (1979) Wildcat strikes in bituminous coal mining, *Industrial and Labor Relations Review*, **32**, pp. 465–83.

BREWER, M.B. (1991) The social self: On being the same and different at the same time, *Personality and Social Psychology Bulletin*, **17**, pp. 475–82.

BREWER, M.B. (1993a) Social identity, distinctiveness and ingroup homogeneity, *Social Cognition*, **11**, pp. 150–64.

BREWER, M.B. (1993b) The role of distinctiveness in social identity and group behaviour, in HOGG, M.A. and ABRAMS D. (Eds) *Group Motivation: Social Psychological Perspectives*, London: Harvester Wheatsheaf, pp. 1–16.

BREWER, M.B. (1994) The social psychology of prejudice: Getting it all together, in ZANNA, M.P. and OLSON, J.M. (Eds) *The Psychology of Prejudice: The Ontario Symposium*, **7**, Hillsdale, NJ: Erlbaum, pp. 315–30.

BREWER, M.B. and SCHNEIDER, S.K. (1990) Social identity and social dilemmas: A double-edged sword, in ABRAMS, D. and HOGG, M.A. (Eds) *Social Identity Theory: Constructive and Critical Advances*, London: Harvester Wheatsheaf, pp. 169–84.

BRIET, M., KLANDERMANS, B. and KROON, F. (1987) How women become involved in the women's movement of the Netherlands, in KATZENSTEIN, M.F. and MUELLER, C.M. (Eds) *The Women's Movement of the US and Western Europe: Consciousness, Political Opportunity and Public Policy*, Philadelphia, PA: Temple University Press, pp. 44–63.

BRISCOE, J. (1994) *Mothers and Other Lovers*, London: Phoenix House. Extract reprinted in *Everywoman*, June 1994.

BROWN, H.P. (1990) The counter-revolution of our time, *Industrial Relations*, **29**, pp. 1–14.

BROWN, R.J. (1988) *Group Processes: Dynamics Within and Between Groups*, Oxford: Blackwell.

BROWN, R.J., CONDOR, S., MATHEWS, A., WADE, G. and WILLIAMS, J.A. (1986) Explaining intergroup differentiation in an industrial organization, *Journal of Occupational Psychology*, **59**, pp. 273–87.

BRUNER, J.S. (1957) On perceptual readiness, *Psychological Review*, **64**, pp. 123–51.

BRUNT, R. (1989) The politics of identity, in HALL, S. and JACQUES, M. (Eds) *New Times: The Changing Face of Politics in the 1990s*, London: Lawrence & Wishart, pp. 150–9.

BYNNER, J. and ASHFORD, S. (1994) Politics and participation: Some antecedents of young people's attitudes to the political system and political activity, *European Journal of Social Psychology*, **24**, pp. 223–36.

CADDICK, B. (1982) Perceived illegitimacy and intergroup relations, in TAJFEL, H. (Ed.) *Social Identity and Intergroup Relations*, Cambridge: Cambridge University Press and Paris: Editions de la Maison des Sciences de l'Homme, pp. 137–54.

CAMPBELL, A., GURIN, G. and MILLER, W. (1954) *The Voter Decides*, Evanston, IL: Row Peterson.

CHARNG, H-W., PILIAVIN, J.A. and CALLERO, P.L. (1988) Role identity and reasoned action in the prediction of repeated behavior, *Social Psychology Quarterly*, **51**, pp. 303–17.

CHASE, J. (1992) The self and collective action: Dilemmatic identities, in BREAKWELL, G.M. (Ed.) *Social Psychology of Identity and the Self Concept*, London: Academic Press/Surrey University Press, pp. 101–27.

CHINESE CULTURE CONNECTION (1987) Chinese values and the search for culture-free dimensions of culture, *Journal of Cross-Cultural Psychology*, **18**, pp. 143–64.

CICOUREL, A.V. (1982) Interviews, surveys and the problem of ecological validity, *American Sociologist*, **17**, pp. 11–20.

CINI, M.A., MORELAND, R.L. and LEVINE, J.M. (1993) Group staffing levels and responses to prospective and new group members, *Journal of Personality and Social Psychology*, **65**, pp. 723–34.

CLARK, R.D., III and MAASS, A. (1988a) Social categorization in minority influence: The case of homosexuality, *European Journal of Social Psychology*, **18**, pp. 347–64.

CLARK, R.D., III and MAASS, A. (1988b) The role of social categorization and perceived source credibility in minority influence, *European Journal of Social Psychology*, **18**, pp. 381–94.

CLAYTON, S. and CROSBY, F.J. (1992) *Justice, Gender and Affirmative Action*, Ann Arbor, MI: University of Michigan Press.

COCHRANE, R. and BILLIG, M. (1982a) Youth and politics in the eighties. *Youth and Policy*, **2**, pp. 31–4.

COCHRANE, R. and BILLIG, M. (1982b) Adolescent support for the National Front: A test of three models of political extremism, *New Community*, **10**, 86–94.

COLMAN, A. (1991) Psychological evidence in South African murder trials, *The Psychologist*, British Psychological Society, Nov. 1991, **4**, pp. 482–7.

CONDOR, S. (1986) Sex role beliefs and traditional women: Feminist and intergroup perspectives, in WILKINSON, S. (Ed.) *Feminist Social Psychology: Developing Theory and Practice*, Milton Keynes: Open University Press, pp. 97–118.

CONDOR, S. (1989) Biting into the future: Social change and the social identity of women, in SKEVINGTON, S. and BAKER, D. (Eds) *The Social Identity of Women*, London: Sage, pp. 15–39.

COOK, T.D., CROSBY, F. and HENNIGAN, K.M. (1977) The construct validity of relative deprivation, in SULS, J.M. and MILLER, R.I. (Eds) *Social Comparison Processes*, Washington, DC: Hemisphere, pp. 307–33.

COOTE, A. and CAMPBELL, B. (1987) *Sweet Freedom: The Struggle for Women's Liberation*, Oxford: Blackwell. 2nd ed.

CREWE, I. and SARLVIK, B. (1983) *Decade of Dealignment*, Cambridge: Cambridge University Press.

CROOK, S., PAKULSKI, J. and WATERS, M. (1992) *Postmodernization: Change in Advanced Society*, London: Sage.

CROSBY, F. (1976) A model of egoistical relative deprivation, *Psychological Review*, **83**, pp. 85–113.

CROSBY, F. (1982) *Relative Deprivation and Working Women*, New York: Oxford University Press.

CROSBY, F. (1984) The denial of personal discrimination, *American Behavioral Scientist*, **27**, pp. 371–86.

CROSBY, F., CLAYTON, S.D., HEMKER, K. and ALKSNIS, O. (1986) Cognitive biases in the perception of discrimination, *Sex Roles*, **14**, pp. 637–46.

CROSBY, F., CORDOVA, D. and JASKAR, K. (1993) On the failure to see oneself as disadvantaged: Cognitive and emotional components, in HOGG, M.A. and ABRAMS, D. (Eds) *Group Motivation: Social Psychological Perspectives*, London: Harvester Wheatsheaf, pp. 87–104.

CROSBY, F., PUFALL, A., SNYDER, R.C., O'CONNELL, M. and WHALEN, P. (1989) The denial of personal disadvantage among you, me and all the other ostriches, in CRAWFORD, M. and GENTRY, M. (Eds) *Gender and Thought: Psychological Perspectives*, New York: Springer-Verlag, pp. 79–99.

DAVIES, J.C. (1969) The J-Curve of rising and declining satisfactions as a cause of some great revolutions and a contained rebellion, in GRAHAM, H.D. and GURR, T.R. (Eds) *The History of Violence in America: Historical and Comparative Perspectives*, New York: Praeger, pp. 411–36.

DELGADO, G. (1986) *Organizing the Poor: The Roots and Growth of ACORN*, Philadelphia: Temple University Press.

DELLA PORTA, D. (1992) Life histories in the analysis of social movement activists, in DIANI, M. and EYERMAN, R. (Eds) (op. cit.) pp. 168–93.

DEWAELE, J.P. and HARRÉ, R. (1979) Autobiography as a psychological method, in GINSBURG, G.P. (Ed.) *Emerging Strategies in Social Psychological Research*, Chichester: John Wiley & Sons, pp. 177–224.

DIANI, M. and EYERMAN, R. (1992a) The study of collective action: Introductory remarks, in DIANI, M. and EYERMAN, R. (Eds) (op. cit.) pp. 1–21.

DIANI, M. and EYERMAN, R. (1992b) (Eds) *Studying Collective Action*, London: Sage.

DONATI, P.R. (1992) Political discourse analysis, in DIANI, M. and EYERMAN, R. (Eds) (op. cit.) pp. 136–67.

DOVIDIO, J.F. and GAERTNER, S.L. (1986) Prejudice, discrimination and racism: Historical trends and contemporary approaches, in DOVIDIO, J.F. and GAERTNER, S.L. (Eds) *Prejudice, Discrimination and Racism*, Orlando, FL: Academic Press, pp. 1–30.

DOWNING, N.E. and ROUSH, K.L. (1985) From passive acceptance to active commitment: A model of feminist identity development for women, *Counseling Psychologist*, **13**, pp. 695–709.

DUBÉ, L. and GUIMOND, S. (1986) Relative deprivation and social protest: The personal–group issue, in OLSON, J.M., HERMAN, C.P. and ZANNA, M.P. (Eds) (op. cit.) pp. 201–17.

DUNN, S. and GENNARD, J. (1984) *The Closed Shop in British Industry*, London: MacMillan.

EAGLY, A.H. and MLADINIC, A. (1994) Are people prejudiced against women? Some answers from research on attitudes, gender stereotypes, and judgements of competence, *European Review of Social Psychology*, **5**, pp. 1–35.

ECHEBARRIA-ECHABE, A.E., ROVIRA, D.P. and GARATE, J.F.V. (1988) Testing Ajzen and Fishbein's attitudes model: The prediction of voting, *European Journal of Social Psychology*, **18**, pp. 181–9.

ELLEMERS, N. (1993) The influence of socio-structural variables on identity management strategies, *European Review of Social Psychology*, **4**, pp. 27–53.

ELLEMERS, N., VAN KNIPPENBERG, A. and WILKE, H. (1990) The influence of permeability of group boundaries and stability of group status on strategies of individual mobility and social change, *British Journal of Social Psychology*, **29**, pp. 233–46.

ELLEMERS, N., WILKE, H. and VAN KNIPPENBERG, A. (1993) Effects of the legitimacy of low group or individual status on individual and collective identity enhancement strategies, *Journal of Personality and Social Psychology*, **64**, pp. 766–78.

ELLEMERS, N., VAN KNIPPENBERG, A., DE VRIES, N.K. and WILKE, H. (1988) Social identification and permeability of group boundaries, *European Journal of Social Psychology*, **18**, pp. 497–513.

EPIC INDUSTRIAL COMMUNICATIONS/IRSF (1987) *Best Practice and Realistic Expectations: The Role of Women in the IRSF*, Report commissioned by the Executive Committee of IRSF.

ESSEVELD, J. and EYERMAN, R. (1992) Which side are you on? Reflections on methodological issues in the study of 'distasteful' social movements, in DIANI, M. and EYERMAN, E. (Eds) (op. cit.) pp. 217–37.

FALUDI, S. (1992) *Backlash: The Undeclared War against Women*, London: Vintage.

FANTASIA, R. (1988) *Cultures of Solidarity: Consciousness, Action and Contemporary American Workers*, Berkeley, CA: University of California Press.

FAZIO, R.H. and ZANNA, M.P. (1981) Direct experience and attitude–behavior consistency, in BERKOWITZ, L. (Ed.) *Advances in Experimental Social Psychology*, **14**, New York: Academic Press, pp. 161–202.

FEATHER, N.T. (1982) *Expectations and Actions: Expectancy-value Models in Psychology*, Hillsdale, NJ: Erlbaum.

FERREE, M.M. (1992) The political context of rationality: Rational choice theory and resource mobilization, in Morris, A.D. and McClurg Mueller, C. (Eds) (op. cit.) pp. 29–52.

Filstead, W.J. (1979) Qualitative methods: A needed perspective in evaluation research, in Cook, T.D. and Reichart, C.S. (Eds) *Qualitative and Quantitative Methods in Evaluation Research*, Beverley Hills, CA: Sage, pp. 33–48.

Fireman, B. and Gamson, W.A. (1979) Utilitarian logic in the resource mobilization perspective, in Zald, M.N. and McCarthy, J.D. (Eds) *The Dynamics of Social Movements*, Cambridge, MA: Winthrop Publishers, pp. 8–44.

Firestone, S. (1970) *The Dialectic of Sex*, London: Paladin.

Fischer, L. (1981) Transitions in the mother–daughter relationship, *Journal of Marriage and the Family*, **43**, pp. 613–22.

Fiske, M. (1980) Changing hierarchies of commitment in adulthood, in Smelser, N.J. and Erikson, E.H. (Eds) *Themes of Work and Love in Adulthood*, Cambridge, MA: Harvard University Press, pp. 238–64.

Fiske, S.T. (1987) People's reactions to nuclear war, *American Psychologist*, **42**, pp. 207–17.

Flood, P. (1993) An expectancy value analysis of the willingness to attend union meetings, *Journal of Occupational and Organizational Psychology*, **66**, pp. 213–23.

Folger, R. and Martin, C. (1986) Relative deprivation and referent cognitions: Distributive and procedural justice effects, *Journal of Experimental Social Psychology*, **22**, pp. 531–46.

Folger, R., Rosenfield, D.D. and Robinson, T. (1983) Relative deprivation and procedural justifications, *Journal of Personality and Social Psychology*, **45**, pp. 268–73.

Folger, R., Rosenfield, D.D., Rheaume, K. and Martin, C. (1983) Relative deprivation and referent cognitions, *Journal of Experimental Social Psychology*, **19**, pp. 172–84.

Fosh, P. (1993) Membership participation in workplace unionism: The possibility of union renewal, *British Journal of Industrial Relations*, **31**, pp. 577–93.

Foster, D. (1991) Social influence III: Crowds and collective violence, in Foster, D. and Louw-Potgieter, J. (Eds) *Social Psychology in South Africa*, Johannesburg: Lexicon, pp. 441–83.

Fox, D.L. and Schofield, J.W. (1989) Issue salience, perceived efficacy and perceived risk: A study of the origins of anti-nuclear war activity, *Journal of Applied Social Psychology*, **19**, pp. 805–27.

Freeman, S.J.M. (1990) *Managing Lives: Corporate Women and Social Change*, Amherst, MA: University of Massachusetts Press.

Gaertner, S.L. and Dovidio, J.F. (1986) The aversive form of racism, in Dovidio, J.F. and Gaertner, S.L. (Eds) *Prejudice, Discrimination and Racism*, Orlando, FL: Academic Press, pp. 61–89.

Gallagher, D.G. and Strauss, G. (1991) Union membership attitudes and participation, in Strauss, G., Gallagher, D.G. and Fiorito, J. (Eds) *The State of The Unions*, Madison, WI: Industrial Relations Research Association, pp. 139–74.

Gallie, D. (1988) Employment, unemployment and social stratification, in Gallie, D. (Ed.) *Employment in Britain*, Oxford: Blackwell, pp. 465–92.

GALLIE, D. (1989) *Trade Union Allegiance and Decline in British Urban Labour Markets*, London: Economic and Social Research Council, Social Change and Economic Life Initiative, Working Paper 9.

GAMSON, W.A. (1992) The social psychology of collective action, in MORRIS, A.D. and McCLURG MUELLER, C. (Eds) (op. cit.) pp. 53–76.

GIDRON, B., CHESLER, M.A. and CHESNEY, B.K. (1991) Cross-cultural perspectives on self-help groups: Comparison between participants and non-participants in Israel and the United States, *American Journal of Community Psychology*, **19**, pp. 667–81.

GILLIGAN, C. (1982) *In a Different Voice: Psychological theory and women's development*, Cambridge, MA: Harvard University Press.

GOLDBERG, P.A., GOTTESDIENER, M. and ABRAMSON, P.R. (1975) Another put-down of women? Perceived attractiveness as a function of support for the women's movement, *Journal of Personality and Social Psychology*, **32**, pp. 113–15.

GORE, P.M. and ROTTER, J.B. (1963) A personality correlate of social action, *Journal of Personality*, **31**, pp. 58–64.

GOULDNER, A. (1954) *Wildcat Strike*, New York: Antioch Press.

GRANBERG, D. and HOLMBERG, S. (1990) The intention–behavior relationship among US and Swedish voters, *Social Psychology Quarterly*, **53**, pp. 44–54.

GRIFFIN, C. (1989) 'I'm not a women's libber but . . .': Feminism, consciousness and identity, in SKEVINGTON, S. and BAKER, D. (Eds) (op. cit.) pp. 173–93.

GRIFFIN, G. (Ed.) (1995) *Feminist Activism in the 1990s* London: Taylor & Francis.

GUIMOND, S. and DUBE-SIMARD, L. (1983) Relative deprivation theory and the Quebec Nationalist Movement: The cognition–emotion distinction and the personal–group deprivation issue, *Journal of Personality and Social Psychology*, **44**, pp. 526–35.

GURIN, P. (1985) Women's gender consciousness, *Public Opinion Quarterly*, **49**, pp. 143–63.

GURIN, P. and MARKUS, H. (1989) Cognitive consequences of gender identity, in SKEVINGTON, S. and BAKER, D. (Eds) (op. cit.) pp. 152–72.

GURIN, P. and TOWNSEND, A. (1986) Properties of gender identity and their implications for gender consciousness, *British Journal of Social Psychology*, **25**, pp. 139–48.

GURIN, P., MILLER, A.R. and GURIN, G. (1980) Stratum identification and consciousness, *Social Psychology Quarterly*, **43**, pp. 30–47.

GURIN, P., GURIN, G., LAO, R. and BEATTIE, H. (1969) Internal–external control in the motivational dynamics of negro youth, *Journal of Social Issues*, **25**, pp. 29–53.

GURNEY, J.N. and TIERNEY, K.J. (1982) Relative deprivation and social movements: A critical look at twenty years of theory and research, *The Sociological Quarterly*, **23**, pp. 33–47.

HAFER, C. and OLSON, J. (1989) Beliefs in a just world and reactions to personal deprivation, *Journal of Personality*, **57**, pp. 799–823.

HAFER, C. and OLSON, J. (1993) Discontent, beliefs in a just world and assertive actions by working women, *Personality and Social Psychology Bulletin*, **19**, pp. 30–38.

HALL, S. (1992) The question of cultural identity, in HALL, S., HELD, D. and McGREW, T. (Eds) *Modernity and its Futures*, Buckingham: Open University Press.

HAMILTON, S.B., KNOX, T.A., KEILIN, W.G. and CHAVEZ, E.C. (1987) In the eye of the beholder: Accounting for the variability in cognitive/affective responses to the threat of nuclear war, *Journal of Applied Social Psychology*, **17**, pp. 927–52.

HARRISON, M. (1979) Participation of women in trade union activities: Some research findings and comments, *Industrial Relations Journal*, **10**, pp. 41–55.

HARTLEY, J., KELLY, J. and NICHOLSON, N. (1983) *Steel Strike: A Case Study in Industrial Relations*, London: Batsford.

HARTMAN, H. and GIDRON, B. (1991) Apples and oranges: The comparability of self-help groups, *Journal of Applied Social Sciences*, **15**, pp. 221–43.

HASELAU, J., FOX-CARDAMONE, D.L., HINKLE, S. and BROWN, R.J. (1991) *The Abortion Controversy: A Look at Activists on Both Sides of the Conflict*. Paper presented at the Annual Conference of the Midwestern Psychological Association, Chicago, IL, May 1991.

HEATH, A., JOWELL, R. and CURTICE, J. (1985) *How Britain Votes*, Oxford: Pergamon.

HEATH, A. and TOPF, R. (1987) Political culture, in JOWELL, R., WITHERSPOON, S. and BROOK, L. (Eds) (op. cit.) pp. 51–69.

HEIRICH, M. (1971) *The Spiral of Conflict: Berkeley, 1964*, New York: Columbia University Press.

HENWOOD, K. and COUGHLIN, G. (1993) The construction of 'closeness' in mother–daughter relationships across the lifespan, in COUPLAND, N. and NUSSBAUM, J. (Eds) *Discourse and Lifespan Identity*, Newbury Park, CA: Sage, pp. 191–214.

HENWOOD, K. and PIDGEON, N. (1992) Qualitative research and psychological theorizing, *British Journal of Psychology*, **83**, pp. 97–111.

HENWOOD, K. and PIDGEON, N. (1994) Beyond the qualitative paradigm: A framework for introducing diversity within qualitative psychology, *Journal of Community and Applied Social Psychology*, **4**, pp. 225–38.

HEWSTONE, M. (1989) *Causal Attribution: From Cognitive Processes to Collective Beliefs*, Oxford: Blackwell.

HEWSTONE, M. and JASPERS, J. (1982) Explanations for racial discrimination: The effect of group discussion on intergroup attributions, *European Journal of Social Psychology*, **12**, pp. 1–16.

HINKLE, S.W. and BROWN, R.J. (1990) Intergroup comparisons and social identity: Some links and lacunae, in ABRAMS, D. and HOGG, M.A. (Eds) *Social Identity Theory: Constructive and critical advances*, London: Harvester Wheatsheaf, pp. 48–70.

HINKLE, S.W., BROWN, R.J. and ELY, P.G. (1990) *Individualism/Collectivism, Group Ideology and Intergroup Processes*, Paper presented at British Psychological Society, Annual Conference, London, Dec. 1990.

HIRSCH, E.L. (1990) Sacrifice for the cause: Group processes, recruitment and commitment in a student social movement, *American Sociological Review*, **55**, pp. 243–54.

Hock, E. (1978) Working and non-working mothers with infants: Perceptions of their careers, their infant's needs and satisfaction with mothering, *Developmental Psychology*, **4**, pp. 37–43.

Hofstede, G. (1980) *Culture's Consequences: International Differences in Work-related Values*, London: Sage.

Hogg, M.A. (1987) Social identity and group cohesiveness, in Turner, J.C., Hogg, M.A., Oakes, P.J., Reicher, S.D. and Wetherell, M.S., *Rediscovering the Social Group: A Self-categorization Theory*, Oxford: Blackwell, pp. 89–116.

Hogg, M.A. (1992) *The Social Psychology of Group Cohesiveness: From Attraction to Social Identity*, London: Harvester Wheatsheaf and New York: New York University Press.

Hogg, M.A. (1993) Group cohesiveness: A critical review and some new directions, in Stroebe, W. and Hewstone, M. (Eds) *European Review of Social Psychology*, **4**, Chichester: Wiley, pp. 85–111.

Hogg, M.A. and Abrams, D. (1988) *Social Identifications: A Social Psychology of Intergroup Relations and Group Processes*, London: Routledge.

Hogg, M.A. and Hardie, E.A. (1991) Social attraction, personal attraction and social categorization: A field study, *Personality and Social Psychology Bulletin*, **17**, pp. 175–80.

Hogg, M.A. and Turner, J.C. (1987) Intergroup behaviour, self-stereotyping and the salience of social categories, *Britial Journal of Social Psychology*, **26**, pp. 325–40.

Holton, R. (1978) The crowd in history: Some problems of theory and method, *Social History*, **3**, pp. 219–33.

Huszczo, G.E. (1983) Attitudinal and behavioral variables related to participation in union activities, *Journal of Labor Research*, **4**, pp. 289–97.

Hui, C.H. (1988) Measurement of individualism–collectivism, *Journal of Research in Personality*, **22**, pp. 17–36.

Hui, C.H. and Villareal, M.J. (1989) Individualism–collectivism and psychological needs: Their relationships in two cultures, *Journal of Cross-Cultural Psychology*, **20**, pp. 310–23.

Ichheiser, G. (1943) Misinterpretation of personality in everyday life and the psychologist's frame of reference, *Character and Personality*, **12**, pp. 145–60.

Inglehart, R. (1990) *Culture Shift in Advanced Industrial Society*, Princeton, NJ: Princeton University Press.

Jacobson, M.B. and Koch, W. (1978) Attributed reasons for support of the feminist movement as a function of attractiveness, *Sex Roles*, **4**, pp. 169–74.

Jardim, A. (1993) From hierarchy to centrachy, *Women's Review of Books*, **10**, pp. 27–8.

Jenkins, P. (1987) *Mrs Thatcher's Revolution: The Ending of the Socialist Era*, London: Unwin Hyman.

Johnson, R.W., Dannenbring, G.L., Anderson, N.R. and Villa, R.E. (1983) How different cultural and geographic groups perceive the attractiveness of active and inactive feminists, *Journal of Social Psychology*, **119**, 111–17.

Jowell, R. and Airey, C. (1984) *British Social Attitudes: The 1984 Report*, Aldershot: Gower.

Jowell, R., Brook, L., Prior, G. and Taylor, B. (Eds) (1992) *British Social Attitudes: The 9th Report*, Aldershot: Gower.

Jowell, R., Witherspoon, S. and Brook, L. (Eds) (1987) *British Social Attitudes: The 1987 Report*, Aldershot: Gower.

Jowell, R., Witherspoon, S. and Brook, L. (Eds) (1990) *British Social Attitudes: The 7th Report*, Aldershot: Gower.

Judd, C.M. and Park, B. (1988) Out-group homogeneity: Judgements of variability at the individual and group levels, *Journal of Personality and Social Psychology*, **54**, pp. 778–88.

Kanter, R.M. (1977) *Men and Women of the Corporation*, New York: Basic Books.

Katzenstein, M.F. (1987) Comparing the feminist movements of the United States and Western Europe: An overview, in Katzenstein, M.F. and McClurg Mueller, C. (Eds) *The Women's Movement of the United States and Western Europe: Consciousness, Political Opportunity and Public Policy*, Philadelphia, PA: Temple University Press, pp. 3–20.

Kavanagh, D. (1971) The differential English: A comparative critique, *Government and Opposition*, **6**, pp. 333–60.

Kavanagh, D. (1989) Political culture in Britain: The decline of the civic culture, in Almond, G.A. and Verba, S. (Eds) *The Civic Culture Revisited*, London: Sage, pp. 124–76.

Kawakami, K. and Dion, K.L. (1992) *Social Identity and Affect as Determinants of Collective Action: Towards an Integration of Relative Deprivation and Social Identity Theories*, Unpub. MS. University of Toronto.

Kawakami, K. and Dion, K.L. (1993) The impact of salient self-identities on relative deprivation and action intentions, *European Journal of Social Psychology*, **23**, pp. 525–41.

Kelly, C. (1988) Intergroup differentiation in a political context, *British Journal of Social Psychology*, **27**, pp. 319–32.

Kelly, C. (1989) Political identity and perceived intragroup homogeneity, *British Journal of Social Psychology*, **28**, 239–50.

Kelly, C. (1990a) Social identity and intergroup perceptions in minority–majority contexts, *Human Relations*, **43**, pp. 583–99.

Kelly, C. (1990b) Social identity and levels of influence: When a political minority fails, *British Journal of Social Psychology*, **29**, pp. 289–301.

Kelly, C. (1993) Group identification, intergroup perceptions and collective action, *European Review of Social Psychology*, **4**, pp. 59–83.

Kelly, C. and Kelly, J.E. (1994) Who gets involved in collective action? Social psychological determinants of individual participation in trade unions, *Human Relations*, **47**, pp. 63–88.

Kelly, J.E. and Kelly, C. (1991) 'Them and us': Social psychology and 'the new industrial relations', *British Journal of Industrial Relations*, **29**, pp. 25–48.

Kelly, J.E. and Kelly, C. (1992) Industrial action, in Hartley, J.F. and Stephenson, G.M. (Eds) *Employment Relations: The Psychology of Influence and Control at Work*, Oxford: Blackwell, pp. 246–68.

Kelly, J.E. and Waddington, J. (1995) Journey up a cul-de-sac: Bassett and Cave on the future of the unions, *Organization Studies* (in press).

Kimiecik, J. (1992) Predicting vigorous physical activity of corporate employees:

Comparing the theories of reasoned action and planned behaviour, *Journal of Sport and Exercise Psychology*, **14**, pp. 192–206.

KLANDERMANS, P.G. (1983) Rotter's IE-scale and socio-political action taking: The balance of 20 years of research, *European Journal of Social Psychology*, **13**, pp. 399–415.

KLANDERMANS, P.G. (1984a) Mobilization and participation in trade union action: An expectancy-value approach, *Journal of Occupational Psychology*, **57**, pp. 107–20.

KLANDERMANS, P.G. (1984b) Mobilization and participation: Social-psychological expansions of resource mobilization theory, *American Sociological Review*, **49**, pp. 583–600.

KLANDERMANS, P.G. (1985) Individuals and collective action: Rejoinder to Schrager, *American Sociological Review*, **50**, pp. 860–1.

KLANDERMANS, P.G. (1986a) Psychology and trade union participation: Joining, acting and quitting, *Journal of Occupational Psychology*, **59**, pp. 189–204.

KLANDERMANS, P.G. (1986b) Perceived costs and benefits of participation in union action, *Personnel Psychology*, **39**, pp. 379–97.

KLANDERMANS, P.G. (1989) Grievance interpretation and success expectations: The social construction of protest, *Social Behaviour*, **4**, pp. 113–25.

KLANDERMANS, P.G. (1992) The social construction of protest and multiorganizational fields, in MORRIS, A.D. and McCLURG MUELLER, C. (Eds) *Frontiers in Social Movement Theory*, New Haven, CT and London: Yale University Press, pp. 77–103.

KLEIN, E. (1984) *Gender Politics*, Cambridge, MA: Harvard University Press.

KOMOROVSKY, A. (1985) *Women in College*, New York: Basic Books.

KONEK, C.W. and KITCH, S. (1994) (Eds) *Women and Careers: Issues and challenges*, London: Sage.

KRAMER, R.M. and BREWER, M.B. (1984) Effects of group identity on resource use in a simulated commons dilemma, *Journal of Personality and Social Psychology*, **42**, pp. 487–96.

KRIESI, H. (1992) The rebellion of the research 'objects', in DIANI, M. and EYERMAN, R. (Eds) (op. cit.) pp. 194–216.

LALONDE, R.N. and CAMERON, J.E. (1994) Behavioral responses to discrimination: A focus on action, in ZANNA, M.P. and OLSON, J.M. (Eds) *The Psychology of Prejudice: The Ontario Symposium*, **7**, Hillsdale, NJ: Erlbaum, pp. 257–88.

LALONDE, R.N. and SILVERMAN, R.A. (1994) Behavioral preferences in response to social injustice: The effects of group permeability and social identity salience, *Journal of Personality and Social Psychology*, **66**, pp. 78–85.

LANE, T. and ROBERTS, K. (1971) *Strike at Pilkingtons*, London: Fontana.

LAWRENCE, E. (1994) *Gender and Trade Unions*, London: Taylor & Francis.

LE BON, G. (1895) (translated 1947) *The Crowd: A Study of the Popular Mind*, London: Ernest Benn.

LEDWITH, S., HAYES, M., JOYCE, P. and GULATI, A. (1985) *Women in SOGAT '82*, Report of a research project into the role of women in the union, Published by SOGAT '82.

LERNER, M.J. (1980) *The Belief in a Just World*, New York: Plenum.

LEVINE, J.M. and MORELAND, R.L. (1985) Innovation and socialization in small groups, in MOSCOVICI, S., MUGNY, G. and VAN AVERMAET, E. (Eds) *Perspectives* on *Minority Influence*, Cambridge: Cambridge University Press and Paris: Editions de la Maison des Sciences de l'Homme, pp. 143–69.

LEVINE, J.M. and MORELAND, R.L. (1990) Progress in small group research, *Annual Review of Psychology*, **41**, pp. 585–634.

LOCATELLI, M.G. and HOLT, R.R. (1986) Anti-nuclear activism, psychic numbing and mental health, *International Journal of Mental Health*, **15**, pp. 143–61.

LOUW-POTGIETER, J. (1989) Covert racism: An application of Essed's analysis in a South African context, *Journal of Language and Social Psychology*, **8**, pp. 307–19.

LYDON, J.E. and ZANNA, M.P. (1990) Commitment in the face of adversity: A value-affirmation approach, *Journal of Personality and Social Psychology*, **58**, pp. 1040–7.

LYKES, M.B. (1983) Discrimination and coping in the lives of black women: Analyses of oral history data, *Journal of Social Issues*, **39**, pp. 79–100.

MAASS, A., CLARK, R.D., III and HABERKORN, G. (1982) The effects of differential ascribed category membership and norms on minority influence, *European Journal of Social Psychology*, **12**, pp. 89–104.

McADAM, D. (1986) Recruitment to high-risk activism: The case of Freedom Summer, *American Journal of Sociology*, **92**, pp. 64–90.

McADAM, D. (1989) The biographical consequences of activism, *American Sociological Review*, **54**, pp. 744–60.

McCARTHY, M.N. and ZALD, J.D. (1979) *The Dynamics of Social Movements*, Cambridge, MA: Winthrop.

McCLURG MUELLER, C. (1992) Building social movement theory, in MORRIS, A.D. and McCLURG MUELLER, C. (Eds) (op. cit.) pp. 3–25.

McCONAHAY, J.B. (1986) Modern racism, ambivalence, and the modern racism scale, in DOVIDIO, J.F. and GAERTNER, S.L. (Eds) *Prejudice, Discrimination and Racism*, Orlando, FL: Academic Press, pp. 91–125.

McDERMOTT, M. (1993) On cruelty, ethics and experimentation: Profile of Philip G. Zimbardo, *The Psychologist*, British Psychological Society, Oct. 1993, pp. 456–9.

McDOUGALL, W. (1921) *The Group Mind*, Cambridge: Cambridge University Press.

McDOWELL, L. and PRINGLE, R. (1992) Women's struggles: Unity and diversity, in McDOWELL, L. and PRINGLE, R. (Eds) *Defining Women: Social institutions and gender divisions*, Cambridge: Polity Press, pp. 246–52.

MacINNES, J. (1987) *Thatcherism at Work*, Milton Keynes: Open University Press.

McILROY, J. (1995) *Trade Unions in Britain Today*, Manchester and New York: Manchester University Press. 2nd ed.

McPHAIL, C. (1971) Civil disorder participation: A critical examination of recent research, *American Sociological Review*, **36**, pp. 1058–73.

McSHANE, S.L. (1986) The multidimensionality of union participation, *Journal of Occupational Psychology*, **59**, pp. 177–87.

MADDEN, T.J., ELLEN, P.S. and AJZEN, I. (1992) A comparison of the theory of planned behavior and the theory of reasoned action, *Personality and Social Psychology Bulletin*, **18**, pp. 3–9.

MARKUS, H. and KITAYAMA, S. (1991) Culture and the self: Implications for cognition, emotion and motivation, *Psychological Review*, **98**, pp. 224–53.

MARQUAND, D. (1988) *The Unprincipled Society: New Demands and Old Politics*, London: Jonathan Cape.

MARSH, A. (1977) *Protest and Political Consciousness*, London: Sage.

MARSH, A. (1990) *Political Action in Europe and the USA*, London: Macmillan.

MARSHALL, G., NEWBY, H., ROSE, D. and VOGLER, C. (1988) *Social Class in Modern Britain*, London: Hutchinson.

MARSHALL, J. (1986) Exploring the experiences of women managers: Toward rigour in qualitative method, in WILKINSON, S. (Ed.) *Feminist Social Psychology*, Milton Keynes: Open University Press, pp. 193–209.

MARTIN, J., BRICKMAN, P. and MURRAY, A. (1984) Moral outrage and pragmatism: Explanations for collective action, *Journal of Experimental Social Psychology*, **20**, pp. 484–96.

MARTIN, R. (1988a) Ingroup and outgroup minorities: Differential impact upon public and private responses, *European Journal of Social Psychology*, **18**, pp. 39–52.

MARTIN, R. (1988b) Minority influence and social catagorization: A replication, *European Journal of Social Psychology*, **18**, pp. 369–73.

MARTIN, R. (1988c) Minority influence and 'trivial' social categorization, *European Journal of Social Psychology*, **18**, pp. 465–70.

MARTIN, R. and MURRAY, A. (1983) Distributive injustice and unfair exchange, in COOK, K.S. and MESSICK, D.M. (Eds) *Theories of Equity: Psychological and Sociological Perspectives*, New York: Praeger.

MARWELL, G. and AMES, R.E. (1979) Experiments on the provision of public goods, I. Resources, interest, group size, and the free-rider problem, *American Journal of Sociology*, **84**, pp. 1335–60.

MARWELL, G. and OLIVER, P. (1993) *The Critical Mass in Collective Action: A Micro-social Theory*, Cambridge: Cambridge University Press.

MELUCCI, A. (1989) *Nomads of the Present*, London: Hutchinson and Philadelphia, PA: Temple University Press.

MELUCCI, A. (1992) Frontier land: Collective action between actors and systems, in DIANI, M. and EYERMAN, E. (Eds) (op. cit.) pp. 238–58.

MIKULA, G. (1993) On the experience of injustice, *European Review of Social Psychology*, **4**, pp. 223–44.

MILBRATH, L. and GOEL, M. (1977) *Political Participation: How and Why do People get Involved in Politics?*, Chicago, IL: Rand McNally. 2nd ed.

MILLER, A., GURIN, P., GURIN, G. and MALUNCHUK, O. (1981) Group consciousness and political participation, *American Journal of Political Science*, **25**, pp. 494–511.

MILLER, J. (1984) Culture and the development of everyday social explanation, *Journal of Personality and Social Psychology*, **46**, pp. 961–78.

MILLWARD, N. (1990) The state of the unions, in JOWELL, R., WITHERSPOON, S. and BROOK, L. (Eds) (op. cit.), pp. 27–50.

MIRELS, H.L. (1970) Dimensions of internal versus external control, *Journal of Consulting and Clinical Psychology*, **34**, pp. 226–8.

MOGHADDAM, F.M. and PERREAULT, S. (1992) Individual and collective mobility strategies among minority group members, *Journal of Social Psychology*, **132**, pp. 343–57.

MONTANO, D.E. and TAPLIN, S.H. (1991) A test of an expanded theory of reasoned action to predict mammography participation, *Social Science and Medicine*, **36**, pp. 733–41.

MORELAND, R.L. (1985) Social categorization and the assimilation of 'new' group members, *Journal of Personality and Social Psychology*, **48**, pp. 1173–90.

MORELAND, R.L. and LEVINE, J.M. (1982) Socialization in small groups: Temporal changes in individual–group relationships, in BERKOWITZ, L. (Ed.) *Advances in Experimental Social Psychology*, **15**, New York: Academic Press, pp. 137–92.

MORELAND, R.L., LEVINE, J.M. and CINI, M. (1993) Group socialization: The role of commitment, in HOGG, M.A. and ABRAMS, D. (Eds) *Group Motivation: Social Psychological Perspectives*, London: Harvester Wheatsheaf, pp. 105–29.

MORRIS, A.D. and McCLURG MUELLER, C. (Eds) (1992) *Frontiers in Social Movement Theory*, New Haven, CT and London: Yale University Press.

MOSCOVICI, S. (1981) On social representations, in FORGAS, J. (Ed.) *Social Cognition: Perspectives on everyday understanding*, London: Academic Press, pp. 181–209.

MOSCOVICI, S. (1984) The phenomenon of social representations, in FARR, R.M. and MOSCOVICI, S. (Eds) *Social Representations*, Cambridge: Cambridge University Press, pp. 3–71.

MOSCOVICI, S. (1985) Innovation and minority influence, in MOSCOVICI, S., MUGNY, G. and VAN AVERMAET, E. (Eds) *Perspectives on Minority Influence*, Cambridge: Cambridge University Press, and Paris: Editions de la Maison des Sciences de l'Homme, pp. 9–51.

MOSCOVICI, S., LAGE, E. and NAFFRECHOUX, M. (1969) Influence of a consistent minority on the responses of a majority in a color perception task, *Sociometry*, **32**, pp. 365–80.

MUGNY, G. (1982) *The Power of Minorities*, London and New York: Academic Press.

MUGNY, G., KAISER, C. and PAPASTAMOU, S. (1983) Influence minoritaire, identification et relations entre groupes: Étude expérimentale autour d'une votation, *Cahiers de Psychologie Sociale*, **19**, pp. 1–30.

MUGNY, G., KAISER, C., PAPASTAMOU, S. and PEREZ, J.A. (1984) Intergroup relations, identification and social influence, *British Journal of Social Psychology*, **23**, pp. 317–22.

MUGNY, G. and PAPASTAMOU, S. (1980) When rigidity does not fail, *European Journal of Social Psychology*, **10**, pp. 43–61.

MULLEN, B. and HU, L. (1989) Perceptions of ingroup and outgroup variability: A meta-analytic integration, *Basic and Applied Social Psychology*, **10**, pp. 233–52.

MULLER, E.N. and OPP, K.D. (1986) Rational choice and rebellious collective action, *American Political Science Review*, **80**, pp. 471–87.

NAGATA, D.K. and CROSBY, F.J. (1991) Comparisons, justice and the internment of Japanese-Americans, in SULS, J. and WILLS, T. (Eds) *Social Comparison: Contemporary Theory and Research*, Hillsdale, NJ: Erlbaum, pp. 347–68.

NETEMEYER, R.G. and BURTON, S. (1990) Examining the relationships between voting behavior, intention, perceived behavioral control and expectation, *Journal of Applied Social Psychology*, **20**, pp. 661–80.

NETEMEYER, R.G., BURTON, S. and JOHNSTON, M. (1991) A comparison of two models for the prediction of volitional and goal-directed behaviors: A confirmatory analysis approach, *Social Psychology Quarterly*, **54**, pp. 87–100.

NICHOLSON, N., URSELL, G. and BLYTON, P. (1981) *The Dynamics of White Collar Unionism*, London: Academic Press.

OAKES, P.J. (1987) The salience of social categories, in TURNER, J., *et al.* (1987) (op. cit.), pp. 117–41.

OAKLEY, A. (1980) *Women Confined*, Oxford: Martin Robertson.

O'CONNOR, P. (1990) The adult mother/daughter relationship: A uniquely and universally close relationship? *Sociological Review*, **38**, pp. 293–323.

OLIVER, P. (1984) 'If you don't do it, nobody else will': Active and token contributors to local collective action, *American Soiological Review*, **49**, pp. 601–10.

OLSON, J.M., HERMAN, C.P. and ZANNA, M.P. (1986) (Eds) *Relative Deprivation and Social Comparison: The Ontario symposium*, **4**, Hillsdale, NJ: Erlbaum.

OLSON, M. (1965) *The Logic of Collective Action: Public Goods and the Theory of Groups*, Cambridge, MA: Harvard University Press.

OTT, E.M. (1989) Effects of the male–female ratio at work: Policewomen and male nurses, *Psychology of Women Quarterly*, **13**, pp. 41–57.

PAICHELER, G. (1988) *The Psychology of Social Influence*, Cambridge: Cambridge University Press and Paris: Editions de la Maison des Sciences de l'Homme.

PAPASTAMOU, S. (1986) Psychologization and processes of minority and majority influence, *European Journal of Social Psychology*, **16**, pp. 165–80.

PAPASTAMOU, S. and MUGNY, G. (1985) Rigidity and minority influence: The influence of the social in social influence, in MOSCOVICI, S., MUGNY, G. and VAN AVERMAET, E. (Eds) *Perspectives on Minority Influence*, Cambridge: Cambridge University Press and Paris: Editions de la Maison des Sciences de l'Homme, pp. 113–36.

PAPASTAMOU, S., MUGNY, G. and KAISER, C. (1980) Echec à l'influence minoritaire: La psychologisation, *Recherches de Psychologie Sociale*, **2**, pp. 41–56.

PARRY, G. (1986) Paid employment, life events, social support and mental health in working class mothers, *Journal of Health and Social Behaviour*, **27**, pp. 193–208.

PARRY, G. (1987) Sex role beliefs, work attitudes and mental health in employed and non-employed mothers, *British Journal of Social Psychology*, **26**, pp. 47–58.

PARRY, G., MOYSER, G. and DAY, N. (1992) *Political Participation and Democracy in Britain*, Cambridge: Cambridge University Press.

PERCY, C. and KREMER, J. (1995) Feminist identifications in a troubled society, *Feminism and Psychology*, **5**, pp. 201–22.

PETTA, G. and WALKER, I. (1992) Relative deprivation and ethnic identity, *British Journal of Social Psychology*, **31**, 285–93.

PISTRANG, N. (1984) Women's work involvement and experience of new motherhood, *Journal of Marriage and the Family*, May, pp. 433–47.

POTTER, J. and WETHERELL, M. (1987) *Discourse and Social Psychology: Beyond Attitudes and Behaviour*, London: Sage.

PURCELL, K. (1979) Militancy and acquiescence amongst women workers, in

BURMAN, S. (Ed.) *Fit Work for Women*, London: Croom Helm, pp. 112–33.

QUATTRONE, G.A. (1986) On the perception of a group's variability, in WORCHEL, S. and AUSTIN, W.G. (Eds) *Psychology of Intergroup Relations*, Chicago, IL: Nelson Hall, pp. 25–48.

RANDALL, V. (1987) *Women and Politics: An International Perspective*, London: Macmillan. 2nd ed.

RAPPAPORT, J. (1977) *Community Psychology*, New York: Holt Rinehart & Winston.

REGAN, D.T. and FAZIO, R.H. (1977) On the consistency between attitudes and behavior: Look to the method of attitude formation, *Journal of Experimental Social Psychology*, **13**, pp. 38–45.

REICHER, S.D. (1982) The determination of collective behaviour, in TAJFEL, H. (Ed.) *Social Identity and Intergroup Relations*, Cambridge: Cambridge University Press and Paris: Editions de la Maison des Sciences de l'Homme, pp. 41–78.

REICHER, S.D. (1984a) Social influence in the crowd: Attitudinal and behavioural effects of deindividuation in conditions of high and low group salience, *British Journal of Social Psychology*, **23**, pp. 341–50.

REICHER, S.D. (1984b) The St Pauls riot: An explanation of the limits of crowd action in terms of a social identity model, *European Journal of Social Psychology*, **14**, 1–21.

REICHER, S.D. (1987) Crowd behaviour as social action, in TURNER, J.C., *et al.* (1987) (op. cit.) pp. 171–202.

REICHER, S.D. (1991) Politics of crowd psychology, *The Psychologist*, British Psychological Society, Nov. 1991, **4**, pp. 487–92.

REICHER, S.D. (1993) The battle of Westminster: Developing the social identity model of crowd behaviour in order to explain the initiation and development of collective conflict, Unpub. MS.: University of Exeter.

REICHER, S.D. and POTTER, J. (1985) Psychological theory as intergroup perspective: A comparative analysis of 'scientific' and 'lay' accounts of crowd events, *Human Relations*, **38**, pp. 167–89.

RENTOUL, J. (1989) *Me and Mine: The Triumph of the New Individualism?*, London: Unwin Hyman.

RENTOUL, J. (1990) Individualism, in JOWELL, R., WITHERSPOON, S., BROOK, L. and TAYLOR, B. (Eds) (op. cit.) pp. 167–82.

RENZETTI, C.M. (1987) New wave or second stage? Attitudes of college women toward feminism, *Sex Roles*, **16**, pp. 265–77.

ROHNER, R. (1984) Toward a conception of culture for cross-cultural psychology, *Journal of Cross-Cultural Psychology*, **15**, pp. 111–38.

ROTTER, J.B. (1966) Generalized expectancies for internal versus external control of reinforcement, *Psychological Monographs*, **80**, (Whole No. 609).

ROTTER, J.B., SEEMAN, M.R. and LIVERANT, S. (1962) Internal versus external control of reinforcements: A major variable in behavior theory, in WASHBURN, W.F. (Ed.) *Decisions, Values and Groups*, **2**, New York: Pergamon, pp. 473–516.

ROWLAND, R. (1984) *Women Who Do and Women Who Don't Join the Women's Movement*, London: Routledge & Kegan Paul.

ROWLAND, R. (1986) Women who do and women who don't join the women's movement: Issues for conflict and collaboration, *Sex Roles*, **14**, pp. 679–92.

RUGGIERO, K.M. and TAYLOR, D.M. (1995) Coping with discrimination: How disadvantaged group members perceive the discrimination that confronts them, *Journal of Personality and Social Psychology*, **68**, pp. 826–38.

RUNCIMAN, W.G. (1966) *Relative Deprivation and Social Justice*, London: Routledge & Kegan Paul.

RYAN, B. (1992) *Feminism and the Women's Movement: Dyanmics of Change in Social Movement, Ideology and Activism*, New York and London: Routledge.

SAMPSON, E.E. (1977) Psychology and the American ideal, *Journal of Personality and Social Psychology*, **35**, pp. 767–82.

SCASE, R. and GOFFEE, R. (1989) *Reluctant Managers: Their Work and Life Style*, London: Unwin Hyman.

SCHENNINK, B. (1988) From peace week to peace work: Dynamics of the peace movement in the Netherlands, in KLANDERMANS, B., KRIESI, H. and TARROW, S. (Eds) *From Structure to Action: Comparing Movements Across Cultures*, International Social Movement Research, **1**, Greenwich, CT: JAI Press, pp. 247–81.

SCHOFIELD, J. and PAVELCHAK, M. (1989) Fallout from 'The Day After': The impact of a television film on attitudes, *Journal of Applied Social Psychology*, **19**, pp. 433–48.

SCHRAGER, L.S. (1985) Private attitudes and collective action, *American Sociological Review*, **50**, pp. 858–9.

SCHWARTZ, S.H. (1992) The universal content and structure of values: Theoretical advances and empirical tests in twenty countries, in ZANNA, M. (Ed.) *Advances in Experimental Social Psychology*, **25**, New York: Academic Press, pp. 1–65.

SCHWARTZ, S.H. and BILSKY, W. (1987) Towards a psychological structure of human values, *Journal of Personality and Social Psychology*, **53**, pp. 550–62.

SCHWARTZ, S.H. and BILSKY, W. (1990) Towards a theory of the universal content and structure of values: Extensions and cross-cultural replications, *Journal of Personality and Social Psychology*, **58**, pp. 878–91.

SEDDON, V. (Ed.) (1986) *The Cutting Edge: Women and the Pit Strike*, London: Lawrence & Wishart.

SIMON, B. (1992) The perception of ingroup and outgroup homogeneity: Reintroducing the intergroup context, *European Review of Social Psychology*, **3**, pp. 1–30.

SIMON, B. and BROWN, R.J. (1987) Perceived intragroup homogeneity in minority–majority contexts, *Journal of Personality and Social Psychology*, **53**, pp. 703–11.

SIMON, B. and MUMMENDEY, A. (1990) Perceptions of relative group size and group homogeneity: We are the majority and they are all the same, *European Journal of Social Psychology*, **20**, pp. 351–6.

SIMON, B. and PETTIGREW, T.F. (1990) Social identity and perceived group homogeneity: Evidence for the ingroup homogeneity effect, *European Journal of Social Psychology*, **20**, pp. 269–86.

SIVACEK, J.K. and CRANO, W.D. (1982) Vested interest as a moderator of attitude–behaviour consistency, *Journal of Personality and Social Psychology*, **43**, pp. 210–21.

SKEVINGTON, S. and BAKER, D. (Eds) (1989) *The Social Identity of Women*, London: Sage.

SMITH, P.B. and BOND, M.H. (1993) *Social Psychology Across Cultures: Analysis and Perspectives*, London: Harvester Wheatsheaf.

SMITH, P. and GASKELL, G. (1990) The social dimension in relative deprivation theory, in FRASER, C. and GASKELL, G. (Eds) *The Social Psychological Study of Widespread Beliefs*, New York: Oxford University Press, pp. 179–91.

SNYDER, C.R. and FROMKIN, H.L. (1980) *Uniqueness: The Human Pursuit of Difference*, New York: Plenum Press.

SPARKS, P. and SHEPHERD, R. (1992) Self-identity and the theory of planned behavior: Assessing the role of identification with 'Green consumerism', *Social Psychology Quarterly*, **55**, pp. 388–99.

SPELMAN, E.V. (1988) *Inessential Woman: Problems of Exclusion in Feminist Thought*, Boston, MA: Beacon Press.

STAGNER, R. and EFLAL, B. (1982) Internal union dynamics during a strike: A quasi-experimental study, *Journal of Applied Psychology*, **67**, pp. 37–44.

STEWART, A.J. and GOLD-STEINBERG, S. (1990) Midlife women's political consciousness: Case studies of psychosocial development and political commitment, *Psychology of Women Quarterly*, **14**, pp. 543–66.

STOUFFER, S.A., SUCHMAN, E.A., DE VINNEY, L.C., STAR, S.A. and WILLIAMS, R.M. (1949) *The American Soldier: Adjustment during army life*, **1**, Princeton, NJ: Princeton University Press.

STRUCH, N. and SCHWARTZ, S.H. (1989) Intergroup aggression: Its predictors and distinctness from in-group bias, *Journal of Personality and Social Psychology*, **56**, pp. 364–73.

SULLIVAN, M. (1983) Introduction to women emerging: Group approaches, *Journal for Specialists in Group Work*, **8**, pp. 3–8.

SWIM, J.K., AIKIN, K.J., HALL, W.S. and HUNTER, B.A. (1995) Sexism and racism: Old-fashioned and modern prejudices, *Journal of Personality and Social Psychology*, **68**, pp. 199–214.

TAJFEL, H. (1975) The exit of social mobility and the voice of social change, *Social Science Information*, **14**, pp. 101–18.

TAJFEL, H. (1978) Interindividual behaviour and intergroup behaviour, in TAJFEL, H. (Ed.) *Differentiation between Social Groups: Studies in the Social Psychology of Intergroup Relations*, New York: Academic Press, pp. 27–60.

TAJFEL, H. and TURNER, J.C. (1979) An integrative theory of intergroup conflict, in AUSTIN, W.G. and WORCHEL, S. (Eds) *The Social Psychology of Intergroup Relations*, Monterey, CA: Brooks Cole, pp. 33–47.

TAJFEL, H. and TURNER, J.C. (1986) The social identity theory of intergroup behaviour, in WORCHEL, S. and AUSTIN, W.G. (Eds) *Psychology of Intergroup Relations*, Chicago, IL: Nelson Hall, pp. 7–24.

TARROW, S. (1991) *Struggle, Politics and Reform: Collective Action, Social Movements and Cycles of Protest*, Ithaca, NY: Cornell University: Western Societies Program, Occasional Paper 21.

TARROW, S. (1994) *Power in Movement: Social Movements, Collective Action and Politics*, Cambridge: Cambridge University Press.

TAYLOR, D.M. and McKIRNAN, D.J. (1984) A five-stage model of intergroup relations, *British Journal of Social Psychology*, **23**, pp. 291–300.

TAYLOR, D.M., MOGHADDAM, F.M., GAMBLE, I. and ZELLERER, E. (1987) Disadvantaged group responses to perceived inequality: From passive acceptance to collective action, *Journal of Social Psychology*, **127**, pp. 259–72.

TAYLOR, D.M., WONG-RIEGER, D., McKIRNAN, D.J. and BERCUSSON, T. (1982) Interpreting and coping with threat in the context of intergroup relations, *The Journal of Social Psychology*, **117**, pp. 257–69.

TAYLOR, D.M., WRIGHT, S.C., MOGHADDAM, F.M. and LALONDE, R.N. (1990) The personal/group discrimination discrepancy: Perceiving my group, but not myself, to be a target for discrimination, *Personality and Social Psychology Bulletin*, **16**, pp. 254–62.

TAYLOR, D.M., WRIGHT, S.C. and PORTER, L.E. (1994) Dimensions of perceived discrimination: The personal/group discrimination discrepancy, in ZANNA, M.P. and OLSON, J.M. (Eds) *The Psychology of Prejudice: The Ontario symposium*, **7**, Hillsdale, NJ: Erlbaum, pp. 233–55.

TAYLOR, R. (1993) *The Trade Union Question in British Politics: Government and Unions Since 1945*, Oxford: Blackwell.

TILLY, C. (1978) *From Mobilization to Revolution*, New York: McGraw Hill.

TOUGAS, F. and VEILLEUX, F. (1988) The influence of identification, collective relative deprivation, and procedure of implementation on women's response to affirmative action: A causal modelling approach, *Canadian Journal of Behavioural Science*, **20**, pp. 15–28.

TOUGAS, F. and VEILLEUX, F. (1989) Who likes affirmative action: Attitudinal processes among men and women, in BLANCHARD, F.A. and CROSBY, F.S. (Eds) *Affirmative Action in Perspective*, New York: Springer-Verlag, pp. 111–24.

TOUGAS, F., BROWN, R., BEATON, A.M. and JOLY, S. (1995) Neosexism: Plus ca change, plus c'est pareil, *Personality and Social Psychology Bulletin*, **21**, pp. 842–9.

TRIANDIS, H.C. (1989) The self and social behaviour in different cultural contexts, *Psychological Review*, **96**, pp. 506–20.

TRIANDIS, H.C., BONTEMPO, R., VILLAREAL, M.J., ASAI, M. and LUCCA, N. (1988) Individualism and collectivism: Cross-cultural perspectives on self–ingroup relationships, *Journal of Personality and Social Psychology*, **54**, pp. 323–38.

TRIANDIS, H.C., LEUNG, K., VILLAREAL, M.H. and CLACK, F.L. (1985) Allocentric vs. idiocentric tendencies: Convergent and discriminant validation, *Journal of Research in Personality*, **19**, pp. 395–415.

TURNBULL, P., WOOLFSON, C. and KELLY, J. (1991) *Dock Strike: Conflict and Restructuring in Britain's Ports*, Aldershot: Avebury.

TURNER, J.C. (1987) A self-categorization theory, in TURNER, J.C., *et al.* (op. cit.), pp. 42–67.

TURNER, J.C. (1991) *Social Influence*, Milton Keynes: Open University Press.

TURNER, J.C. and BROWN, R.J. (1978) Social status, cognitive alternatives and intergroup relations, in TAJFEL, H. (Ed.) *Differentiation Between Social Groups: Studies in the social psychology of intergroup relations*, London: Academic Press, pp. 201–34.

TURNER, J.C., HOGG, M.A., OAKES, P.J., REICHER, S.D. and WETHERELL, M.S. (1987)

Rediscovering the Social Group: A Self-categorization Theory, Oxford: Blackwell.

TYLER, T.R. and McGRAW, K.M. (1983) The threat of nuclear war: Risk interpretation and behavioral response, *Journal of Social Issues*, **39**, pp. 25–40.

UNESCO (1981) *Youth in the 1980s*, Paris: Unesco Press.

VAN DE VALL, M. (1970) *Labor Organizations: A Macro- and Micro-sociological Analysis on a Comparative Basis*, Cambridge: Cambridge University Press.

VAN KNIPPENBERG, A. and ELLEMERS, N. (1990) Social identity and intergroup differentiation processes, *European Review of Social Psychology*, **1**, pp. 137–69.

VAN KNIPPENBERG, A. and ELLEMERS, N. (1993) Strategies in intergroup relations, in HOGG, M.A. and ABRAMS, D. (Eds) *Group Motivation: Social Psychological Perspectives*, London: Harvester Wheatsheaf, pp. 17–32.

VANNEMAN, R.D. and PETTIGREW, T.F. (1972) Race and relative deprivation in the urban United States, *Race*, **13**, pp. 461–86.

WADDINGTON, D., WYKES, M. and CRITCHER, C. (1991) *Split at the Seams? Community, Continuity and Change after the 1984–5 Coal Dispute*, Milton Keynes: Open University Press.

WALKER, I. and MANN, L. (1987) Unemployment, relative deprivation and social protest, *Personality and Social Psychology Bulletin*, **13**, pp. 275–83.

WALKER, I. and PETTIGREW, T.F. (1984) Relative deprivation theory: An overview and conceptual critique, *British Journal of Social Psychology*, **23**, pp. 301–10.

WALSH, E. (1988) *Democracy in the Shadows: Citizen Mobilization in the Wake of the Accident at Three Mile Island*, Westport, CT: Greenwood.

WANDERSMAN, A. (1981) A framework of participation in community organizations, *Journal of Applied Behavioural Science*, **17**, pp. 27–58.

WERTHEIMER, B.M. and NELSON, A.H. (1975) *Trade Union Women: A Study of Their Participation in New York City Locals*, New York: Praeger.

WETHERELL, M., STIVEN, H. and POTTER, J. (1987) Unequal egalitarianism: A preliminary study of discourses concerning gender and employment opportunities, *British Journal of Social Psychology*, **26**, pp. 59–73.

WICKER, A.W. (1968) Undermanning, performances, and students' subjective experiences in behavior settings of large and small high schools, *Journal of Personality and Social Psychology*, **10**, pp. 255–61.

WICKER, A.W. (1969) Size of church membership and members' support of church behavior settings, *Journal of Personality and Social Psychology*, **13**, pp. 278–88.

WICKER, A.W. and KAUMA, C. (1974) Effects of a merger of a small and large organization on members' behaviors and experiences, *Journal of Applied Psychology*, **59**, pp. 24–30.

WICKER, A.W., KIRMEYER, S.L., HANSON, L. and ALEXANDER, D. (1976) Effects of manning levels on subjective experiences, performance and verbal interaction in groups, *Organizational Behavior and Human Performance*, *17*, pp. 251–74.

WICKER, A.W. and MEHLER, A. (1971) Assimilation of new members in a large and a small church, *Journal of Applied Psychology*, **55**, pp. 151–6.

WILDER, D.A. (1984) Predictions of belief homogeneity and similarity following social categorization, *British Journal of Social Psychology*, **23**, pp. 323–33.

WILLIAMS, J.A. (1984) Gender and intergroup behaviour: Towards an integration, *British Journal of Social Psychology*, **23**, pp. 311–16.

WILLIAMS, J.A. and GILES, H. (1978) The changing status of women in society: An intergroup perspective, in TAJFEL, H. (Ed.) *Differentiation Between Social Groups: Studies in the Social Psychology of Intergroup Relations*, London: Academic Press, pp. 431–46.

WINTERTON, J. and WINTERTON, R. (1989) *Coal, Crisis and Conflict: The 1984–85 miners' strike in Yorkshire*, Manchester: Manchester University Press.

WOLF, S., GREGORY, W.L. and STEPHAN, W.G. (1986) Protection motivation theory: Prediction of intentions to engage in anti-nuclear war behaviors, *Journal of Applied Social Psychology*, **16**, pp. 310–21.

WOOLFSON, C. and FOSTER, J. (1988) *Track Record: The Story of the Caterpillar Occupation*, London: Verso.

WRIGHT, S.C., TAYLOR, D.M. and MOGHADDAM, F.M. (1990) Responding to membership in a disadvantaged group: From acceptance to collective protest, *Journal of Personality and Social Psychology*, **58**, pp. 994–1003.

YAHNE, C.E. and LONG, V.O. (1988) The use of support groups to raise self-esteem for women clients, *Journal of American College Health*, **37**, pp. 79–84.

YOUNG, A. (1990) *Femininity in Dissent*, London: Routledge.

ZIMBARDO, P.J. (1969) The Human Choice: Individuation, reason, and order versus deindividuation, impulse and chaos, in ARNOLD, W.G. and LEVINE, D. (Eds) *Nebraska Symposium on Motivation*, Lincoln, NB: University of Nebraska Press, pp. 237–307.

Index

Note: 'f' and 't' after a page reference indicate figures and tables.

Abeles, R.D. 39
Abrams, D. and Hogg, M.A. 143
activist identity 53–4 (*see also*
    non-activism)
    psychologization 143, 144, 149
    women's movement 65, 72, 78, 94–5,
    173
Adams, J.P. Jr and Dressler, W.W. 101
affluence 4, 5
Ajzen, I. 25, 26, 27, 28
Ajzen, I. and Fishbein, M. 26
Ajzen, I. and Madden, T.J. 26, 27, 74, 174
Allen, P.T. and Stephenson, G.M. 58
allocentrism 23, 24
Almond, G.A. and Verba, S. 139
Al-Zahrani, S.S. and Kaplowitz, S.A. 44
Andrews, M. 16, 17, 22, 48, 54, 83, 94, 122,
    125, 173
anti-nuclear campaigning 21–2, 173
anti-war movement 1
apathy 140, 165 (*see also* non-activism)
Appelgry, A.E. and Niewoudt, J.M. 39
Archer, J. 52
Arnold, D. and Greenberg, C. 113
Ashworth, G. 178

Bagozzi, R.P. 28
Bagozzi, R.P. and Yi, Y. 28
Bagozzi, R.P., Yi, Y. and Baumgartner, J.
    28
Baker, D. 103
Banister, P. *et al.* 16
Banks, M. *et al.* 140
Banks, O. 89, 107
Bargad, A. and Hyde, J.S. 130
Barling, J., Kelloway, E.K. and Fullager, C.
    56
Barnes, S. *et al.* 22
Baruch, G. and Barnett, R.C. 90

Bassett, P. and Cave, A. 3, 5
Beaumont, P.B. and Elliott, J. 107
Becker, H.S. and Geer, B. 83
Beckwith, K. 21
Beer, S.H. 139
behavioural control 72–6, 77–8
beliefs, *see* social beliefs
Benokraitis, N.V. and Feagin, J.R. 97
Berkowitz, L. 21
Beynon, H. 33
Bhavnani, K.K. 140
Biddle, B.J., Bank, B.J. and Slavings, R.L.
    29, 50, 54
Billig, M. 177
Birt, C. and Dion, K.L. 39, 40, 99
blood donation 28, 29
Blumer, H. 17
Boyd, C.J. 90
Breakwell, G.M. 51, 52
Breinlinger, S. and Kelly, C. 51
Brett, J.M. and Goldberg, S.B. 31
Brewer, M.B. 49, 139, 164, 174
Brewer, M.B. and Schneider, S.K. 35
Briet, M., Klandermans, B. and Kroon, F.
    99, 166
Briscoe, J. 90
Brown, H.P. 4, 5
Brown, R.J. 89
Brown, R.J. *et al.* 132
Bruner, J.S. 34
Brunt, R. 141
Bynner, J. and Ashford, S. 140

Caddick, B. 110
Campbell, A., Gurin, G. and Miller, W. 21
causal attribution 42, 44
Charng, H-W, Piliavin, J.A. and Callero,
    P.L. 28–9, 50, 54
Chase, J. 13, 35

childcare 129, 146, 178
Chinese Culture Connection 137
Cicourel, A.V. 16
Cini, M.A., Moreland, R.L. and Levine, J.M. 113
civil rights campaigns 1
Clark, R.D. III and Maass, A. 143
class de-alignment 2
Cochrane, R. and Billig, M. 140
collective action
 group processes
  deindividuation and crowd behaviour 36–8
  five-stage model intergroup relations 42–8
  gender relations 51–3
  group membership and self-stereotyping 34–6
  moderating role of group identification 48–51
  relative deprivation theory 38–40
  social identity and low status 40–42
 growth 1
 incentives 11–13
 individual decision-making 25
  expectancy-value model 30–34
  reasoned action and planned behaviour 26–30
  individualist-collectivist orientation 23–5
 individual personality characteristics
  locus of control 20–21
  political efficacy 21–3
 methodology and study 16–18
 micro-sociological approaches 14–16
 perceived inappropriateness 171 (*see also* non-activism)
 Olson's theory 11–13, 14, 15
 resource mobilization theory 13–14
 social psychological approaches 19–20
collective bargaining 4
collectivism
 decline 2, 4
 multi-dimensional 10–11
 political attitudes 9–11
 shared cultural values 9
collectivist orientation 23–5
 participation in women's groups 68, 70, 71, 73, 80, 174
 union participation 59–60, 80
Colman, A. 37
community organizations 113, 173
Condor, S. 41, 51, 152–3, 174

consciousness-raising 7–8, 52–3, 113–18, 124
consensus mobilization 30, 32–3
conservatism 155–6
contraception 6
Cook, T.D., Crosby, F. and Hennigan, K.M. 39
Coote, A. and Campbell, B. 7, 124
Crewe, I. and Sarlvik, B. 2
Crook, S., Pakulski, J. and Waters, M. 2
Crosby, F. 38, 99
Crosby, F., Còrdova, D. and Jaskar, K. 99, 166, 172
Crosby, F. *et al.* 99
crowd behaviour 36–8
cultural values 9, 23
 individualism 136–41, 155–7
cycle of protest 1
cynicism 139–40

data-gathering 18
Davies, J.C. 89
decision-making 25
 expectancy-value model 30–34
 reasoned action and planned behaviour 26–30
deindividuation 36–8
Delgado, G. 114
della Porta, D. 17
demonstrations 2, 10
depersonalization 35
deprivation 4, 5 (*see also* inequality)
 causal attribution 42, 44
 relative 38–40
  group identification 49, 50
  participation in women's groups 68, 69, 71, 73, 80, 89, 104, 135, 172–3, 174
  permeability of group boundaries 44–6
  union participation 61
DeWaele, J.P. and Harre, R. 83
Diani, M. and Eyerman, R. 17
disadvantage, *see* deprivation
discrimination 95–101
Donati, P.R. 17
Dovidio, J.F. and Gaertner, S.L. 97
Downing, N.E. and Roush, K.L. 130
Dube, L. and Guimond, S. 39, 48
Dye, T.R. and Zeigler, L.H. 42

Eagly, A.H. and Mladinic, A. 98
Echebarrio-Echabe, A.E., Rovira, D.P. and Garate, J.F.V. 28

Ellemers, N. *et al.* 45, 49
Ellemers, N., Van Knippenberg, A. and
    Wilke, H. 45
employees
    discrimination 95–7
    individualism 4, 5
    women's status and earnings 178
empowerment 122, 124, 175
EPIC Industrial Communications/IRSF 146
Esseveld, J. and Eyerman, R. 17
expectancy-value models 25, 30–34, 57, 74
    reasoned action and planned
    behaviour 26–30, 174

Faludi, S. 7
family values 7
    gender relations 86–90
Fantasia, R. 33, 114–15, 116
Fazio, R.H. and Zanna, M.P. 28
feasibility 49
Feather, N.T. 25
feminism (*see also* women's movement)
    definitions 163–4
    developmental model 130
    stereotyping 151–2, 157–60, 171–2
Ferree, M.M. 15
Filstead, W.J. 16
Fireman, B. and Gamson, W.A. 13, 14–15
Firestone, S. 6
Fischer, L. 90
Fiske, S.T. 22, 95
Flood, P. 32
Folger, R. and Martin, C. 38
Folger, R., Rosenfield, D.D. and Robinson,
    T. 38
Folger, R., Rosenfield, D.D., Rheaume, K.
    and Martin, C. 38
Fosh, P. 56, 147
Foster, D. 36
Fox, D.L. and Schofield, J.W. 22
Freeman, S.J.M. 103
free-riding 11, 12, 107

Gaertner, S.L. and Dovidio, J.F. 97, 98
Gallagher, D.G. and Strauss, G. 56
Gallie, D. 3, 9, 10, 12
Gamson, W.A. 15
gender (*see also* women)
    identity 68–9, 71, 78
        social 51–3
    stereotypes 35, 103
Gidron, B., Chester, M.A. and Chesney,
    B.K. 113

Gilligan, C. 52
goal motives 30, 57, 74, 175
Goldberg, P.A., Gottesdiener, M. and
    Abramson, P.R. 152
Gore, P.M. and Rotter, J.B. 20
Gouldner, A. 33
Granberg, D. and Holmberg, S. 29, 50, 54
Greenham Common peace group 151
Green movements 14
Griffin, C. 17, 151, 171
group boundaries 44–6
group hierarchies 119, 124, 162, 175
group identification 48–51
    optimal distinctiveness 139, 164–5, 174
    trade unions 61–2
    women's groups 70–72, 76–8, 79
group membership 34–6, 139, 164–5
group socialization 111–13
group staffing levels 112–13
Guimand, S. and Dube-Simard, L. 39, 40
Gurin, P. 53
Gurin, P. and Markus, H. 53
Gurin, P. and Townsend, A. 51, 52
Gurin, P., Miller, A.R. and Gurin, G. 52, 53
Gurney, J.N. and Tierney, K.J. 40

Hafer, C. and Olson, J. 44, 99
Hall, S. 140, 176
Hamilton, S.B. *et al.* 21
Harrison, M. 146
Hartley, J., Kelly, J. and Nicholson, N. 32,
    116
Hartley, J.F. and Stephenson, G.M. 31f
Hartman, H. and Gidron, B. 113
Haselau, J. *et al.* 50, 61, 79–80
Heath, A. and Topf, R. 139, 140
Heath, A., Jowell, R. and Curtice, J. 2
Heirich, M. 114
Henwood, K. and Coughlin, G. 90
Henwood, K. and Pidgeon, N. 16
Hewstone, M. 44
Hewstone, M. and Jaspers, J. 44
hierarchies 119, 124, 162, 175
Hinkle, S.W. and Brown, R.J. 24, 41, 109
Hinkle, S.W., Brown, R.J. and Ely, P.G. 24
Hirsch, E.L. 33, 115, 124, 134, 175
Hock, E. 103
Hofstede, G. 9, 23, 137
Hogg, M.A. 112
Hogg, M.A. and Abrams, D. 40
Hogg, M.A. and Hardie, E.A. 112
Hogg, M.A. and Turner, J.C. 35, 103
Holton, R. 37

Hui, C.H. 23
Hui, C.H. and Villareal, M.J. 24
Huszczo, G.E. 56

Ichheiser, G. 44
identity 28–9
    activist 53–4
        women's movement 65, 72, 78, 94–5
    gender 68–9, 71, 78
    groups 48–51
        trade unions 61–2
        women's movement 70–72, 76–8
    optimal distinctiveness 139, 164–5, 174
    social, *see* social identity
idiocentrism 23, 24
INDCOL scale 23, 24
individualism 1, 2
    causal attribution 44
    employees 4, 5
    non-activism 136–41, 155–7
individual mobility 5, 41, 42, 44-5, 46, 47,
    48, 138, 156
individualist-collectivist orientation 23–5
industrial action, *see* strike action
industrial relations 1
    attitudes 58
inequality 38–40, 46, 49, 50 (*see also*
    deprivation)
    gender relations 87–8, 105
Inglehart, R. 141
injustice, *see* inequality
intended behaviour 59, 72–6
interdependence 23, 24
intergroup relations 42–8
interviews 18, 82, 85–6, 153–5

Jacobson, M.B. and Koch, W. 152
Jardim, A. 124
Jenkins, P. 140
Johnson, R.W. *et al.* 152
Jowell, R. and Airey, C. 10t
Jowell, R. *et al.* 10t
Judd, C.M. and Park, B. 35

Kanter, R.M. 103
Katzenstein, M.F. 7
Kavanagh, D. 139
Kawakani, K. and Dion, K.L. 49, 80
Kelly, C. 34, 35, 41, 53, 59, 132–3, 139, 143
Kelly, J.E. and Kelly, C. 5, 31f, 32, 50, 141,
    175
Kelly, J.E. and Waddington, J. 5, 10
Kimiecik, J. 28

Klandermans, P.G. 15, 20, 22, 30–34, 40,
    53, 61, 74, 113–14, 145, 175
Klein, E. 6
Komorovsky, A. 152
Konek, C.W. and Kitch, S. 6, 124
Kramer, R.M. and Brewer, M.B. 35
Kriesi, H. 17

labour relations 1
    attitudes 58
Lalonde, R.N. and Cameron, J.E. 40, 101
Lalonde, R.N. and Silverman, R.A. 47
Lane, T. and Roberts, K. 114
Lawrence, E. 56, 145, 146, 169
Le Bon, G. 36, 37
Ledwith, S. *et al.* 146
legitimacy 45–6
Lerner, M.J. 44, 99
lesbianism 151
Levine, J.M. and Moreland, R.L. 111, 112,
    113
life-cycle changes 94–5, 126, 128–9
life-histories 83
Locatelli, M.G. and Holt, R.R. 21
locus of control 20–21
Louw-Potgieter, J. 101
Lydon, J.E. and Zanna, M.P. 53
Lykes, M.B. 101

Maass, A., Clark, R.D. III and Haberkorn,
    G. 143
McAdam, D. 117
McCarthy, M.N. and Zald, J.D. 13
McClurg Mueller, C. 15
McConahay, J.B. 98
McDougall, W. 36
McDowell, L. and Pringle, R. 177
McIlroy, J. 178
MacInnes, J. 141
McPhail, C. 40
McShane, S.L. 56, 58
Madden, T.J., Ellen, P.S. and Ajzen, I. 28
Markus, H. and Kitayama, S. 23
Marquand, D. 140
Marsh, A. 139, 140
Marshall, G. *et al.* 9, 10, 12
Marshall, J. 17
Martin, J., Brickman, P. and Murray, A. 40
Martin, R. 143
Martin, R. and Murray, A. 40
Marwell, G. and Ames, R.E. 13
Marwell, G. and Oliver, P. 13, 19
maternity rights 96–7, 178

Melucci, A. 15, 17
Mikula, G. 99
Milbrath, L. and Goel, M. 22, 53
militancy
    trade unions 148–9
    women's groups 152, 158, 163
Miller, A. *et al.* 52, 53
Miller, J. 44
Millward, N. 5, 10, 12
miners' strike 1984–85 3, 115–17, 171
minority influence 141–5, 172, 179
Mirels, H.L. 20
mobility 5, 41, 42, 44–5, 46, 47, 48, 138, 156
Moghaddam, F.M. and Perreault, S. 47, 48
Montano, D.E. and Taplin, S.H. 28
Moreland, R.L. 112
Moreland, R.L. and Levine, J.M. 111
Moreland, R.L. *et al.* 111, 112, 134
Morris, A.D. and McClurg Mueller, C. 14, 15
Moscovici, S. 44, 114, 142
Moscovici, S. *et al.* 142
Mugny, G. 143, 172, 179
Mugny, G. and Papastamou, S. 143
Mugny, G. *et al.* 143
Mugny, G., Kaiser, C. and Papastamou, S. 143, 144
Mullen, B. and Hu, L. 35
Muller, E.N. and Opp, K.D. 12

Nagata, D.K. and Crosby, F.J. 99
NALGO (National and Local Government Officers' Association) 56, 147
neighbourhood collective action 113, 173
neosexism 98
Netemeyer, R.G. and Burton, S. 28
Netemeyer, R.G., Burton, S. and Johnston, M. 28
Nicholson, N., Ursell, G. and Blyton, P. 57, 58, 147
non-activism 136, 168–70
    individualist cultures 136–41
    perceptions of political minorities and activists 141–5
    political cynicism 139–40
    trade unions 145–51
    women's groups
        apathy 165
        beliefs about feminism 157–62, 163–4
            cultural and political context 155–7
            data-gathering 153–5

denial of personal disadvantage 166
fear of negative stereotyping 151–2
feelings of disloyalty to the family 163
    individual aversion to group membership 164–5
    lack of confidence 165
    perceived inappropriateness of collective action 152–3, 167–8
    practical constraints 167
    structure and organization of women's groups 162

Oakes, P.J. 34
Oakley, A. 103
O'Connor, P. 90
Oliver, P. 32, 173
Olson, J.M., Herman, C.P. and Zanna, M.P. 38
Olson, M. 11–13, 14, 15, 106
optimal distinctiveness 139, 164–5, 174
Ott, E.M. 103
outgroup homogeneity effect 138

Paicheler, G. 144
Papastamou, S. 143
Papastamou, S. and Mugny, G. 142
Papastamou, S., Mugny, G. and Kaiser, C. 143
Pareto, V. 42
Parry, G. 103
Parry, G., Moyser, G. and Day, N. 19, 21, 22, 140
participation studies
    outcomes 110
        consciousness raising 7–8, 52–3, 113–18
        group socialization 111–13
    trade unions
        factor analysis 58, 59t
        moderating role of group identification 61–2
        predicting participation 59—61
        questionnaire 57–8
        setting and respondents 56–7
    women's groups, *see* women's movement
perceived behavioural control 72–6, 77–8
Percy, C. and Kremer, J. 152, 163, 171
Petta, G. and Walker, I. 40, 50
picketing 12
Pistrang, N. 103
planned behaviour 26–30, 74, 77, 174

political conservatism 155–6
political cynicism 139–40
political efficacy 21–3, 53, 54
    participation in women's groups 68, 69,
    70, 71, 73, 80, 174
    union participation 61, 80
political minorities 141–5,172, 179
Potter, J. and Wetherell, M. 177
psychologization 143, 144, 149
Purcell, K. 146

qualititative research 16–18, 82, 153
Quattrone, G.A. 138
questionnaires 18, 57, 62–4, 82, 85, 153–5

racism 97
Randall, V. 6, 64
Rappaport, J. 44
Reagan, Ronald 2
reasoned action 26–30, 74, 77–8
Regan, D.T. and Fazio, R.H. 28
Reicher, S.D. 35, 36, 37
Reicher, S.D. and Potter, J. 36, 37
Rentoul, J. 9, 10, 140, 141
Renzetti, C.M. 152, 155
research methodology 16–18
resource mobilization theory 13–14
reward motives 30, 58, 74
Rohner, R. 23
Rotter, J.B. 20
Rotter, J.B., Seeman, M.R. and Liverant, S.
    20
Rowland, R. 151, 152
Ruggiero, K.M. and Taylor, D.M. 100
Runciman, W.G. 5, 38, 89
Ryan, B. 6, 7

safe space 119–20, 124, 134, 175
Sampson, E.E. 48, 139
Scase, R. and Goffee, R. 103
Schenninck, B. 114
Schofield, J. and Pavelchak, M. 22
Schrager, L.S. 33
Schwartz, S.H. 137
Schwartz, S.H. and Bilsky, W. 137
Seddon, V. 115, 116
self-advancement, *see* individual mobility
self-categorization 34–6, 103, 112
self-concept 29 (*see also* identity)
self-interest 13
sex discrimination 95–101
sex sterotypes 35, 103
sexual harassment 97

Simon, B. 35, 138
Simon, B. and Brown, R.J. 35
Simon, B. and Mummendey, A. 35
Simon, B. and Pettigrew, T.F. 138
Sivacek, J.K. and Crano, W.D. 28
Skevington, S. and Baker, D. 51, 177
Smith, P. and Gaskell, G. 40
Smith, P.B. and Bond, M.H. 23, 24, 137
Snyder, C.R. and Fromkin, H.L. 138
social beliefs
    participation in women's groups 67–70,
    104–6
    self-reported changes 125–31, 133–4,
    135
    union participation 59
social change 41–2, 128, 129–30, 156
    women's groups 62
social class 2
social constructs 15
social identity (*see also* status)
    causal attribution 42, 44
    fragmentation 176
    gender 51–3
    low status 40–42
    optimal distinctiveness 139, 164–5,
    174
    permeability of group boundaries 44–6
social motives 30, 57, 74
social norms 13
solidarity 114–15
Sparks, P. and Shepherd, R. 29, 50, 54
Spelman, E.V. 8, 64, 161, 179
Stagner, R. and Eflal, B. 117
status 40–42 (*see also* social identity)
    women 51–3, 105
stereotypes
    feminists 151–2, 157–60, 171–2
    gender 35, 103
    political minorities 144, 172
Stewart, A.J. and Gold-Steinberg, S. 89, 94
Stouffer, S.A. *et al.* 38
strike action 1, 2, 3
    consciousness raising 114–17
    consensus mobilization 32–3
    expectancy-value model of
    participation 31–2
    miners' strike 1984–85 3, 115–17, 171
    picket lines 12
Struch, N. and Schwartz, S.H. 50
student groups 111–12
student unrest 1
Sullivan, M. 113
Swim, J.K. *et al.* 98

Tajfel, H. 41
Tajfel, H. and Turner, J.C. 41, 42, 47
Tarrow, S. 1
Taylor, D.M. and McKirnan, D.J. 42, 43f, 106, 138
Taylor, D.M. *et al.* 45, 46, 47, 99, 100, 108, 172
Taylor, R. 10
Thatcherism 2, 140, 156, 157
Tilly, C. 9, 10
Tougas, F. and Veilleux, F. 40, 50
Tougas, F. *et al.* 98
trade unions (*see also* strike action)
    coercion 12
    decline 2, 3–4
    growth 1, 3
    intimidation 150
    militancy 148–9
    non-activism 145–51
    quantitative study of participation
        factor analysis 58, 59t
        moderating role of group
        identification 61–2
        predicting participation 59–61
        questionnaire 57–8
        setting and respondents 56–7
    role conflict 150
    silent majority 149, 150–51
    women's participation 145–7
Triandis, H.C. 4, 9
Triandis, H.C. *et al.* 23, 24, 45, 137
Turnbull, P., Woolfson, C. and Kelly, J. 32
Turner, J.C. 142, 143
Turner, J.C. and Brown, R.J. 42
Turner, J.C. *et al.* 35, 103, 143
Tyler, T.R. and McGraw, K.M. 21, 22, 173

unemployment 2
Unesco 140
unlawful behaviour 65, 78

van de Vall, M. 148
Van Kippenberg, A. and Ellemers, N. 45
Vanneman, R.D. and Pettigrew, T.F. 39
voluntary organizations 112–13
voting behaviour 28, 29

Waddington, D., Wikes, M. and Crichter, C. 116
Walker, I. and Mann, L. 39
Walker, I. and Pettigrew, T.F. 38, 39
Walsh, E. 114
Wandersman, A. 113

welfare state 4
Wertheimer, B.M. and Nelson, A.H. 145
Wetherell, M., Stiven, H. and Potter, J. 101
Wicker, A.W. 113
Wicker, A.W. and Kauma, C. 113
Wicker, A.W. and Mehler, A. 113
Wicker, A.W. *et al.* 113
Wilder, D.A. 35
Williams, J.A. 52
Williams, J.A. and Giles, H. 51
Winterton, J. and Winterton, R. 3, 33, 116
Wolf, S., Gregory, W.L. and Stephan, W.G. 22
women (*see also* gender)
    employment statistics 178
    mothers and daughters 90–93
    status 51–3, 105
    working class 161–2
women's movement 1 (*see also* feminism)
    consciousness raising 7–8, 52–3, 124
        miners' strike 1984–85 115–16
    criticism of group members 132–3
    developmental model of feminism 130
    diversity 8, 129, 176–9
    divisions 6–7
    employment 6
    exclusion of some categories of
    women 8, 160–62
    higher education 6
    militancy 152, 158, 163
    non-activism
        apathy 165
        beliefs about feminism 157–62, 163–4, 171–2
            cultural and political context 155–7
            data-gathering 153–5
            denial of personal disadvantage 166
            fear of negative stereotyping 151–2
            feelings of disloyalty to the family 163
            individual aversion to group
        membership 164–5, 174
            lack of confidence 165
            perceived inappropriateness of
        collective action 152–3, 167–8
            practical constraints 167
            structure and organization of
    women's groups 162
    non-hierarchical structures 119, 124, 162, 175
    outcomes of participation 118–19
        changes in social beliefs 125–31, 133–4, 135, 176

empowerment 122, 124, 175
new recruits and longstanding
members 131–3
    personal development 122–3
    political 121–2
    professional development 123–4
    social 119–21, 175
post-feminism 7
quantitative study of participation
    groups and respondents 62–4
    impact of identification as an activist
72
    identity and behavioural expression
78
    intentions, behaviour and perceived
control 72–6
    measuring prospective and
potential participation 64–5, 65f, 66f
    moderating role of group
identification 70–72, 76–8, 79
    using social beliefs to predict
participation 67–70
reasons for involvement 82–6
    activist identity 94–5, 173
    belief in collective action 106
    belief in political efficacy 70, 71, 73,
80, 174

chance 107
    collective relative deprivation 68,
69, 71, 73, 80, 89, 104, 135, 172–3, 174
    collectivist orientation 68, 70, 71, 73,
80, 174
    discrimination 95–101, 172
    feminist consciousness 105–6
    gender relations in the family 86–90,
172
    group services 106–7
    isolation 102–4
    life-cycle changes 94–5, 126, 128–9
    meeting and helping others 104
    mothers and daughters 90–93
separatism 160
Woolfson, C. and Foster, J. 33
working class 4, 5
    women 161–2
Wright, S.C., Taylor, D.M. and
Moghaddam, F.M. 19, 46, 47, 108

Yahne, C.E. and Long, V.O. 113
Young, A. 151

Zimbardo, P.J. 35, 36–7